JOHN COTTER
70 years of HARDWARE

by
Edward R. Kantowicz

Regnery Books
Chicago   Washington, DC

"This book is dedicated to the 25 charter members of Cotter & Company, whose faith in John Cotter and the future of dealer-ownership helped establish a sound, low-cost company."

Regnery Books is a Division of Regnery Gateway, Inc.
All inquiries concerning this book should be directed to
Regnery Books, 950 N. Shore Drive, Lake Bluff, IL 60044.

Library of Congress Cataloging-in-Publication Data

Kantowicz, Edward R.
    True Value.

    1. Cotter & Company—History.   2. Cotter,
John, 1904–   .   3. Hardware industry—United States—
History.   4. Businessmen—United States—Biography.
I. Title.
HD9745.U5C655   1986   381′.45683′0924   [B]   86-42795
ISBN 0-89526-580-X

CONTENTS

INTRODUCTION
JOHN M. COTTER
AND THE INDEPENDENT
HARDWARE DEALER

**"The Entrepreneur —
Artist of the Business World"**

"In a sense we can view the entrepreneur in business today as a man who practices the *art* of business. He constantly seeks new relationships with his environment. He conjures up new configurations of facts and ideas. He dreams and he makes his dreams into realities. And in the process, he leads. He convinces others of the value of his goals. His energy and dedication attract others to join in his undertakings."

"The entrepreneur is intellectually and emotionally oriented to the future. To him, what is, is obsolete. He seeks to control his environment, not to resist it. He initiates change and thrives on it. He works harder and longer than other men but he doesn't call it work because he enjoys it so much. He is a risk-taker but he can relax amid tension because his security lies in his confidence in his ability to think creatively and constructively. He is likely to be indifferent to the pipe and slippers concept of security, and to create havoc in an environment where systems, procedures and work measurement techniques are prized."

—Roy Ash,
Harvard Business Bulletin (1966)

On a foggy evening in mid-July of 1947, John Cotter and Ed Lanctot pulled up to the Fargo Hotel in the small northern Illinois town of Sycamore. They had invited hardware store owners from the surrounding territory to a meeting, and were wondering if anyone would show up. By 7 o'clock, twelve had arrived, one of them flying over from Lake Forest in his own plane and touching down just before the fog closed in completely over the cornfields. Cotter got up and told them that he wanted to save them money, by organizing a wholesale company they themselves would own. The dealers liked what they heard, but they adopted a cautious, "prove it to me" attitude.

The next morning, Cotter set out to organize the company and raise the money. He needed 25 dealers to put up $1500 each before he could start a dealer-owned wholesale firm. He drove to McHenry and convinced Bill Althoff, a former-president of the Illinois Retail Hardware Association, to write a check for $1500, over the vehement protests of his wife. Then he made a beeline for Elgin and signed up Roy Baseman at Westside Hardware, returning again to Sycamore to persuade Stan Staskey of Sycamore Hardware. He started home to Chicago with three checks in his pocket, but his car died in Elmhurst, stranding him with a broken fuel pump. It had been an eventful twenty-four hours.

Cotter spent the next six months putting on dealer meetings and signing up members. He opened a tiny office in Chicago's South Loop on January 15, 1948 and moved into rented warehouse space the following June 1. He began the year with 25 dealers and ended it with 84, shipping $385,000 worth of goods. He himself made less than $5000 his first year as manager. In the nearly forty years since then, Cotter & Company has grown to a nationwide company with 6900 Members doing over one and a half billion dollars worth of business. If the firm were publicly owned, it would rank among the 500 largest corporations in the U.S. on the *Forbes* and *Fortune* lists. Dealer-owned wholesalers supply just about half of all the hardware sold through hardware stores today; Cotter alone enjoys a market share of about 20%.

Few people outside the hardware industry know the name of John Cotter or of the business he founded in 1947; but most Americans instantly recognize his brand name, True Value Hardware. Over 200 million copies of True Value catalogues are distributed yearly; and dozens of times each day, Pat Summerall and Paul Harvey take to the air to proclaim the latest bargain of the month, or simply the everyday low prices and high quality of True Value. Paul Harvey's commercials have even been parodied on "Saturday Night Live."

Paradox surrounds the history of John Cotter and his company. Direct mail and national advertising have made True Value a household name, yet it is not Cotter & Company's original brand. Hibbard, Spencer, Bartlett & Co. of Chicago, Cotter's first major competitor, coined the trademark in 1932; Cotter acquired it for $2500 when he bought out Hibbard's in 1962. The average customer often considers his neighborhood True Value Hardware a chain store; but, in reality, an independent businessman owns each individual store and these hardware dealers together own the wholesale distributor. John Cotter runs that wholesale distributor like a family firm; he started it, he gave it his name, he guided it to success. Now that he has moved aside as chairman of the board, his son, Dan Cotter, carries on as company president and his son-in-law, Paul Fee, executive vice president. Yet the Cotters do not own the firm; the individual dealers do. Cotter & Company is a dealer-owned, mutual or cooperative, corporation; the Cotters are salaried managers. The word "cooperative" conjures up visions of long-haired socialist theorists or radical prairie farmers. Cotter & Company, however, could not be more practical, down-to-earth, or profit-oriented.

John Cotter is an entrepreneur, a bold risk-taker who gave up a secure, good-paying job to explore new methods of distribution. He started a company with $37,500 of capital contributed by dealers and shook up a tradition-bound industry from top to toe, eventually building a nationwide firm doing $1.8 billion of business annually. He is also an old-fashioned man, with conventional attitudes and traditional moral values, a cautious businessman who measures every step carefully, a devoted family man with an "Ozzie and Harriet" home life, a religious man who quietly aids his church without fanfare or publicity.

Roy Ash's apt characterization of an entrepreneur fits John Cotter well in most particulars. He initiates change, thrives on the excitement of competition and company takeovers, works harder and longer than other men, plays hunches and takes risks; yet he can relax amid tension, taking a daily nap at lunchtime and awakening refreshed and clear-headed. The rapid growth of Cotter & Company created havoc and jealousy in hardware wholesaling; the major trade association blacklisted Cotter's company for 25 years and its president blasted him publicly, and by name, at its 1966 national convention. Yes, John Cotter practiced the *art* of business, turning his dreams into reality and making others uncomfortable in the process.

Still, in one crucial respect, Ash's vignette falls short of describing John Cotter. He is not by temperament or intention a disturber of systems, procedures, or orderly work habits. On the contrary, he preaches that "hardware is a business of repetition" — a retailer has to place orders on a seasonal schedule, pay his bills weekly, send out ad circulars regularly, attend semi-annual merchandise markets, and do the same things again next year. Cotter furnishes each True Value hardware store with a management calendar detailing what needs to be taken care of every day of the year. Once he found the formula for low-cost distribution and put it into practice, he did not alter it significantly in forty years.

John Cotter, then, is a conservative entrepreneur, a risk-taker who appreciates routine, a persuasive salesman and leader without a hint of personal flamboyance. Besides his caution, Cotter is conservative in another sense; his major achievement has been to conserve, to preserve, to save the independent hardware retailer from a slow process of extinction.

Probably, the independent hardware store will never literally go out of existence. Many American men (and, increasingly, women) feel an almost primitive urge to tinker with tools and implements, and to be their own boss. Yet, in the years following World War II, the hardware dealer did undergo a severe crisis of confidence, as new competition put a sharp squeeze on his profits. Mass merchandisers of all sorts — discount houses, catalogue stores, national department store chains, even drug stores and supermarkets — competed for the hardware dollar. The wholesale level of the trade suffered even greater trials, as a "profitless prosperity" of greater volume but lower profits drove many 100 year old firms out of business. Many experts predicted that the independent retailer would soon follow.

Indeed, if John Cotter, and others, had not developed new methods of low-cost distribution, the independent dealer would have become an increasingly marginal part of the hardware business. Cotter & Company brought the dealer-owned cooperative movement, pioneered by others, to a high state of efficiency and helped the hardware dealer survive and flourish. Cotter spearheaded a major transformation of the hardware industry in the last forty years.

Dealer-ownership, a kind of franchise system in reverse, forms the heart of this transformation. Americans have become increasingly familiar with franchising. McDonald's, Burger King, and their many imitators dot the landscape from Maine to California, homogenizing Americans' taste in food and promoting business opportunities for "semi-independent businessmen." In a typical franchise deal, the central organization, such as McDonald's, owns the name and the formula, leasing the right to use them to independent operators. Frequently, McDonald's owns the land and the building as well, renting them back to the franchisee. The central organization earns a hefty profit; typical service and rental fees run to 10% of sales volume on each outlet. In a cooperative or mutual organization, however, the dealers or store owners themselves own the central organization; they are its only shareholders. Profits made at the wholesale level get rebated back to them at the end of the year. Though the middleman's functions are not eliminated, for they are essential, dealer-ownership eliminates the middleman's profit, allowing the independent retailer to compete with integrated, nation-wide merchandisers, such as Sears or K-Mart.

Why is saving the independent hardware store important? Service is the key. You can buy an adjustable wrench at Sears or K-Mart, but will the teenage girl at the checkout counter teach you how to use it? A department store will sell you a lawn mower, but will they fix it if it needs service? A warehouse store may advertise lower prices, but do you want to tramp around a warehouse to find what you need to complete a job?

So consider Smith & Jones True Value Hardware, Anytown, USA. On a sunny spring Saturday, home do-it-yourselfers may pay several visits to Smith & Jones for fencing, hose, wood screws, or maybe just socializing. Mr. Smith will patiently explain the difference between male and female pipe fittings to a blushing housewife, while Jones tactfully suggests to an apartment dweller that his new mousetrap would work better with some bait in it. Both firmly insist that gardeners who buy a potent weed-killer read the directions before leaving the store. Smith & Jones are do-it-yourself consultants as much as salesmen. Thousands of retailers like them might not be there unless Cotter & Company got them the same price on tools and appliances that the chain store buyer gets.

Most True Value hardware stores are family operations, some in their third generation of ownership; but forget the usual image of the "mom and pop" store. If mom and pop slave away 12 hours a day, seven days a week in a profitless little hole-in-the-wall, never making any headway against giant competitors in the shopping mall, their son or daughter is unlikely to consider taking over the store. They will go off to college and study medicine, law, engineering, or business administration and never come back. But if the college boy or girl sees his parents making a good living, expanding their store, taking a vacation once in a while, he or she may consider hardware retailing a decent way of life. True Value dealer-ownership makes possible the perpetuation of family businesses, it preserves a piece of the American Dream.

Hardware is not a glamorous business, and its history has gone largely unchronicled. The wholesale level of the trade remains particularly obscure, for no one loves the middleman. Mass production has long been America's glory. The famous entrepreneurs, from Carnegie and Rockefeller to Henry Ford and Lee Iacocca, have been primarily men who made things. Mass production, of course, is worthless without mass distribution, so the great merchant retailers — Field, Sears, Macy, even L.L. Bean — have found their chroniclers. But no one praises the middleman, the wholesaler; few even acknowledge his existence, except when advocating his elimination. Yet the old adage still applies — "You can eliminate the jobber but you cannot eliminate the job." Someone needs to perform the intermediate functions of storage, transportation, finance, and sales. Wholesalers can be entrepreneurs too; studies of business and enterprise have too long neglected them.

John Cotter is a wholesaler who "thinks retail." He has helped thousands of small retailers provide a good living for their families and service for their customers. In the process, he created havoc among the old-line, higher-cost wholesalers, took over one of the largest of their number, Hibbard, Spencer, Bartlett, and transformed the industry.

CHAPTER ONE
THE OLD-LINE
HARDWARE
WHOLESALER

"For forty years I have constantly heard about the elimination of the jobber in business. I have heard about the manufacturer going direct to the retail trade and still today after all this time, I find that the jobber still exists and is still doing business at the old stand."

—Saunders Norvell,
Forty Years of Hardware (1924)

"If you can't eat it, and it don't pour or fold, it's hardware." Hardware is a necessity of life, like food, clothing, and medicine; and the hardware industry is an ancient one. Books about hardware or housewares all start with an obligatory Stone Age chapter relating how some unknown cave man created the first tool, a crudely chipped hunk of bone or rock. The company history of one hardware firm pompously intones on its first page: "The story of hardware is the story of mankind." Be that as it may, the production of hardware does trace an ancient lineage in America. "Ironmongery," as the English colonists called it (and the English still do), began with the Saugus Iron Works outside Lynn, Massachusetts in 1642. The manufacture of cutlery and other iron and steel implements flourished throughout New England, but especially in the Connecticut Valley, during colonial times. Until well into America's first century of independence, however, the lion's share of U.S. hardware was imported from England or continental Europe. Whether imported or domestic, nearly all hardware passed through wholesalers before reaching the retailer and the consumer.

GENESIS OF THE JOBBER

In its earliest years, the wholesale hardware trade remained in the hands of importers, commission agents, and unspecialized general wholesalers in the seaboard cities. Yankee peddlers, who hawked their wares on foot or from wagons, and small town storekeepers from the hinterlands made buying trips to the great mercantile centers twice a year to choose their stock. In a ritual little changed from the medieval trade fairs of Europe, merchants set up displays in hotels, staged dinners and tours for the buyers, arranged for the slow laborious shipping of goods by barge and wagon, and provided extended credit terms. Relations between city merchant and country storekeeper were long-term and stable, based on personal acquaintance and mutual trust.

This placid and traditional process changed as production quickened and transportation improved in the mid-nineteenth century. What we now think of as the "old-line" wholesaler was himself once new, a product of the railroads and a response to the manufacturers' need to move a greatly increased volume of goods. As railroads leapt over plains and mountain ranges, spanning the continent, wholesale merchants set up shop in major rail centers, such as Chicago, St. Paul, and St. Louis, and at smaller junction points along the roads. In order to relieve the bottlenecks of trade and keep the manufacturers from choking on the products of mass production, these regional wholesalers usually specialized in one of the staples — hardware, groceries, drugs, dry goods.

The hardware wholesalers who opened shop in the mid-nineteenth century at regional marketing points took title to the goods they handled (unlike commission agents or brokers), they specialized only in hardware (unlike general merchants and importers in the seaboard cities), they carried a large assortment or "full-line," and they provided "full-service" to retailers by sending out travelling salesmen and extending credit. They were also called jobbers, because they bought goods in large quantities and sold them in small "jobs." Such wholesalers or jobbers furnished storage, credit, and salesmanship to the emerging system of mass distribution.

Full-line, full-service wholesalers proliferated rapidly after the Civil War. Retailers no longer needed to make long buying trips, since travelling salesmen from the wholesale houses came to them to "drum up" business. Fierce competition between the salesmen of various houses allowed the retailers to drive hard bargains and get lower prices. Railroads brought speedy delivery of goods. Saunders Norvell, in his memoir *Forty Years of Hardware,* recalled the excellent service the Burlington road gave him during his years as a salesman in Colorado for the E. C. Simmons Hardware firm of St. Louis:

"I could place orders in the mail on Saturday, they would arrive in St. Louis Monday morning, they would usually be shipped on Tuesday or Wednesday and in the majority of cases our customers would have the goods in their stores by the following Saturday, or within one week."

Retailers ordered more frequently, but they placed smaller orders and were able to carry leaner inventories. In return for their many services, though, the wholesalers demanded shorter credit terms. Standard payment terms in the trade became "2% 10 days, net 30 days," that is, if a retailer paid within 10 days of billing he could deduct a 2% cash discount, otherwise the full balance was due in 30 days, or at the end of the month. Most wholesalers, however, were not too rigorous in adhering to these terms, and allowed the cash discount if payment was made by the 10th of the following month. They also offered extended credit terms (or "dating") on seasonal goods such as garden tools for spring, screen cloth for summer, stove pipe for fall, and toys for Christmas. Payment for such goods would come due after the harvest of local crops. In the South, for example, they were commonly referred to as cotton terms or tobacco terms.

Many wholesale houses were family firms. Joseph Orgill, for example, came to the U.S. from England to open an importing business in New York in 1830. His younger brother, William, joined him, then opened a wholesale house in the Mississippi River town of Memphis, which promised to be a thriving transportation hub upon completion of the Memphis and Charleston Railroad in 1853. Finally, in 1857 three Orgill brothers pooled their talents and money with the Memphis firm, which is still doing business today under their name. More common than family connections were partnerships, with each partner bringing substantial capital to the firm. Many jobbing houses had three partners, such as Farwell, Ozmun, Kirk in St. Paul; Kelley-How-Thomson in Duluth; or Hibbard, Spencer, Bartlett in Chicago. Triple partnerships reflected the nature of the wholesale trade. A well-run wholesale house required a man on the road (sales and marketing), a man in the warehouse (buying, personnel, operations), and a man in the office (finance, accounting). In the industry's premier Chicago firm, William Gold Hibbard did most of the buying, Franklin F. Spencer was the "bean-counter," or accountant, and Adolphus Clay Bartlett shepherded the sales force on the road. (Interestingly, Sears, Roebuck & Co., the pioneer mass merchandiser, also followed this triple leadership pattern. Richard Warren Sears was the sales genius, Julius Rosenwald the bean-counter, and Otto Doering the man in the warehouse. Alvah Roebuck had left the firm early on.)

Most wholesalers served a regional clientele, limiting their sales to a radius of about 350 miles in order to ensure prompt delivery; but some sales regions were larger. Minnesota houses, such as Marshall-Wells in Duluth and Janney, Semple, Hill in Minneapolis, served the whole Upper Midwest and Northern Plains. A few houses in major rail centers, such as Hibbard's in Chicago, Simmons in St. Louis, and Belknap in Louisville, aspired to a national market.

Middlemen are never popular, and no sooner did the full-line wholesaler establish himself than he came under attack. Why have a middleman at all? Why not shorten the distribution chain and let manufacturers of goods sell direct to retailers, or even to consumers? Some manufacturers did exactly that. Large producers of steel rails for the railway industry were the first to sell direct. Since their market was concentrated among a handful of large railroads with specialized, expert buying staffs, no middleman proved necessary. By the end of the nineteenth century, many suppliers of producers' goods and industrial supplies sold directly to the ultimate users. Some manufacturers of consumers' goods did likewise, particularly if their product was perishable, expensive, or technically complicated. So, Swift & Co. operated a huge network of refrigerated rail cars and depots to distribute meat from the Chicago Stockyards; Singer Sewing Machine sold only through company-owned retail outlets; the Hoover Sweeper Company originally sold its novel electric sweeper door to door. Makers of technically complex or perishable goods desired a close and continuing relationship between producer, retailer, and consumer.

But in those industries where many small manufacturers produced a great variety of simple, standard items for sale through a host of small retail outlets, the wholesale middleman endured. In such industries as groceries, drugs, hardware, jewelry, liquor, furniture, and dry goods, no special marketing problems required the manufacturer to sell direct, and the great number of retailers would have made direct selling prohibitively expensive. As one economic historian has aptly stated: "If the jobber was to be eliminated, each sale had to be either large in volume or high in value in order to make freight and handling costs lower than those the middleman could set." For example, the U.S. Playing Card Co. of Cincinnati could send 3 gross (432 decks of cards) to a jobber in Chicago for 40 cents, but if the company shipped in small lots to retailers, a shipment of just five decks would cost 30 cents. Not surprisingly, then, most hardware manufacturers remained content to sell through jobbers, even when other, more technologically advanced firms had integrated vertically all the way from raw materials to point of sale.

Indeed, hardware wholesalers flourished in the nineteenth century, servicing 95 to 98 per cent of the retail hardware market. The maturing industry organized a National Wholesale Hardware Association in 1895. As one of its first acts, the fledgling association attempted to define the industry by working up an "approved list" of full-line, full-service wholesalers and urging manufacturers to sell only to them. The first list counted 178 such approved jobbers.

THE COMMERCIAL TRAVELLER

In wholesale hardware, the travelling salesman was the locomotive who pulled the train. Indeed, when the NWHA devised its first definition of the trade, it required that a house send out a corps of travelling salesmen in order to make the approved list. Fanning out across the country after the Civil War, commercial travellers, or "drummers," considered themselves the "ambassadors of supply and demand," the advance couriers of the latest fashions. There were only about 1000 salesmen, from all industries, in 1860, but by 1870 they numbered 7000, and at the turn of the century 93,000. Mostly young and well-dressed, self-confident gladhanders, aggressive without being pushy, travelling salesmen succeeded mainly through sheer endurance. Saunders Norvell, who spent nine years on the road and another nine supervising salesmen, remarked that "the man who could travel the hardest, sell goods the longest number of hours every day, and write the fastest, was the best salesman."

As the wholesale trade developed, most salesmen worked a well-defined territory on a regular basis. The salesman knew his territory the way a precinct captain knew his neighborhood or the cop his beat. He generally visited each hardware store every two weeks, on the same day. He inspected the "want book," where the owner had jotted down any items he had run out of, he then showed the new goods and prices from his huge leather-bound, valise-handled catalogue, and gave the merchant his most persuasive pitch. The storekeeper greeted many salesmen each week and often played one man's prices off against another's. In order to meet this competition, experienced drummers enjoyed considerable leeway from their houses to cut prices if necessary to make a sale. The real bane of the salesman, however, was the "Russian buyer," who after listening to an extended sales pitch, bought "one-of-ich," or, if he was feeling generous, 2/12 of a dozen.

A travelling salesman often built up close friendships with storekeepers and their families and employees. If the owner was busy when he called, he would go in and tidy up the stock, take a rough inventory, and write up the sales himself. He often ended up knowing the owner's store better than the owner himself. The personal connection between storekeeper and travelling salesman was hard to break. Many a retailer threw a few orders to a favorite salesman even when he could get a better price elsewhere. The wise salesman did not plan to carry his grip until he dropped, but saved his money to buy a store of his own. If he had squandered his sales commissions, he could usually find a final resting place as a clerk for one of his former customers.

Travelling salesmen were the stuff of legends, an inspiration for old men's jokes and young men's fantasies. Saunders Norvell recalled the perfect freedom of the road:

> "My first year as a sales manager . . . was one of the most unhappy years of my life. I had been accustomed to almost absolute freedom. I had worked exactly according to my own ideas. Nothing had been asked of me except results. I had led a life of perfect individualism."

Historian Gerald Carson, in his classic study, *The Old Country Store,* wrote:

> "To a country boy hanging around the little store at a four corners, the drummer was a gay bird of passage, his home where his hat hung, a hero to be compared favorably with the engineers on the fast freight."

Yet despite the legendary romance of the road, fatigue, loneliness, and sometimes real danger dogged the drummer's steps. After working all day, his hours of sleep depended on the train schedule. One drummer recalled leaving a 4 A.M. wake-up call with the hotel owner. At the appointed time, a fierce thunderstorm was raging, so the salesman sleepily muttered: "I believe I won't go out in this storm." The innkeeper blazed back: "Oh yes, you will. I have been sitting up all night to call you and you *will* go." On other occasions, train wrecks and hotel fires took their toll. Many victims of the Great Chicago Fire of 1871 were believed to be out-of-town drummers trapped in their downtown lodgings.

But worst of all was the loneliness. A salesman stayed out on the road continuously, except for a week or two of sales meetings at his wholesale house towards the end of the year. Train stations, single hotel rooms, and bars were his home. Not surprisingly, many salesmen became alcoholics and some wasted all their free time building up huge gambling debts. No matter what town or city they stayed in at night, the red light district always seemed to be right around the corner from the hotel and train station. To deal with such problems, religious salesmen formed the Commercial Travelling Mens Association in 1898. The Gideons, as they were popularly known, organized religious services in hotel lobbies and distributed a copy of the Bible to every hotel room in the country.

Along with the loneliness went a concern for the wife and family left behind. One of the few printable travelling salesman jokes deals with this worry. "A travelling salesman wired his wife that he would be home that evening. When he arrived he found her in another man's arms. He was despondent. His friends suggested that he talk it over with another woman, perhaps his mother. 'Mother, I was out on the road selling. Yesterday I wired my wife I'd be home last night, and when I got home I found her in another man's arms. Why? Mother, you're a woman. Tell me why?' His mother was quiet for a long time. Finally, she broke the silence. 'Maybe she didn't get your telegram.'"

Commercial travellers proved to be a mixed blessing for the wholesale houses. Jobbers depended upon them to drum up trade and beat the competition. Yet at the same time, they feared the drummers' free and easy ways and thought them too eager to cut prices. Of necessity, the jobber had abdicated one of the essentials of his business — control over prices. Even more important in the long run was the cost of keeping salesmen on the road. Sales costs represented a steady 5 to 10 per cent of total sales, and eventually this proved too heavy a burden to bear. Yet, for almost a century, during the long heyday of the full line, full-service wholesaler, the commercial traveller remained "king of the road."

THE OLD-FASHIONED HARDWARE STORE

Retailers had begun to specialize about the same time jobbers did, in the early nineteenth century, as the production of goods and the volume of trade quickened. By 1850 or so, the general store, where a farm family could buy everything from collar buttons to Jamaica rum, remained only in the smallest crossroads hamlets, or on the frontier;

every town of any size boasted one or more independent grocery, drug, clothing and hardware stores. Still, many merchants hedged their bets by continuing in more than one line of trade; so combination stores of "hardware and dry goods," "hardware, furniture and undertaker," "hardware and implements," or, later, "hardware and automobile dealer" surrounded many a courthouse square.

Hardware stores normally filled long and narrow storefronts on Main Street, covering little more than 1000 square feet of floor space, with windows kept to a minimum thus providing maximum shelf space. One or two bare electric bulbs cast a dim illumination; and a pot-bellied stove, surrounded by men telling stories, chewing, and spitting, graced the entrance. The atmosphere was decidedly masculine, with pervasive odors of paint, oil, turpentine, and tobacco; few women dared to enter.

Hardware consisted largely of demand merchandise, useful tools and implements which farmers, craftsmen, or homeowners needed to build or repair things. A man came in and asked for what he needed. The owner, who stored his goods in closed boxes, drawers, or bins, or else on shelves lining both side walls, then had to locate the items, count them out, and determine the price. The storekeeper usually marked his goods with the wholesale price in code. One common code read like this:

R E P U B L I C A N   Another used a
1 2 3 4 5 6 7 8 9 0
tic-tac-toe motif:

$$\begin{array}{c|c|c} 1 & 2 & 3 \\ \hline 4 & 5 & 6 \\ \hline 7 & 8 & 9 \end{array}$$

So a wholesale price of $1.59 read either RBA or ⌐ ▯Γ. The owner figured a standard mark-up of 50% in his head and sold the goods for $2.39, producing a 33⅓% margin of profit. (Mark-up is a percentage of the wholesale price; margin a percentage of the final sales price.)

An 1892 hardware magazine listed the following inventory of a Connecticut retail store as typical of the range of goods carried:

"The first department of enumerated goods covers a line of buckboards, carriages, buggies, phaetons, surreys, rockaways, road wagons and sleighs; followed, in turn, by agricultural implements, hardware, paints, oils, varnishes and woodenware; then comes all kinds of brushes, artists' materials, lamps and fixtures, Astral oil, gasoline, naptha, turpentine, tar, rope, barb wire fencing, fish hooks, lines, pocket and table cutlery, scissors, razors, straps, refrigerators, sash weights, rock and gun powder, shot, fuse, drain pipe, sheathing paper, mowers, reapers, horse rakes, hay tedders, horse power machines, fruit jars, rubber bucket pumps, guns, ammunition, lawn tennis and croquet sets; the next list embraces slat, butter workers, fertilizers, ground bone, organs, Colley's creamery, Hoyt and Son's nursery, Bradley mowers, birds, bird cages, carving knives, forks, spoons, nut crackers, knives, revolvers, carpet sweepers, rocking horses and toy wagons."

An astute observer will notice that, despite some unfamiliar terms, the list of goods resembles the stock of today's hardware store — tools, transportation supplies (then buggies, today automotive), paint housewares, garden supplies, sporting goods, toys. The difference lay not so much in the choice of goods but in how the goods were sold. Little attempt was made to display merchandise attractively, to advertise it, or to encourage impulse buying. A hardware store was essentially a small, cluttered storehouse, with the stock arranged for the convenience of the owner and his clerks.

The hardware store owner hung his own name on the storefront, cherished his independence, and paid no allegiance to any organization. He bought from many different wholesalers; and he spent as much time haggling with drummers for an extra few pennies a dozen, as he did selling merchandise. When he snared an especially good price, he would try to compound his advantage by insisting that the drummer not sell to his local competitor down the street. Though he might be attached to an individual salesman, he felt little loyalty to any jobbing house. Until well into the twentieth century, brand names meant little in hardware so the retailer felt free to stock the goods he could get at the lowest price. A few of the larger wholesale houses developed their own brands of merchandise which established such a reputation that most retailers had to carry them. Simmons Hardware first applied the Keen Kutter name to edge tools in the 1880's and Hibbard's followed suit not long after with the OVB—Our Very Best lines of merchandise.

Sharp retailers noticed that they made more profit on specialty goods, such as stoves, lawn mowers, bicycles, and cutlery, than on nuts and bolts, hammers and nails, or other staples. Wholesale houses pushed specialty items hard, often employing extra specialty salesmen, for cutlery and sporting goods. Pocket cutlery was an important commodity until well into the twentieth century (and has recently made a comeback among collectors and nostalgia buffs). Out West, pocket knives were important tools for cowboys and farmers, while nationwide, a knife was an indispensable companion for most males. Young boys eagerly looked forward to getting their first personal pocket knife.

Specialty salesmen did not travel a fixed territory but rather accompanied the regular salesmen once or twice a year on special sales trips. Pocket knives, firearms, and fishing tackle were all small in size but high in value, and they required special handling and expert demonstration. So specialty salesmen carried trunkloads of samples, not just a catalogue, set up shop in a local hotel, and called in the local retailers to view the goods. The store owners, then, aware of the high value and the profit possibilities of pocket cutlery and sporting goods kept them in locked cases in their stores, much like jewelry. Hibbard's not only put their OVB label on pocket knives, they also would etch the storekeeper's name on the blades for advertising purposes. Gradually modern salesmanship was penetrating the world of the traditional hardware store, and none too soon. By the early years of this century, the hardware retailer no longer had the marketing of hard lines all to himself.

COMPETITION APPEARS

The same forces of mass production and rapid transportation which called the hardware wholesaler into existence also produced his competition. Railroads brought travelling salesmen to every hardware store in America, but they also carried mail order catalogues to every farm house. In 1872, Aaron Montgomery Ward began selling direct by catalogue from the country's rail capital of Chicago. Buttressed by an endorsement from the Patrons of Husbandry, popularly known as the Grange, Ward built a direct relationship of trust and profit with farm families across the country. Then, in 1886, a young railroad station agent in Minnesota named Richard Warren Sears peddled an unclaimed lot of pocket watches to other agents up and down the line. Discovering a natural talent as a salesman, Sears moved to Chicago in 1887 to follow Ward's example. After Sears' first partner, Alvah Roebuck, left in frustration over his unorganized business practices, Julius Rosenwald signed on and changed him from "a huckster of watches and junk jewelry to the buyer for the American farmer."

Sears first passed Ward's with $10 million in sales in 1900, and Ward's never caught up. By 1907, Sears was printing 3 million catalogues a year. As historian Daniel Boorstin points out:

> "The farmer kept the Bible in the frigid parlor but . . . the mail order catalogue was kept in the cozy kitchen. That was where the farm family ate and where they really lived . . . In rural schoolhouses, children were drilled in reading and spelling from the catalogue. They tried their hand at drawing by copying the catalogue models, and acquired geography by studying the postal zone maps."

Boorstin doesn't mention it, but the farm boy also saw his first "pornography" in the women's underwear pages of the catalogue.

As the mail-order houses threatened small town merchants, department stores competed for big-city sales dollars. Merchant princes, such as R. H. Macy in New York, John Wanamaker in Philadelphia, and Marshall Field in Chicago, built "Palaces of Consumption" in the downtown centers of every major city. Commuter railroads and electric streetcars brought patrons from throughout the city and surrounding suburbs, and even, on special occasions, from the rural hinterlands. Department stores added to their magnetic power by advertising heavily, with full page ads in big-city daily newspapers.

Through newspapers and catalogues, then, both city and country folks discovered a cornucopia of goods beyond the capacity of the local neighborhood or small town merchant to stock. Fortunately for the hardware store, and its wholesale suppliers, hard lines did not predominate at either the mail-order houses or department stores. The Sears catalogue appealed more to the farm wife, starved for fashion or luxury, than to her hardbitten husband. Department stores carried many housewares items, indeed they gave home furnishings and kitchen utensils a separate marketing identity for the first time; but they did not feature traditional tools and implements. Furthermore, though Sears and Ward's eliminated the middleman, most department stores did not.

Huge stores, such as Field's and Macy's, purchased many goods direct from manufacturers; but they also relied on numerous local jobbers for marginal items like hardware. Hibbard's in Chicago maintained a separate sales force to service Field's, Carson's, and other downtown department stores.

Nevertheless, the new mass merchandisers clearly worried traditional hardware retailers and wholesalers. Retail dealers began forming state hardware associations just before the turn of the century. The earliest association resolutions emphasized the threat from catalogue supply houses and department stores and urged member retailers to compete by upgrading their stores, improving the lighting and fixtures, and installing systematic bookkeeping and accounting practices. With twelve state associations already in existence, a National Retail Hardware Association organized in 1900 to pursue the same ends. In 1902, fifty-one hardware wholesalers, under the leadership of E.C. Simmons from St. Louis, attempted to form a giant hardware buying combine in order to secure lower prices from the manufacturers. This national distribution scheme proved premature and foundered on financial and organizational difficulties. A more modest effort by the NRHA and NWHA in 1904, a joint committee to fight mail order competition, likewise failed. The committee urged manufacturers to boycott Sears and other catalogue houses, but fear of anti-trust action in this era of the trust-buster aborted the effort.

New threats to the traditional manufacturer-wholesaler-retailer nexus appeared in the 1920s when both Ward's and Sears opened retail outlets. In the last two years before the Great Depression settled in, 1928 and 1929, the two mass merchandisers opened 757 retail stores between them. By 1931, retail stores generated more than 51% of Sears total sales volume. Sears' new stores gave equal emphasis to hard lines and soft lines and consciously attempted to draw men and women together in a family shopping experience. Under the leadership of General Robert Wood, Sears had gone further than anyone else in developing a smooth, dependable, low-cost flow of goods from manufacturer to retailer, with no middleman.

Though Sears worried him, the old-line hardware wholesaler, and the traditional hardware stores he supplied, continued to do business in the old way, as if nothing had happened. The depression temporarily slowed the expansion of mass merchandisers and it brought the cost of borrowed money down to 2% or less, so the wholesaler felt little pressure to turn over his inventory more rapidly. Then the artificial shortages of World War II assured high profits for anyone with goods to sell.

Throughout the nearly 100 years of its heyday, old-line hardware wholesaling had proven consistently profitable. Hibbard, Spencer, Bartlett, for example, from the time of its incorporation in 1882, never suffered an unprofitable year, never missed a cash discount from its suppliers, and always paid a dividend. Closely held firms, to be sure, were very closemouthed about their profits and often cried poor all the way to the bank. A marketing professor once summed up this situation perfectly: "A well-run family business doesn't make money. It just keeps breaking even at a higher and higher level."

The hardware industry carried an air of eternity about it. The same old-stock, Anglo-Saxon families dominated, sales figures were closely held secrets but profits remained good, the inventory carried a layer of dust, tried-and-true methods prevailed. There had been changes, to be sure. Salesmen no longer relied on the railroad and horse-drawn buggies to visit the trade, but made their rounds by automobile. Newer warehouses, such as the plant Hibbard's constructed on North Water Street in 1926, bristled with conveyor belts, chutes, oversize elevators, and pneumatic tubes to speed orders on their way. Color and style had invaded the drab world of kitchen utensils, transforming them into modern housewares. Well-known brands and national advertising did much of the salesman's work for him, turning him into more of an order-taker and less of a salesman. Still, nothing fundamental seemed to have altered. When critics recited the threat from Sears and Ward's, the tycoons and pundits of the trade replied, "We've heard it all before," and then quoted Saunders Norvell's reassuring phrase (at the head of this chapter): "The jobber still exists, and is still doing business at the old stand."

Wide-awake wholesalers realized that high overhead costs threatened their long-range prospects, but few did anything about it. In 1934, Ray Higgins, a shrewd, tough credit manager who had worked his way up to general manager of Kelley-How-Thomson in Duluth, had a brainstorm. He refurbished several baggage cars and filled them with merchandise displays, then sent his "Hardware Train of Progress" on a 1300 mile tour of 29 towns in Minnesota, Wisconsin, the Dakotas, and Montana. The Hardware Train's encore tour in 1935 covered 3800 miles. Higgins considered this train the promotional event of the century and circulated a glossy brochure describing it to every wholesaler in the country. Shannon Crandall, president of California Hardware, a courtly gentleman right out of the previous century, who always dressed in a black string tie and a wing collar, wrote back to Higgins:

"The train is nice. But what we really should be worrying about in this industry is how to get our damn costs down. Some of the younger people are going to do it, and when they do I don't want to be in the business any longer."

Higgins exploded, and never did see the point; but Crandall was right. One of the younger men who would take heed and change the industry was Higgins' young housewares buyer, John Cotter.

CHAPTER TWO
AN
APPRENTICESHIP
IN HARDWARE

"I think I was blessed with the ability to see when a change was necessary."
—John Cotter

Twenty-nine years old when the Hardware Train of Progress first rolled out of Duluth, John Cotter had grown up in the seemingly eternal world of hardware. Nearly fifteen more years would pass before he found and applied the formula for low-cost distribution which would rock the wholesale hardware industry on its foundations. But in the meantime, he served a full apprenticeship in all phases of the hardware trade, retail and wholesale; and, just as important, he got to know a wide range of hardware people.

BOYHOOD IN ST. PAUL

John Matthew Cotter was born in St. Paul, Minnesota on July 8, 1904. His father, Daniel Joseph Cotter, had emigrated from County Cork, Ireland as a young man. Landing in Boston in 1881, he came west by rail to stay with a friend by the name of Barry in Dubuque, Iowa. He hired out for a time as a farmhand near the little town of Farley, Iowa; then, as so many Irish immigrants did, he went to work for a railroad contractor, grading roadbeds. One of his biggest jobs, the construction of the Chicago and Eastern Illinois R.R. from Chicago to Danville, helped him survive the depression of 1893.

One day at a country dance back in Farley, Daniel Cotter met Mary Agnes Garrigan, one of six children born in the U.S. of Irish immigrant parents. The young couple fell in love, but immediate marriage was out of the question for neither had any money. Mary Agnes left the farm and headed north to St. Paul to find work as a domestic, joining a girlfriend who had landed a position with the family of Mr. Bunn, general counsel for the Northern Pacific Railroad. Mary Agnes became cook for the family, and Daniel followed her to St. Paul. The couple married at the relatively late ages of 35 or 36 (there are some discrepancies surrounding their birthdates) on April 27, 1897. Mary Agnes gave birth to a daughter, Julia Mary, in May, 1899; but Julia died three years later of what the doctors called "summer complaint." The grieving mother bore a second child, John Matthew, in 1904.

"We were always well-fed and well-clothed," John Cotter recalls of his boyhood. "I never saw a bill collector at our house." Nevertheless, the Cotter family's origins were very humble. Census records reveal that in 1900 Daniel and Mary Cotter and their infant daughter, Julia, shared one-half of a rented duplex at 909 Fauquier St. (now named Bush St.) with another family, Thomas and Margaret Cullen, their one-year old son, a seventy-two year old mother-in-law, and one boarder — eight people in all in the household. A family with six children occupied the other half of the house. The census lists Daniel Cotter's occupation in 1900 simply as "contractor (grading)." Ten years later, the family's fortunes had advanced considerably. In 1910 the Cotters still lodged one boarder, but they owned their own house at 919 Fauquier, free of any mortgages. Daniel had found steady construction work with the St. Paul City Railway (streetcar company); when the company named him foreman, he sold his team of horses and remained with this job until he retired on a pension in 1930.

"My father was an opinionated tough Irishman who got off the streetcar after work, went to the saloon and had a couple of schnapps before he came home," John Cotter recalls. His mother ran the house with "no fear of soap and water" and with the deft, efficient touch of a born manager. "Hell, my mother could make a dollar go farther than any two people I ever saw in my life." In short, the Cotter family can best be described as working-class by origin and income, but middle-class by aspiration and behavior.

Dayton's Bluff, the area of east St. Paul where the Cotters lived, must have seemed more like a small town in some ways than a big city. Daniel Cotter had chosen the lightly-settled, industrial area, down near the Northwestern railroad tracks, because the city allowed him to keep his horses there in a barn behind the house. He had sold the horses shortly after John came along, but the family still kept almost one hundred chickens and John remembers doing the sort of chores he might have done if he had grown up on a farm. "I had to bring in the wood and feed the chickens and clean out the damn chicken coop on Saturdays. That was the worst job I ever had. I hated it." John also sold eggs house to house for 10¢ a dozen.

The neighborhood was more German than Irish. The 1910 census listed fifteen families on the Cotters' block of Fauquier St. — 6 German, 5 Swedish, 2 Irish, 1 English, and 1 New England Yankee. Only three families, including the Cotters, owned their own house; typical occupations were "foreman in an ice house," "driver for a wholesale house," "laborer in a brewery," and "carpenter in a factory." The 3-M company built a factory just around the corner on Forest St., and numerous small shops and factories dotted the area. The Cotters worshipped at St. John's Catholic Church, a few blocks away in the more Irish end of Dayton's Bluff; the Germans went to Sacred Heart Catholic Church or one of several Lutheran congregations. John attended St. John's parochial grammar school (he remembers the tuition was 50¢ per month) and, later, Cretin Catholic High School, conducted by the Christian Brothers at 6th and Main, in downtown St. Paul.

As a boy, John Cotter was "always a stringbean, who didn't weigh nothing, and had to walk twice to make a shadow." And he was sickly. His mother suffered from a "bilious stomach," and the family assumed John had inherited this condition from her. Every six weeks or so he got terribly sick, threw up green bile, and felt like he was going to die. In between, he felt OK, but he never could put on any weight. Years later, as an adult, he suffered an acute attack of appendicitis; and when the doctors operated on him they found that his appendix had been the culprit all along. His appendix was porous and had been leaking poison which accumulated every six weeks or so, thus making him ill. His bilious condition disappeared after his appendectomy (at age 34).

John was always mechanically inclined, a "closet engineer" one of his sons calls him, fascinated by automobiles and machines; and he spent much of his free time hanging around the blacksmith's or one of the machine shops in the neighborhood. Late in the summer of 1916, when he was twelve years old, he happened to be in Dayton's Bluff Hardware at 967 E. 7th St., about a block away from his house. He noticed several pieces of change lying loose on a shelf and brought the money to the attention of the store manager, Harold Chamberlain. "You ought to put it in a safe place," he said. Chamberlain apparently was impressed by the boy's honesty, for two months later he offered him a part-time job after school, starting at a dollar a week. This story sounds almost too good to be true, recalling, as it does, Honest Abe Lincoln clerking in a store at New Salem and hiking a mile or two to return a widow's change. Cotter swears to its truth, though, and he has the ledger from Dayton's Bluff Hardware to document it. Mr. Chamberlain paid him his first week's wages on October 21, 1916. He has been in hardware for all of the seventy years since then.

Dayton's Bluff Hardware was owned by the Groetsch family, Ger-

man hardware people from Henderson, Minnesota. Harold Chamberlain, Mr. Groetsch's son-in-law, ran the store. John Cotter remembers:
"I would go up there in the morning and start the furnace, then sweep out one aisle, and when Mr. Chamberlain would get there, I'd go to school. They gave me a key to the store, after the first week, so I could open up — imagine a twelve year old with a key to the store. After school I worked until about six every day."
"I'll never forget the first Christmas I was there. Mr. Chamberlain said, 'Now, what do you want for Christmas? You can have anything in the store.' I took a pocket knife. Then he said, 'You got to have more than that.' So I took a pair of skates. But he still insisted I take something else, so I took a hockey stick too. When I got home, my parents thought I stole all that stuff."

The twelve-year-old's ardor for hardware soon cooled, however, and long about February he got tired and quit. But he found that he soon missed the $2.50 a week that Chamberlain had been paying by then. Now if he wanted to buy an ice cream cone or go to a movie, he had to ask his mother for money. So after about six weeks he casually sauntered by Dayton's Bluff Hardware Store. Harold Chamberlain spotted him and asked: "John, would you like to come back here and work for me again?" He readily agreed. John Cotter had found the best incentive for work — to be financially independent. He and three or four other local boys formed the neighborhood elite. John Sullivan and George Schafer worked in drugstores, Pierre Herrmann in his father's haberdashery, and John Cotter at Dayton's Bluff Hardware — they all had their own money.

John worked at the hardware store during 7th and 8th grades and all through high school. He did everything in the store except pay the bills, "the boss always wrote the checks." Without knowing it, he was receiving a grassroots, from-the-ground-up education in the hardware business; and he was making good money for a teenager. At Cretin High School, many of the students worked after school, mainly as errand boys in downtown banks and offices. One day the principal conducted an informal survey of the students' earnings. Most boys raised their hands when he got to $3 a week; a few waited until he said 4 or 5 dollars. Then, the principal barked, "Cotter, you're working, why haven't you raised your hand?" John replied, "Because you didn't name the figure yet." He was earning $7 a week. Still, he had no thought of making hardware his career. Many tasks at the store were dirty and tedious. He particularly hated threading pipe, before electric thread cutters, replacing window glass, and polishing stoves. "We had ten or twelve wood stoves we took out of houses in the spring and stored in the basement. In the fall we cleaned and polished them, put in new mica windows (I've got scars all over my hands to prove it), then helped deliver them." At times like that he thought, "Anything but hardware."

He would have liked to go to St. Thomas College in St. Paul, but his family did not have the money to send him. He showed an aptitude for drawing and had taken some commercial illustration courses in high school, but he found no outlet for this talent. When he looked around for jobs at 3-M or other factories in the area, they offered him less than he was making at the hardware store. So he stayed on full-time at Dayton's Bluff Hardware for a year after high school. The Groetsch family, meanwhile, had sold the store to another German, Mr. Adolph Blazing, a grouchy bachelor, who rarely talked to the customers or to him. John realized that Blazing might well run the store out of business; and besides, he felt he had outgrown the job. What Blazing needed was another young boy, like he had once been. It was time for him to move on.

All in all, John Cotter enjoyed a pretty ordinary childhood for a son of immigrant, working-class parents at the turn-of-the-century. He learned the value of money and the necessity of working hard to earn it. He savored the ordinary joys of boyhood and suffered the usual small humiliations, the latter occasionally intensified by his sickliness and by the fact that he was the "dumb Irish kid" in a German neighborhood. He learned to keep his religion and ethnicity private: "Sure, you didn't go around professing the fact you were a Catholic. You kept your mouth shut. . . You didn't have a big Shriner pin on, or a K.C. pin, or a ring, or anything else. You kept your private life to yourself." The only psychological hint of his later ambition and drive for success lies in a comparison between John and his older sister, Julia, who died at age three, before he was born. As John tells the story: "Julia was the smart one, I was the dumb one. She could read the signboards when she was three. Mother wanted another girl. She wanted another Julia.'' Perhaps it's not too Freudian to suspect that John Cotter tried a little harder in order to compete with his dead sister's memory for his mother's esteem and affection.

ST. PAUL'S LARGEST HARDWARE STORE

Raymer's Hardware, St. Paul's largest hardware store, hired John Cotter as a salesclerk in the sporting goods department in 1923. His first day on the job, the man breaking him in complained that this was the toughest department in the store because the clerk spent so much time assembling merchandise he had little time left to sell. Coaster wagons were hot sellers, the store sold at least 3 or 4 a day, but they took forever to assemble. When he got to the storeroom, Cotter saw why — the only tools in sight were a hammer and a pair of pliers. Now, he knew how to put together a coaster wagon, the German had showed him how at Dayton's Bluff. So he hunted up some proper tools — a drift punch to line up the bolt hole, socket wrenches of various sizes and a spinner handle — and got to work. It took him only 30 minutes to assemble each wagon, and he got back on the sales floor by 9:30 that morning. He was on his way.

He "built a good sales book" at Raymer's, working from 7:30 AM to 6:00 PM, often waiting on 100 or more customers a day, six days a week. He eventually became the No. 2 salesman in the store in volume of sales. He also found an outlet for his artistic abilities, moonlighting as window trimmer in the evenings. He did not consider Raymer's window displays very imaginative, so he often took a 10¢ streetcar ride on Sundays to get ideas from the windows at Warner's Hardware in downtown Minneapolis. By the time he finished at Raymer's five years later, he was earning $125 per month in salary and $25 more for window-trimming. He paid for his first car, a 1926 Chevy, out of window trim earnings.

Raymer's offered him a promotion to housewares department manager, but Cotter turned it down since he didn't feel he knew enough about housewares. The store then hired W. C. "Bill" Hoffmann, a former housewares buyer for a St. Paul department store, who had been let go due to personal problems. Showing him around the first day, Cotter discovered that Hoffmann knew his business, so he asked to be assigned as his assistant. Bill Hoffmann was John Cotter's first real mentor and teacher, and something of a father figure. Hoffmann widened the younger man's horizons, took him to meetings and trade shows, exposed him to the latest ideas in merchandising, and convinced him that "in this business you can make a better living than working by the week." For the first time, perhaps, Cotter started thinking of hardware as a lifetime career.

Bill Hoffmann also introduced John to his future wife. Cotter states it very matter-of-factly: "We needed a cashier and Alice walked in and got the job. I went down there, and she was there, and he (Hoffmann) said, 'This is Alice Germain.' She was sitting there cashiering, and my desk was over here next to hers, and that was that." Alice Germain came from a French Canadian farm family in Somerset, Wisconsin, about 30 miles outside St. Paul. After finishing high school and clerking in a Somerset store for a while, she went to work at Raymer's in 1926. John Cotter impressed her as "light-hearted and full of fun and endowed with a tremendous amount of surplus energy. He was always in some kind of contest with the other salespeople to see who could sell the most." John and Alice dated for nearly six years before marrying in 1932.

In the meantime, Cotter had been keeping his eyes open and thinking about the future of the hardware business. The same wholesale salesmen who had sold to Dayton's Bluff also called on Raymer's — they were mostly from Janney, Semple, Hill; Farwell, Ozmun, Kirk; and Hackett, Gates, Hurty in the Twin Cities. But they usually knocked 10% off the price for Raymer's, and other large accounts. "I got to thinking," Cotter says, "that ain't fair that my little neighborhood hardware store always paid 10% more than Raymer's." Cotter filed this discovery away for future reference; many years later, he found a way to right the balance and help the average hardware dealer get a better price.

He also saw new competition coming into the Twin Cities. "Montgomery Ward opened a store in St. Paul and they did an enormous hardware and paint business. And then the variety chains — Newberry and Woolworth's — they came in with a pretty good selection of housewares. And Western Auto started up, and they branched out into tools. The last year I was at Raymer's they put me in charge of the tool department, and I told them 'You're trying to get too much margin; Ward's is killing us.' ' '

Cotter was also thinking about his immediate future. He made good money at Raymer's, but he saw little prospect of advancement. Three Raymer sons and two long-time employees blocked any high-level management promotions. Besides, he wasn't sure Raymer's could meet the new competition and stay in business much longer. Then, when his doctor suggested that outside work might improve his bilious stomach, he made up his mind to look for a job as a travelling salesman for a wholesale house.

ON THE ROAD

Cotter wanted to get out on the road, but he also wanted to stay near St. Paul so he could "protect his territory" with Alice on weekends. He knew the youngest salesman with any wholesale house would get sent to the boondocks, so he didn't apply to any of the Twin Cities firms. Instead, he talked to a salesman-friend of his, H. T. McDonald, who travelled for Kelley-How-Thomson of Duluth, and got a job with them. He asked for and was assigned to the Eau Claire, Wisconsin territory, starting in June, 1928. Eau Claire lay at the southern fringe of Kelley-How's selling range, but it was only 80 miles from St. Paul. John could live at home with his parents on weekends and see Alice on Friday, Saturday, and Sunday nights. He went out on Monday mornings and visited the cities of Eau Claire and Menominee every week, swinging around to smaller towns such as River Falls, Durand, Neillsville, and Black River Falls every two weeks. He came home Friday evening. Three or four times a year he had to drive 160 miles to Duluth on Saturdays for meetings with the department managers, but he always got back for a date with Alice on Saturday night. The specialty salesmen who sometimes travelled with him said he had the cleanest car of any salesman. He cleaned it before his date every Friday.

Kelley-How-Thomson was a middle-sized, regional hardware wholesaler, travelling about 60 salesmen throughout the 9th Federal Reserve District — northern Wisconsin, the upper peninsula of Michigan, Minnesota, the Dakotas, and Montana. Marshall-Wells, the dominant wholesaler in Duluth and one of the largest hardware wholesalers in the country, had encouraged Messrs. Kelley, How, and Thomson to come together in 1899, thus forestalling a possible entry into the area by Simmons or one of the other larger firms. Kelley had started a blacksmith supply company previously, How was a hardware store owner from Sauk City, Minnesota, and the real merchandising dynamo of the partnership, and Thomson the finance man. By the time John Cotter joined the company, the original partners had all died; Ray W. Higgins ran the house as general manager and George Taylor supervised the salesmen as sales manager.

Kelley-How specialized in logging and mining supplies for the Mesabi Iron Range and specialty consumer items, such as stoves, refrigerators, and electrical appliances. Cotter travelled one of their worst territories and could not compete with wholesalers from Wisconsin, the Twin Cities, or Chicago because of the freight differential. Merchandise had to be shipped by rail to Duluth, then back again to the customer around Eau Claire, raising the price prohibitively. Furthermore, as a rookie salesman, Cotter did not enjoy the privilege of cutting prices and making his own deals. Kelley-How did, however, have good lines of radios, stoves, and other specialties, so Cotter took advantage of this and made himself a self-appointed specialty salesman. Sometimes he didn't even bring his big catalogue with him into a store, but just his specialty brochures. Cotter sold a lot of Philco radios his first year on the road; one retailer in Eau Claire bought 150 of the big floor model Philcos from him. Cotter says it was the "first easy money he ever made."

A monthly sales report for October, 1929 shows that John Cotter sold $10,632 worth of goods that month, $7,817 of it in the electrical department. He sold only $86 worth of general hardware and $50 of builders' hardware. George Taylor, his sales manager, wrote him: "Your total volume to date shows a wonderfully nice increase over last year, which pleases all of us... While your increased sales in Radio brings your total well over last year's sales, I am worried because of your loss of sales in some of the other departments... After all we are hardware jobbers and for you to allow a falling behind in your general sales is a very dangerous thing to do. Watch this closely, John." Cotter replied from the Durand Hotel, in Durand, Wisconsin ("Steam Heated and Electric Lighted—First Class Commercial Hotel" — $2.50 per night) in a neatly handwritten note: "I am going to make a real try to show a good total increase and not a loss in a single Dept."

Thanks largely to Philco radios, Cotter won a sales contest his first six months on the road, earning a $600 bonus on top of his $175 per month salary. His father, who probably never earned $100 per month in his life, thought John had it pretty soft and said "the company has spoiled you, you'll never be any good for anything else." The Great Depression settled in, however, Kelley-How-Thomson lost the Philco radio line, and sales came hard on every territory. Cotter recalls that his most consistent customers were the county highway shops. He sold them lots of shovels, tools, belts, and chains; and they always wanted the best quality goods. "I didn't bribe anybody," he says. "Hell, I didn't know enough to do that. But if a guy wanted something for his home, I damn well took care of him."

After three years on the road, John Cotter decided he wanted to settle down and get married. He had proven he could sell; but constant travelling had not improved his health, and he found that carrying the massive hardware catalogue had permanently lengthened his right arm by ½ inch. So, like many commercial travellers before him, he went into partnership in a retail hardware store. Armin Kohlhepp, one of his better retail accounts in Eau Claire, had been badgering him for some time to join him. When Kohlhepp offered him a partnership in the store for no capital investment, Cotter resigned from Kelley-How-Thomson in March, 1931. He threw himself like a whirlwind into the store, completely refurbishing it and upgrading the fixtures and the merchandise. He continued to handle a few sales accounts for Kelley-How in the Eau Claire area, and for about a year he also cut a deal with Hibbard, Spencer, Bartlett in Chicago. In return for writing his own orders on merchandise purchased from Hibbard's, he received a salesman's commission (in effect, a rebate or cut price for the store, much like at Raymer's). In order to justify the deal, Hibbard's asked him to drum up additional business in the area in his spare time. He never had any spare time, so less than a year later Hibbard's cancelled the arrangement.

On May 24, 1932, John Cotter married Alice Germain in Alice's home town of Somerset. They rented a small house near the store in Eau Claire for $30 a month. Shortly thereafter, John's father, who had been retired about two years, died of cancer on October 23, 1932, and John's mother came to live with them in Eau Claire. The Depression was sinking down to its lowest point, and Cotter and Kohlhepp reduced their own salaries at the store to $40 per week each. But they managed to stay in business. John and Alice "always had a Ford, in good condition, always had good tires on it, always took a vacation, and even came down to the Chicago World's Fair." They survived the Depression.

FIRST COUSIN TO GOD

George Taylor, sales manager at Kelley-How-Thomson, had kept in touch with Cotter while he was at Kohlhepp's in Eau Claire. In 1933, Taylor's boss, Ray Higgins, decided to ease out his housewares buyer who had let his department become the orphan of the house. Taylor prompted Higgins that the young man "who had been a salesman on one of their worst territories and managed to survive" might be just the man to inject some life into housewares. On November 1, Higgins wired Cotter "Going Through Your Town Four Today Like To See You." That afternoon, he pulled up in front of Kohlhepp's in his chauffeured Lincoln, poked around the store a bit, and must have liked what he saw; for he offered John the job.

Cotter was flattered. As clerk, salesman, and hardware retailer, he had always thought a "wholesale hardware buyer and God were first cousins." But he kept his wits about him and interrogated Higgins on the ground rules before he accepted. Higgins said he would like a 10% annual growth in the housewares department and a profit margin of 20%. Cotter asked if he could run things his own way, set some specials and cut prices, just so long as average margin worked out to 20%.

Higgins agreed. Then he asked about turnover. Higgins said not to worry too much about turnover since he could borrow all the money he needed in New York at 2%. Cotter accepted the job, beginning in December, 1933.

He arrived in Duluth just in time to help put the finishing touches on Higgins' beloved Hardware Train of Progress. More importantly for him, he had to generate some activity in his housewares department. He had learned something about human nature out on the road and in his store, about the need for personal attention, so he wrote all 60 salesmen a personally signed letter introducing himself and asking for their suggestions. In his own mind, the needs of the department seemed obvious — "It was a case of getting competitive on price."

He put together an assortment of nine enamel kitchenware utensils to retail for 69¢. This was the first real housewares special Kelley-How's salesmen had to push in years. Cotter bought a carload of enamelware, with an option for another car; they eventually moved six carloads. He put out other specials, convinced manufacturers to take back poor selling items that were clogging up the warehouse if he agreed to buy 2 or 3 times as many good sellers from them. "I got turnover, I got margin, I got activity," Cotter recalls, "and when I made mistakes, which I did, I got rid of them quick." Instead of the ten percent growth Higgins had set as a target, Cotter doubled housewares sales in his first year.

Three years after Cotter came to Duluth, Ray Higgins and George Taylor fell out and Higgins fired Taylor. The stove buyer, a cadaverous fellow named I. W. "Inky" Wold, moved up to sales manager; and Cotter took over the stove department in addition to housewares. Then after three more years, in 1939, Higgins created a new position of head buyer, or merchandise manager, and leapfrogged the 35-year-old Cotter over nine other buyers, eight of whom where old enough to be his father. Needless to say, this made him, in his own words, "as popular as a skunk at a Sunday picnic."

For the first time, now, John Cotter faced the problem of high costs in wholesaling head-on. Many factors contributed to high overhead — the care and feeding of sixty salesmen, too many bad credit risks among the retail accounts, overstocking and low turnover in the warehouse, repacking and other costly services on small orders. As merchandise manager, the only one he could do much about was overstocking. So, with the help of Ed Lanctot, who had joined Kelley-How right out of high school in 1936 and was now assigned as Cotter's clerk, he started to whittle down the 68,000 item inventory. Overstocking had many causes. The wholesale house had plenty of warehouse space, money was cheap, and few were concerned. Cotter recalled that during his whole tenure as housewares buyer, he never ordered a single "hank" of clothesline. His predecessor had purchased a lot just before the Depression; when cotton prices sagged, he bought more in order to average his costs lower; when the price continued down, he bought even more. Salesmen, too, added to the problem. They wanted their house "to stock every item that ever sold anywhere,'' so they would never be caught unable to fill a retailer's order. As a result, merchandise piled up in the warehouse. Cotter and Lanctot pared the stock down to about 40,000 items, but other elements of high cost escaped their control.

When he was named head buyer, Cotter bought a six room red brick house in a pleasantly wooded area at 1421 Vermillion Road in Duluth. John and Alice had begun to have children — Dan arrived in December, 1934, Mary in July, 1939; Patricia would come along in June, 1942, then, finally, Michael was born in December, 1944, after the Cotters had left Duluth. In the late 30s, Cotter looked like a fixture in Duluth; and, as a result, Ray Higgins apparently started to take him for granted. Cotter held one of the top three posts at Kelley-How, but he thought he had reached a dead end before he was forty.

Some people cling to the same job for life, enticed by the security; others flit from job to job like a bumblebee in a daisy bed, never finding a permanent home. John Cotter did neither. His father had once advised him that whatever he did with his life, he should stay on any job for five years or else people will think he's a floater. John took this advice; he stayed at Raymer's exactly five years, and at Kelley-How nine years. Yet he also sensed when it was time to move on. He followed no master plan, simply taking on each situation as it came along. But he had an instinctive ability to see when a change was needed, both in his own life and in the hardware business, and the courage to make the change.

When he was working at Dayton's Bluff Hardware after high school and the cantankerous Mr. Blazing took over the store, John told his mother he had to get out of there because Blazing was going to go out of business. She accepted that as reasonable. After five years at Raymer's, he told her they were going to go broke some day too, because they had too many family members to support and they weren't keeping up with the times. She thought he was crazy; Raymer's was the biggest store in St. Paul. Shortly before his mother died in 1936, John told her of his fears that Kelley-How-Thomson might close up. Now she knew he was crazy for sure.

Yet, there were straws in the wind. A CIO union organized the warehouse in the late 30s and Kelley-How took a costly six-week strike. At one point, Higgins threatened to ''turn the key in the door'' and go out of business. That was fine for Higgins, who was independently wealthy, having married a millionaire heiress from Superior, Wisconsin; but Cotter had a growing family to support. Then, when the war broke out, Higgins convinced himself that the wholesale hardware business would shrink away to almost nothing. Finally, after Pearl Harbor, the federal government clamped down controls on all parts of the economy, including a salary freeze.

John Cotter was fed up:

"I wasn't buying the fact that Kelley-How-Thomson was going out of business; I wasn't buying the fact that my salary was frozen. Besides, by then I had become aware that Duluth was not a center of commerce. I was in Chicago every month. They knew me at the Palmer House. And the winters in Duluth were absolutely atrocious. They had terrible springs too. The northeast wind comes off Lake Superior and there's no summer at all until after the Fourth of July."

Fortunately, Red Oakes offered Cotter an alternative, and he had the nerve to take it.

SEARCHING – FOR A BETTER LIFE, AND A BETTER WAY

Lawrence L. "Red" Oakes had started the Tru-Test Marketing & Merchandising Corporation in Chicago in 1936. Red Oakes fit the classic model of an entrepreneur much more than John Cotter did; he was wild, volatile, tossing off an idea a minute. Like many entrepreneurs, he came from a comfortable, even privileged background. Contrary to the popular rags-to-riches myth, entrepreneurs often come from secure, well-to-do families. They need the financial and psychological security in order to take the risks they do. Oakes was born in Kansas to a successful business family in 1894, he played football at the Virginia Military Institute in 1913 and 1914, graduating with the class of 1919 after service in the war. He worked for a time in his father's lumber and hardware business, but then began a series of entrepreneurial ventures and plunges. He started an automotive jobbing house in Oklahoma City, represented several rubber companies in Akron, lost his shirt selling a new kind of rubber-filled golf ball, bounced back to Oklahoma Tire & Supply in Tulsa, then filed for personal bankruptcy in 1933. In 1936, he organized Tru-Test, a pioneering attempt at low-cost hardware wholesaling.

Oakes borrowed the Tru-Test idea from the grocery trade. Small regional wholesalers across the country federated together into a centralized buying and advertising group, each retaining its own independent identity and selling to its traditional accounts, but all enjoying the benefits of volume buying, brand name identification, and national advertising. In Oakes' own words, "We believe if the independent merchant can buy his merchandise on a proper cost factor that because of his independence he can profitably meet any competition provided he is furnished with proper tools advertising-wise." The Independent Grocers Association (IGA) had used this formula with great success to meet chain store competition in the 1920s and 30s. One other central marketing organization, Liberty Distributors, had preceded Oakes' venture in the hardware industry. As it later turned out, wholesalers' federations with voluntary chains of retailers (generally called "merchandising groups" today) proved to be one of the two major proposals for low-cost distribution in hardware.

John Cotter first met Red Oakes when Kelley-How-Thomson joined the Tru-Test group in the late 30s. Oakes couldn't find the right man to manage the basic hardware lines, so he initiated an effort to recruit Duluth's upcoming young merchandise manager. Oakes shrewdly sized up Cotter's situation, writing him on November 3, 1941:

"You have one of the few good jobs left in the hardware business. . .I fully realize it. You also have a family and home to think about. The thing I do see, John, is that you are at the crossroads — you are 37 — and you have 6 or 7 more years to get yourself set where you can go places. People are not taking men over 43 or 45 to build organizations with. . ."

"As I see your problem — whether it is with us or someone else — you are going to have to make up your mind pretty shortly to stick out your chest and get out and make somebody pay for the knowledge and ability you have developed over the last few years. You are not going to get paid for this if you stay in a groove past a certain age."

Cotter didn't jump at the bait immediately. First, he wanted to prove something to his present employer. He convinced Higgins that the hardware trade wouldn't disappear during the war and that they better start stockpiling any goods they could find. "I told Mr. Higgins, you got the shipyards to supply, you got the iron mines to supply, and I don't care what the government says but they got to put the crop in the ground and they got to take it out, so you got to have some tools." Higgins bought a 60,000 sq.ft. building, for $10,000, right next to the existing warehouse. Cotter went out on the road to buy up closeouts and any other merchandise that wasn't nailed down. He started for Minneapolis on a Saturday morning and called up a rep. for a manufacturer of electrical appliances. "John, I'm glad you called," the salesman greeted him. "I've been ordered to report at Ft. Snelling Monday morning. I just got my allotment of appliances in the mail this morning, but the wholesalers in Minneapolis are closed today." Cotter asked him down to the Nicollet Hotel and wrote a hand order for the whole allotment. "The rep didn't give a damn about other wholesalers. He had just gotten his army commission and was leaving."

Cotter moved on to St. Louis, Chicago, Milwaukee, and Cleveland. "For two weeks I bought everything that anyone would sell me," he reports. He bought up a carload of dairy pails with slight defects for $1.20 a dozen, got them painted for 60¢ a dozen, and sold them as wastebaskets. No one else had metal wastebaskets. He filled Higgins' new warehouse with goods, got his wife mad because he missed Good Friday church service at home, but arrived back in Duluth late on Saturday in time for Easter.

Now he thought about himself. "I didn't want my salary froze and that's the reason I left," Cotter told me, pounding the table for emphasis. Oakes offered him a partnership with a $12,000 a year salary, nearly double what he was making with Kelley-How, plus 25% of any profits. By changing jobs and tying his future prospects to profit-sharing, he could beat the government salary controls. Oakes' proposition, however, posed many risks. Oakes had run through 3 or 4 men in this same job in less than six years, and Cotter had no guarantee of lasting any longer. Furthermore, with the war on, the volume of a new buying organization might nosedive and there would be no profits to share. But Cotter wanted to leave Duluth, he wanted a raise, and he knew that even if Tru-Test failed, he would make numerous contacts with the top men at many hardware manufacturers. And, he believed in what Oakes was trying to do. When he signed on at Tru-

Test in December, 1942, he wrote a friend at the Barton Corporation of West Bend, Wisconsin: "When things get back to normal, I am confident that a great deal can be accomplished through this office. As a matter of fact, I firmly believe that it is the only salvation for the distributor and individually-owned dealer."

Tru-Test provided a stimulating atmosphere—Cotter says, "You needed a tin hat" when you went to work, since Oakes bombarded you with so many new ideas. One such idea was a proposal to set up a low-cost hardware wholesaler in Chicago, as a yardstick for the other Tru-Test wholesalers. Oakes and Jules Kirsten, a smooth-talking manufacturer's rep selling rope and cordage from New Orleans, hatched this plan in the mid-40s. They broached the idea separately to John Cotter and to Edmund S. Kantowicz, who was then the buyer of plumbing supplies and heavy hardware at Hibbard, Spencer, Bartlett in Chicago. Both men turned down the offer to jointly manage the new firm, and indeed Cotter and Kantowicz never met at this time, though their fortunes would be intertwined later.

Cotter learned to preach the gospel of low-cost distribution from Red Oakes, and he brought friends into the fold with him. He returned to Duluth in 1944 and convinced Herb Haller, his successor as stove buyer at Kelley-How, to join Tru-Test. When his former-clerk, Ed Lanctot, got out of the service in January, 1946, Cotter made a place for him as well. They did good business after the war, and Cotter's personal financial gamble paid off. In 1946, his last full year with Oakes, he made $38,000.

Yet Tru-Test never quite took off. After Oakes arranged good deals with manufacturers, the individual wholesalers took the low prices and too often didn't pass them on to the retailers. Then, too, the buyers for each wholesaler would use Oakes' deals as benchmarks, bargaining points, and try to beat them elsewhere. "You see," John Cotter explains, "the buyer is trying to protect his domain. He doesn't want to be showed up. If he's got a factory he's working with and you come in with a deal, he's going back to his supplier and say, 'You SOB, you got to meet this.'" Even when the deals went through, Tru-Test took a commission and wholesalers still had to make a profit; so the independent retailer didn't get the best possible price. Gradually, Cotter began to lose faith; Tru-Test did not provide the best formula for low-cost distribution, the best way of keeping the independent retailer competitive.

Red Oakes, himself, eventually lost interest. He struck oil on one of his ventures down in Oklahoma, then in the early 1960s, he folded Tru-Test and devoted the rest of his life to ranching and real estate near Palm Springs, California. To this day, John Cotter has nothing but good to say about Red Oakes. But in 1947 he had finally realized that his apprenticeship was over; and with Oakes' blessing and assistance, he went out on his own. He had found a better way.

CHAPTER THREE
THE DEALER-OWNED COOPERATIVE MOVEMENT

"Our entire cost of selling during 1925 was exactly nine-tenths of one per cent. We did a gross business considerably in excess of $3,000,000, which is the approximate volume that would be brought in under ordinary circumstances by forty high-grade salesmen traveling among the trade. We did it with a catalogue, a weekly bulletin, three development and two specialty salesmen . . . Selling only for cash . . . we spare ourselves the long chain of griefs that come from dealing with the inefficient retailers. Finally, this is a cooperative company, which pays each dealer member his share of its profits, supplying him with plenty of incentive to center his purchases here."
—George E. Hall,
Printer's Ink Monthly (1926)

During the course of his long hardware apprenticeship, John Cotter discovered the dealer-owned cooperative movement the first day he went on the road for Kelley-How-Thomson in June, 1928. This movement had arisen early in the twentieth century as a response by independent retailers to the threat of mail-order houses and price-cutting chain stores.

THE CHAIN STORE CHALLENGE

Independent retailers started fretting when the first Ward's and Sears catalogues sped through the mails. Their worries intensified as chain stores proliferated during the first decades of this century. There were only about 500 chain stores in the whole U.S. at the turn of the century, but this number jumped to well over 37,000 by 1930. Chain stores spread more rapidly in some commodity lines than others. Led by A & P, the oldest chain operation in the country, giant chains handled about 40% of the grocery business in 1930. Woolworth's and its imitators dominated variety retailing, with 90% of total sales. By contrast, chains accounted for only 10% of all hardware stores and 13% of total sales. Still, the mushroom growth of chains terrified all retailers; and new entrants on the scene, such as Western Auto and Coast-to-Coast stores, began encroaching on traditional hardware lines. Frightened store owners viewed this as a battle to the death between "Chain Street and Main Street."

Chains enjoyed inherent price advantages over small retailers due to their huge collective buying power, their ability to average losses over a number of stores, and their elimination of costly wholesaling functions, such as credit departments and salesmen. As an astute observer of chain stores noted: "The wholesaler has to guess what he can sell to retailers; the retailer guesses what he can sell to customers. The chain store system eliminates one of the guesses." In addition, chain stores generally initiated progressive merchandising practices — clean, well lighted stores, easily accessible locations with lots of parking, attractive displays, careful stock control, and rapid turnover. Yet, above all, lower prices, through "loss-leading" specials and overall cost advantages, attracted the customers and posed the greatest threat to other retailers.

Faced with this threat, independent merchants did what free enterprisers always do first; they ran to the government for help. In 1922 the National Association of Retail Grocers yelled "There oughta be a law" to ban or limit chain operations. The state of Maryland actually passed a law in 1927 flatly prohibiting chain stores, but the courts quickly struck it down as unconstitutional. Thereafter, 28 states placed special taxes on multiple unit retailers, hoping to slow their growth if they could not ban them entirely. Two federal statutes in the mid-30s brought the legislative blitz against chains to a climax. The Robinson-Patman Act of 1936 attempted to end the price discrimination which John Cotter had noticed as a young salesclerk at Raymer's. The law forbade manufacturers or wholesalers to grant quantity discounts to large retailers unless these discounts reflected actual cost savings and greater efficiency. The Miller-Tydings Act of 1937 gave a federal blessing to numerous state Fair Trade laws, legalizing price-fixing agreements between manufacturers and retailers. Fair Trade permitted manufacturers of national brands to sign minimum price maintenance agreements with the leading retailers and enforce them against other retailers who didn't sign.

All of these legislative remedies proved slippery to enforce and easy to evade; they didn't hamper chain operations appreciably or slow price competition. So independent retailers realized they would have to rely on their own efforts. A 1938 book, entitled *The Chain Store Problem*, summed up the situation well: "In order to meet chain store competition local merchants adopted chain store practices in the conduct of their own business... This is probably the most notable contribution of the chains — the awakening of the independent merchant from his lethargy." The history of American merchandising since then chronicles the struggle of retailers to act like chains without losing their own independence.

Beginning in the 1930s, Red Oakes and a few others tried to link wholesalers together in federations and sponsor voluntary chains of retailers to obtain greater buying and advertising power. A group of upstart hardware retailers in Chicago, under the dynamic and authoritarian leadership of Richard Hesse and Gunnar Lindquist, organized in 1925 a new kind of "lean and mean" wholesale operation, a program wholesaler. Trying to operate as much as possible like Sears, while retaining individual ownership of stores, the group, named Ace Hardware, sold only to dealers "on the program," arranging for direct shipment from factory to store wherever possible, keeping wholesale inventory minimal and overhead low. Some old-line wholesalers, most notably Marshall-Wells and Hibbard, Spencer, Bartlett, tried to follow suit with stores programs of their own; but their high traditional overhead costs made this difficult. A leading manufacturer, the Winchester Repeating Arms Company, also attempted to foster a chain of independently-owned dealer-agencies. In 1919 the firm unveiled the Winchester Stores plan and began manufacturing a select line of hardware items as well as its traditional arms and ammunition. This overly-ambitious plan, however, failed during the Depression. Ultimately, the most creative and most successful response to the chain store challenge came from the dealer-owned cooperative movement.

THE COOPERATIVE IDEA

Though men and women have cooperated together by pooling their resources since the dawn of time, the modern cooperative movement usually traces its origins to the Rochdale experiment in England in 1844. The same sorts of craftsmen and artisans who, earlier in the Industrial Revolution, earned the name of Luddites by smashing the machines which threatened their jobs adopted a more sophisticated approach this time. Hoping to pioneer a "third way," neither socialistic nor capitalistic, the Rochdale artisans came together to purchase supplies for their trades and consumer goods for their families cooperatively. They formulated a set of ten principles which most cooperatives still adhere to today. Three of these Rochdale Principles capture the essence of the cooperative idea: 1) One Man, One Vote — democratic control of coop business; 2) Cash Trading — no credit; 3) Net Margins Distributed to Members According to Patronage — that is, operation at cost with any profits rebated to member-patrons. The standard, modern-day textbook on cooperatives defines a coop as "a business voluntarily organized, operating at cost, which is owned, capitalized and controlled by member-patrons as users, sharing risks and benefits proportional to their participation."

Following Rochdale, both producers' and consumers' cooperatives spread throughout Europe, particularly in England and Scandinavia. The Swedes made coops the foundation of their non-Marxian socialism which is so often admired by liberals in the U.S. today, and northern Europe still leads the world in number of coops per capita. Many Scandinavian immigrants, particularly the Finns, brought the cooperative idea to America with them and organized numerous farm coops in Northern Minnesota, Wisconsin, and upper Michigan.

The first purely American cooperative dates back long before Rochdale, to 1752, when Benjamin Franklin started a mutual insurance company in Philadelphia. For a long time, mutual insurance remained the most common type of cooperative endeavor in the United States. Particularly in steam-powered industries, where the high risks of fire and accidents made commercial companies leery of insuring factories, the factory mutual system flourished. Farmers and other high risk producers followed suit by orgardzing their own mutuals. In the late 19th century, the American cooperative movement became closely identified with farmers and agrarian issues, as the National Grange promoted cooperatives and Scandinavian immigrants perfected them. Congressman Andrew J. Volstead of Minnesota, most famous for his 1919 act prohibiting the sale of alcohol in the U.S., also sponsored the 1922 Capper-Volstead Act, which gave a federal charter to farm cooperatives by exempting them from the anti-trust acts.

Despite the popular identification of coops with prairie farmers, only about 20% of American coops are agricultural; and cooperative enterprise is more widespread today than most people realize. Cooperatively-owned wholesalers supply about 30% of all grocery stores; and producers' coops market many common food items, such as Diamond Walnuts, Sunkist oranges, and Land-O-Lakes dairy products. Mutuals ensure about one-third of American autos; the American Automobile Association (AAA), which helps guide and service those autos, is also a cooperative. Many small town Americans owe their electric power to the Rural Electrification Administration (REA), a government-sponsored cooperative; and significant numbers of Americans keep their money in credit unions. Economists point out that, even when cooperatives don't dominate in their product line (and they rarely do), they tend to ''discipline the markets'' they compete in. That is, cooperative enterprises operating at cost serve as yardsticks in a capitalist economy, meeting or beating their profit-making competitors' prices, keeping them honest, and benefitting all consumers.

The first hardware merchants who forged a cooperative response to mail-order and chain-store competition, probably didn't know most of this history and economics, and they may have never heard of Rochdale. But they certainly knew about mutual insurance. Like steam-powered factories or combustible lumberyards, hardware stores suffered from specialized fire risks which made it hard for their owners to buy insurance. Since they sold paint, linseed oil, and turpentine, hardware dealers paid excessive premiums to commercial insurance companies. In April, 1897, a group of hardware dealers in the Upper Midwest, led by Charles F. Ladner of St. Cloud, Minnesota, organized the Minnesota Retail Hardware Association and began discussing their insurance problems. Two years later, on May 25, 1899, they chartered the first hardware mutual, the Retail Hardware Dealers Mutual Fire Insurance Company (now called American Hardware Mutual). Two other mutual insurance societies for hardwaremen soon organized in the same geographic area, one at Stevens Point, Wisconsn and another in Owatonna, Minnesota. The hardware mutuals, then, furnished a key model for the first cooperative experiments in hardware merchandising. (Similar trends had earlier led to coop experiments in the wholesale grocery trade. The Frankford Grocery of Philadelphia, organized in 1888, is generally credited as the oldest grocery cooperative in the U.S.)

Some hardware retailers expressed a sense of urgency. George Hall, who helped organize the first successful dealer-owned group, recalled in a 1929 magazine article:

"About 20 hardware retailers attended the meeting. The discussion grew heated. All were in accord in denouncing the new form of competition. They agreed that something had to be done quickly to prevent the independent dealer from being driven out of business... 'They're able to get much lower prices because they place big orders and buy direct. To get our business back we've got to meet their prices, and we can't do it as long as we buy individually from jobbers. So we must get together, pool our orders, and go direct to the manufacturers and demand their lowest prices.'"

The old manufacturer-to-wholesaler-to-retailer system had become increasingly costly and inefficient. Dealers spent too much time talking to travelling salesmen and wound up overstocked in the process. A 1930 survey of 85 Wisconsin hardware dealers revealed that they stocked 35 different brands of parlor furnaces, 32 different brands of basement furnaces, 26 brands of paint, and 17 lines of washing machines. Seventy-six jobbing salesmen made regular calls on these dealers.

Dealer-ownership of a wholesale house, with dealers writing their own orders, thus dispensing with salesmen, paying promptly and keeping their overhead low, promised to remedy these problems.

THE FIRST DEALER-OWNED HARDWARE WHOLESALERS

No one knows for sure who organized the first dealer-owned hardware wholesale house. The earliest recorded hardware cooperative group was the Franklin Hardware Co. of Philadelphia, organized in 1906; but this informal buying club most probably did not operate its own warehouse facilities and function as a complete wholesale operation until much later. The oldest, fully-functioning cooperative wholesalers, then, were American Hardware & Supply Co., founded in Pittsburgh in 1910, the Hardware Merchants Syndicate (later renamed Southwest Hardware Co.) organized in Los Angeles in 1912, closely followed by the Hall Hardware Co. (now known as Our Own) of Minneapolis in 1913.

Retailer-owned cooperatives did not catch on as quickly in the hardware trade as they did in groceries. The early appearance of A & P and other grocery chains, as well as the traditionally low margins of the grocery trade, put a more severe squeeze on grocery store profits demanding a swifter response. In the early 1930s, the Federal Trade Commission, making a wide-ranging inquiry into chain stores and their competitors, sent questionnaires "to 15 hardware organizations that were supposed to have cooperative features. Of this number, six returned completed schedules while another six reported they had no cooperative features." In addition to the four wholesalers just mentioned, the other two dealer-owned houses active in the 1920's were Northern Hardware Co., founded in Portland, Oregon in 1923, and Wisconsin Hardware Co., organized at Madison, Wisconsin in 1925. Pioneers of dealer-ownership, then, had organized hardware wholesale coops on both coasts and in the Midwest by the time of the stock market crash. Only one of these firms, however, Hall Hardware Co. of Minneapolis, flourished in the early days, whereas most others floundered.

The early dealer-owned cooperatives all seemed to follow a standard script. Usually, one or two strong dealers took the initiative and pulled the first organization together. In Pittsburgh, for instance, Charles W. "Uncle Charlie" Scarborough provided the push, serving as president of American Hardware until his death in 1949 at age 87. In Minnesota, Charles Ladner and Amos Marckel took the lead. These energetic dealers, however, had no wholesale experience; so they, reluctantly, hired a full time general manager to run the operation. Since the whole purpose of the coop was to cut costs, the retailers usually did not pay well enough to secure competent managerial talent. As a result, all the early dealer-owned houses suffered a crisis of leadership and flirted with bankruptcy. Wisco at Madison, for instance, had been organized primarily by farm implement dealers; so a salesman from Moline Implement Manufacturing Co. hired on as first manager. A 1929 audit of the books discovered that the company had a negative net worth, so the manager was dismissed. John A. Fitschen, a former employee of Hall Hardware, who had handled Wisco's sales promotions and advertising since 1927, took over as general manager. Fitschen held off the creditors until the firm showed a profit, then guided Wisco until its dissolution nearly fifty years later. Similarly, Harry F. Izenour took over at Southwest Hardware in 1932 and put them on a firm financial footing, William Stout turned around American Hardware in 1933, and F. Leon Herron, Sr. reinvigorated Franklin of Philadelphia in 1939.

Inadequate financing hampered nearly all the early cooperatives. Dealer-members wanted to cut corners everywhere, do everything on the cheap, and immediately rebate all wholesale profits back to themselves. As John Cotter explains: "The theory was to get the merchandise to the dealer on a low-cost basis, but there was no thought of perpetuation, no thought of building a company structure, a financial institution." The second generation of general managers — Stout, Izenour, Fitschen, Herron — had to convince retailers to reinvest wholesale profits in order to buy a wider selection of merchandise, expand the advertising, and increase business.

Besides the problems of inadequate management, too little capital accumulation, and too much interference by dealer-members, early dealer-owned hardware wholesalers faced fierce opposition from the old-line wholesalers and the National Wholesale Hardware Association. Some of this they brought upon themselves by billing well-known brand merchandise at lower-than-usual prices to their dealers, thus earning a reputation as price-cutters, discounters, and disrupters of the market. The traditional hardware industry treated coops the way it did other new entrants into the marketplace — as enemies. Under pressure from old-line wholesalers who sold goods at a standard price, many manufacturers refused to sell to the cooperative wholesalers. Consequently, they often sold the lines of merchandise that other wholesalers rejected, and they could not service their members as a complete source of supply.

With the exception of one firm, Hall Hardware in Minnesota, the dealer-owned hardware wholesaler made little progress before World War II. The last time the U.S. Census of Business enumerated dealer-owned cooperatives separately from other wholesalers, in 1939, the handful of coops recorded less than $9 million annual sales for a 1.7% share of total wholesale hardware sales. Hall Hardware alone did more than half of this total volume. (Unfortunately, the Census Bureau stopped recording hardware coop sales just before they became an important part of the industry. The periodic business censuses still record grocery cooperative sales separately, but not hardware or drugs.)

GEORGE E. HALL AND OUR OWN HARDWARE

In the early summer of 1913, George E. Hall of Fargo, North Dakota was nearly 50 years old and out of a job. Hall-Robertson hardware wholesalers of Fargo had failed and Hall owed several thousand dollars to creditors. He applied for the sales manager's position at Kelley-How-Thomson in Duluth; but, since he was requesting a $5000 annual salary, they refused to hire him. John Cotter recalls that years later this became a standing joke: "Kelley-How would have been better off to pay him $5000 a year, give him an office, and tell him to go fishing." Duluth's loss was the hardware world's gain, as Hall went on to help organize and manage the first truly successful dealer-owned hardware wholesale house.

A group of 24 hardware dealers who were active in the Minnesota Retail Hardware Association and the Hardware Mutual Insurance Co. had earlier attempted to start a cooperative. Following the standard script closely, however, the first manager they hired proved unable to coax the company to life. When Amos Marckel, a retailer in Perham, Minnesota over near the North Dakota line, heard that George Hall was available, he suggested to Charles Ladner that they talk to him about making another try. Marckel, Ladner, and a handful of other Minnesota retailers met with Hall at Marckel's summer home on Little Pine Lake, near Perham. Though Hall needed a job, he told the dealers frankly that they couldn't do enough business with only 24 dealers to support a cooperative wholesaler. So Ladner, who was president of Hardware Mutual, assigned one of his insurance salesmen to canvass the state's retailers and increase the number of members to 75 before commencing wholesale business. In the meantime, Hall and six of the dealers incorporated the Hall Hardware Co. on June 25, 1913, with Ladner as president and Hall as general manager. They acquired a sufficient number of dealers and moved into rented quarters in a public warehouse before the end of the year.

Hall gave his name to the legal title of the firm, but early on he and his associates developed the brand name "Our Own" for store identification and advertising purposes in order to emphasize the dealer-ownership feature. (On February 17, 1949, long after Hall's retirement, the firm officially changed its corporate title from Hall Hardware Co. to Our Own Hardware Co.) Hall made little effort to sign up retailers in the Minneapolis-St. Paul area, for his low-cost operation couldn't compete with the quick delivery and many other services the old line wholesalers offered through their city sales departments. Instead, Hall built his base among the small town dealers in places like Wadena, St. Cloud, Perham and Henderson. These country dealers suffered keenly from mail-order competition, and they received little help and no concessions from traditional wholesalers. Members' purchases from their own wholesaler grew from $280,000 in the company's first full year, 1914, to nearly $2,000,000 by 1919. That year, Hall Hardware moved into a new eight story warehouse in northwest Minneapolis, built and owned by the Hall Building Co., a separate publicly-held corporation. The hardware company expanded panded rapidly to over 470 members purchasing $4,185,910 worth of merchandise in 1929.

The 1926 interview with George Hall, quoted at the head of this chapter, accurately summarizes the key elements in Hall Hardware's early success. "Our entire cost of selling during 1925 was exactly nine-tenths of one percent," whereas the industry average for wholesalers who travelled salesmen stood at 5.6% that year. An Our Own dealer wrote his own orders from a merchandise catalogue which Hall issued twice a year. To keep the retailer current on prices and market conditions and supply him with some of the gossip and inside "dope" he used to get from salesmen, the general manager wrote a weekly market letter to all dealer-members. Elimination of travelling salesmen was the crucial economy in the dealer-owned system. Hall sent out three development men to sign up new dealers; they sold the program, not merchandise. He also made two specialty men available to teach dealers and their salesclerks how to sell stoves, washing machines, paint, and other big-ticket items. But these 5 travellers replaced more than 40 necessary to do business in the old high-cost way.

"Selling only for cash (or what amounts to cash, since every dealer buying from us must discount his bill in eight days)" formed another key feature of Our Own's system. By not extending credit, Hall eliminated another level of wasteful expense and stretched the slender capital of the cooperative further. Hall discovered that the discipline of an inflexible, cash-only rule at the wholesale level made dealers better businessmen at the retail level. "The rule has forced them to become good collectors and to be more careful about extending credit to customers who do not deserve it."

"Finally, this is a cooperative company which pays each dealer-member his share of its profits." Our Own dealers truly did own the wholesale house. Each new member paid a $100 membership fee to cover the costs of signing him up, then subscribed for 5 shares of common (voting) stock at $100 each, and 1 share in the Hall Building Co. for an additional $100. No dealer, whether large or small, ever owned more than 5 shares of voting stock, so each member of the cooperative company enjoyed an equal say at stockholders' meetings and in the election of directors. Though voting rights were allocated on the "one man, one vote" principle, year-end profits were distributed in proportion to each dealer's purchases from the coop. In the distribution of profits, however, Hall Hardware's management and directors made a crucial decision which set them apart from the other dealer-owned houses. Charles Ladner's experience with the mutual insurance company had taught him the importance of capital accumulation for a business' survival and expansion; so at his urging, Hall Hardware did not rebate cash to the members each year. Rather, the company issued preferred (non voting) stock, paying an annual 6% dividend, and retained the capital in the firm. This decision to build a firm financial structure, accumulate a capital reserve, and reinvest profits distinguished Our Own Hardware from the struggling dealer-owned coops.

Hall Hardware pioneered many other features of the developing dealer-owned system. Since most dealers attended the yearly convention of the Minnesota Retail Hardware Association in St. Paul or Minneapolis each February, Hall decided to set up hardware displays at the same time at the warehouse, allowing Our Own's members to view the latest goods, pick up more information, and facilitate their order-writing. These annual displays developed into the first wholesaler-sponsored merchandise shows in the industry. In 1922, Hall instituted a store modernization service to give members competent, experienced assistance in planning store displays, remodeling store fixtures, and making the independent's store as attractive as the new chain outlets. He also encouraged member stores to hang Our Own Hardware signs outside, giving the appearance of a chain; but many members resisted this. Then, in 1933, Our Own began distributing advertising catalogues or circulars which the retailer could mail out to his customers — the first direct-mail advertising program in the industry. Reportedly, George Hall had come up with this idea in a long brainstorming session with Rivers Peterson, the managing director of the National Retail Hardware Association.

Finally, Hall avoided one major pitfall which other dealer-owned coops had fallen into. He did not cut the dealer price on nationally-known merchandise. "There is no inside price advantage to be had. Every member pays the regular market price for his merchandise." This avoided the cutthroat competition which manufacturers feared, defused some of the opposition from other wholesalers, and made it easier for the company to acquire full lines of acceptable merchandise from manufacturers.

To sum up, the essentials of dealer-ownership, common to all firms, were: a) selling for cash, b) to dealers who wrote their own orders, and c) received patronage rebates at the end of the year. But Hall Hardware developed the formula further into a mature system, by 1) building a firm financial structure with reinvested dealers' profits; 2) avoiding cutthroat competition by selling members at the current wholesale price; 3) holding annual merchandise shows for the dealers; and 4) introducing a direct-mail advertising program.

It's probably no accident that this mature system of hardware dealer-ownership blossomed first in Minnesota, a hotbed of cooperative enterprise. With Swedes and Finns in the lead, Minnesota and Wisconsin counted more cooperatives than any other American state. The cooperative idea was "in the air" of the Upper Midwest; and as John Cotter has remarked, only half-jokingly, "the air is cold up there, it clears your sinuses and lets you think clearly." Yet the only direct link between Our Own Hardware and other Minnesota cooperatives was Charles Ladner, founder of the hardware mutual insurance company. As long as Ladner lived (he died in 1937), the relationship between hardware company and insurance society remained very close. The officers of the two organizations were virtually interchangeable, and Our Own always held its annual stockholders' meeting the day after the hardware mutual's insurance meeting.

Hall and Ladner and Our Own's dealers, however, did not relish too close an identification with cooperatives, other than the insurance mutuals. In fact, in many small towns of Minnesota and the Dakotas, Our Own Hardware stores competed directly with farmers' coops, which not only marketed crops but also sold tools and farm implements. An element of ethnic animosity spiced this competition between largely Anglo-Saxon hardwaremen and "the damn Finlanders with their coops." George Hall went out of his way to emphasize the profit motive animating the dealers he served:

"The project was thought to be visionary at the time and perhaps rightfully so. But it was a matter of cold business with us...We are not Socialists. We do not have a great deal of patience with the ideas of those well-meaning people who think they can revolutionize society and make the whole world ideally happy through promulgating radical theories."

Visionary or not, Hall Hardware provided the most important model for dealer-ownership in hardware wholesaling. John Fitschen, for example, who rescued Wisco Hardware, had apprenticed first with Hall Hardware and he applied George Hall's ideas when he took over in Madison. The general managers of all the fledgling dealer-owned hardware firms, though they lacked any ideological consciousness and avoided radical theorizing, did feel a certain kinship for each other and shared some sense of belonging to a new movement in the industry. Beginning in 1935, the managers of dealer-owned firms met annually for an informal exchange of ideas and information. At these meetings, George Hall (and later Steve Duffy, who succeeded him as general manager of Hall Hardware in 1936) always enjoyed a special voice of authority as the leader, the pioneer, the guru of the movement.

JOHN COTTER DISCOVERS DEALER-OWNERSHIP

John Cotter discovered the dealer-ownership movement his first morning out on the road as a travelling salesman in June, 1928. "Hell, the first town I went to, the best damn store was an Our Own store. Nelson-Suennen at Hudson, Wisconsin was the first store I ever called on," he recalls. Cotter adds in amazement, "I can't understand how after 12 years in the hardware business, and all the people I knew, that no one ever said anything about Hall Hardware Co. I didn't know anything about it in St. Paul." As previously mentioned, Hall had practically no dealers in the Twin Cities so Cotter didn't encounter Our Own stores until he got out in the country.

Cotter couldn't sell Nelson-Suennen any merchandise that day, and when he got to the next town he found out why. "In River Falls, Wisconsin, on a Friday afternoon, I walked into A. W. Lund's store. A short, slight, little man in a straw hat stood behind the counter, so I introduced myself and asked to speak with Mr. Lund. 'You're talking to him,' he said. 'And you can't sell me anything. I'm a member of Our Own Hardware. I write my own orders and I get your 5% commission.'" Then realizing that the gangly youngster standing before him was perfectly green, the 75 year-old Swedish immigrant, who had done business in River Falls since 1873, explained the Our Own system. Cotter did manage to make a sale after all; Lund ordered some Florence kerosene stoves, and Coleman gasoline lamps and lanterns, lines Hall Hardware didn't carry. But Cotter came away from the store with his head swimming from what he had heard. "I went out of there and said, 'This is the way to do business.'"

As the young salesman made the rounds and learned his territory, it gradually dawned on him that the best, the busiest, the cleanest hardware store in every town on his territory belonged to Our Own Hardware. In a typical Wisconsin town of the late 20s and early 30s, a number of independent hardware stores still lined Main Street or surrounded the courthouse square. Cotter found the Our Own store the most modern and progressive; if Coast-to-Coast, an aggressive auto supply and hardlines chain founded in 1929 by the Melamed brothers of Minneapolis, had moved into that town, its store would rank no. 2; if not, a Marshall Wells franchise store held the second position. Stores which purchased from old line wholesalers, such as Janney, Semple, Hill, or Farwell, Ozmun, Kirk ranked farther down; and Cotter's accounts with Kelley-How-Thomson brought up the rear.

Cotter relates another discovery he made on the road:

"I'm sitting in the Commercial Hotel in Eau Claire, Wisconsin one night, the second fall I was out in 1929, and I started to count up, and in the city of Eau Claire, a town of 25,000 people, that day there had been 16 hardware salesmen calling on about 6 hardware stores. And I said, hey, I don't care how hard you work, you can't make it."

This horde of salesmen competed fiercely against each other, of course; but they also occupied a lot of the retailer's time during the day, time he could use more profitably selling to customers or managing his stock. This further pointed up the genius of the Our Own system; the dealer chased the salesmen away, spent his time making sales, and did his own stock ordering in odd quiet moments throughout the day or at home in the evening. Cotter never forgot this lesson, and he continually urges retailers to say "No, No, No" to "itinerant peddlers."

When Cotter went into partnership with Armin Kohlhepp in Eau Claire, they couldn't join the Our Own cooperative, though they would have liked to. Our Own protected each member's trading area by accepting only one dealer in each town, and Our Own already had an Eau Claire store. But Cotter appreciated the advantages of dealer-ownership; and, over the next fifteen years, as he wrestled with the problem of reducing wholesale distribution costs, he kept returning to the idea. When Red Oakes' experiment with a merchandising group failed to meet his expectations, Cotter finally decided to start a dealer-owned organization himself. In the course of his extensive travels for Tru-Test, he had visited various dealer-owned firms around the country and introduced himself to their managers. Bill Stout, in particular, who had built American Hardware of Pittsburgh into the second largest dealer-owned wholesaler, behind Our Own, took a liking to Cotter and rendered him invaluable personal advice, counsel, and assistance as he started up. Yet, always, in John Cotter's mind, the general model and the outstanding example of a successful dealer-owned hardware company was Our Own Hardware of Minneapolis.

CHAPTER FOUR
THE ENTREPRENEURIAL MOMENT—THE BIRTH OF COTTER & COMPANY

"I was like the non-Catholic guy who was going with a Catholic gal, and she sold him so intensely on the Catholic Church that he broke the engagement and went on to be a priest. Red Oakes sold me so intensely on low-cost distribution that I left him."
—John Cotter

In February, 1947, John Cotter was attending Our Own Hardware's winter convention in Minneapolis as a representative of Tru-Test, when he ran into Bill Stout. "In those days it was the custom of the dealer-owned managers, if they could possibly fit it in, to go and attend the shows of the other dealer-owned companies." They started talking about postwar needs and opportunities in hardware, and Stout grew enthusiastic and persuasive about the potential of dealer-ownership. "Why couldn't this job be done in Chicago," he challenged Cotter, "if it could be done in Minneapolis, Pittsburgh, and Los Angeles? If you could get 100 dealers together, you could do pretty well."

Cotter recollects, "I had this idea in the back of my mind since 1928, but I had no way to implement it. I had the fear of God in me that I had to make a living." But now, "having in mind that dealer-owned managers earned 1% of shipments (this was Stout's compensation arrangement), I thought that I could develop something here that would do 6 or 7 million. . . I was making $35,000 then and was looking for 60 to 70." Cotter and Stout, talking long into the night, looked up the *Hardware Age* dealer listing for Illinois, Michigan, Iowa, and Indiana and determined that there was room for a dealer-owned wholesaler in Chicago. Ace Hardware, an innovative low-cost operation (though not dealer-owned at that time), was headquartered in Chicago; but they had rigid requirements for membership in their program so many dealers couldn't qualify. Rehm Hardware, a Tru-Test wholesaler, aspired to be another Ace; but Cotter felt they "were very poorly managed and poorly financed." After his marathon gabfest with Stout, Cotter made up his mind — "It seemed like there was a potential here in Chicago."

The next day, Cotter continues:

"I came back to Chicago on one of the fast trains from Minneapolis and I talked at a Rehm show that evening. Then I drove home with Herb Haller, and I guess he was the first one I broached it to. . . There was a hell of a snowstorm. I started up the Outer Drive and couldn't make it. Somehow or other I turned off, got a tank of gas, and found I could make it up Western Avenue. I got home about 12 o'clock, woke up Alice, and told her what I was going to do."

The entrepreneurial moment had arrived.

TAKING THE PLUNGE

Deciding to take the plunge and go out on his own, Cotter knew he could count on help from his friends. Bill Stout had crystallized Cotter's decision, and he continued to impart practical advice and aid. Shortly after returning from Minneapolis, Cotter boarded a train for Pittsburgh to look over American Hardware's operation. As Red Oakes had done earlier, when he hired Cotter for Tru-Test, Stout both cautioned and challenged Cotter: "Give this your most serious consideration but bear in mind you now have a pretty good position, but of course there is a lot of pride, personal pleasure in starting something and making it successful." Oakes himself gave Cotter his blessing, even though he would be losing the heart and soul of his own organization; and he let Cotter use Oakes & Co. offices and resources for nearly six months to launch the new operation.

Ed Lanctot, John Cotter's sidekick off and on for about ten years, signed on immediately in the new venture. A native of Duluth, Edward E. Lanctot had joined Kelley-How-Thomson in 1936 straight out of high school. About a year and a half later, when Cotter was named merchandise manager, Lanctot served as his clerk. Cotter claims that Lanctot has the most terrific memory God ever granted anyone. "The only things he don't remember are things he don't want to." At Kelley-How, Lanctot could unravel a stock mix-up or reconstruct a complicated transaction months later from memory. The two men went separate ways for a time, when Lanctot was assigned to city sales at Kelley-How, then went into the Army in 1942. As soon as Uncle Sam released him, though, in January, 1946, Lanctot headed straight for the Cotter home in Evanston, lllinois. He was considering two options, returning to Kelley-How or reenlisting in the military; but he didn't want to do either. Cotter, therefore, made a place for him at Tru-Test; and the two men have worked together ever since.

A tall, heavy-set, prematurely balding man, Ed Lanctot remained a bachelor until 1952; so, for a time, he became virtually a member of the Cotter family. The Cotter children recall fondly that Lanctot ate Sunday dinner with them frequently, and one of the children claims that he took them out to Kiddieland more often than their father did. A gourmet and bon vivant, Lanctot remembers his trip to Chicago in January, 1946 as the time he ate his first meal on Rush Street. Yet he always earned his good times by working longer hours than anyone else except John Cotter. Lanctot possessed an instinctive flair for advertising and marketing; and to this day, he works the telephone constantly, hammering out one deal or another.

In 1947, Ed Lanctot threw himself into the planning of John Cotter's new organization. He pored over a Dun & Bradstreet credit rating book, which Cotter had scrounged from his friend Frank O. Maharey, of the Athens Stove Works, Athens, Tenn., and listed on $3'' \times 5''$ cards all the hardware dealers with a good credit rating within a 200 mile radius of Chicago, but excluding Chicago city dealers. Following George Hall's example, Cotter had decided to avoid the big city for a time and build his base in the small towns and the booming postwar suburbs. Lanctot found about 3000 dealers who fit the specifications. In the meantime, Cotter had obtained another "mysterious list" of 50 hardware dealers who were disgruntled with their present wholesale source of supply. Charlie Gilbert, then secretary of the Illinois Retail Hardware Association, who had an office in the Merchandise Mart down the hall from Tru-Test, had secretly passed this list on to him.

Armed with both lists, Cotter, Lanctot, Herb and Margaret Haller, and the whole Cotter family spent the hot Memorial Day weekend of 1947 preparing a mailing. Cotter wrote a 7½ minute letter, copying much of its content from Russ Cook, another Oakes disciple who had just gone off to Kansas City to start a dealer-owned wholesale firm there. "Mr. Independent Hardware Dealer," the letter read, "This is a long letter but it is worth reading — it may change your entire future. If acted upon it will double your net profit!...Let's keep the Hardware Business for the Hardware Man! Act now! Fill in the card attached or write us a letter." Cotter ran off 3000 letters on Red Oakes' mimeo machine, then the whole group adjourned to the Cotter home to address them. Typing names on gummed paper, they started to cut them into labels, but discovered a shortage of scissors. So Margaret Haller pulled out her pinking shears, and some of the address labels went out with fancy serrated edges. The two oldest Cotter children, Dan and Mary, stuffed the envelopes all weekend in Dan's room.

Cotter did not sign this initial pre-organization letter, but sent it out anonymously, with a postal box number for the returns. Since this was a fishing expedition to test the waters, he did not want to reveal his own identity too soon. He received replies from about 300 dealers, a 10% response to the mailing; so on July 10, he mailed a signed follow-up letter: "The interest has been so great that it has been definitely decided upon to proceed with the actual organization of this dealer-owned hardware house." Cotter satisfied his final obligations to Red Oakes in early July, helping him conduct the regular midsummer Tru-Test convention. He didn't reveal his own plans at the convention, but preached the gospel of low-cost distribution as fervently as ever, even breaking a podium with his fist at one point. Immediately after the convention, on July 15, he officially tendered his resignation. Red Oakes wrote to all the Tru-Test distributors: "To our mind, John Cotter is the best equipped hardware man in the United States. He has been of untold value to our organization . . . We wish him every success in his new endeavor."

Cotter wanted to visit every prospective dealer personally in his store, but to save time and spread the word more effectively, he also organized meetings for groups of dealers in the evening. The first pre-organization meeting took place on Thursday, July 17, 1947 at the Fargo Hotel in Sycamore, Illinois. Cotter knew the country dealers he had targeted would never drive into Chicago, so he picked the first good town he could think of about 50 miles west of the city. A dense fog settled over the Illinois cornfields that night and only 12 hardware dealers showed up. Joe O'Neill from Lake Forest flew over in his own plane, just touching down before the fog closed in completely.

"The reaction was complimentary, but cautious. They said, 'Young man, you got a good idea, and we need it, but it's not the time to do it. You won't be able to get the dealers to write their own orders, you won't get them to pay weekly. Merchandise is still in short supply. We could be cut off by our regular wholesalers if we join you.' But I was too determined, and too dumb, to listen. I said something like this, 'Well, the program is good, and it's being done in other parts of the United States, and I think I can do it here, and I want to start tomorrow morning and I'll be around to see you.'"

At this first meeting, Cotter settled on a name for his new company. Again following George Hall's example, he planned to use his own name, figuring, "Hell, I'm known in the hardware business and I'm going to make every effort to keep it from failing." He put the question to a vote at the Sycamore meeting, also offering more neutral alternatives, such as "mid-states" or "consolidated" hardware. Ten of the twelve dealers in attendance chose Cotter & Company by secret ballot, and several later straw votes confirmed the choice. The new firm would rise or fall on John Cotter's name and John Cotter's efforts. "We might fail," he told the dealers, "but I ain't gonna run away with the money."

Cotter sought a $1500 stock subscription from each dealer. To simplify matters, he aimed at signing only 25 dealers initially, as it was unnecessary under Illinois securities laws to register a company with 25 or fewer stockholders. Cotter didn't ask for money at Sycamore, but confined himself to preaching the message. The very next day, however, after staying overnight at the Fargo Hotel, Cotter and Lanctot set out to raise Cotter & Company's initial capital.

"I went up to McHenry and signed up Bill Althoff, got a check for $1500, much against the better judgement of his wife who was the bookkeeper. Then I made a beeline for Elgin, and we signed up Westside Hardware. Then I made a beeline back to Sycamore and signed up Stan Staskey. So I signed up 3 in one day. That's about as good as I ever did...I had a new Dodge car, but it died on us coming back home. In Elmhurst, the fuel pump broke."

For the next six months, John Cotter stayed on the road continuously. He scheduled four meetings a week, Monday through Thursday evenings, and spent each day buttonholing dealers individually. Ed Lanctot remained on the payroll at Tru-Test temporarily, but devoted every spare moment to aiding Cotter. Bill Stout loaned Cotter a fifteen minute film strip about American Hardware's dealer-owned operation which Cotter used to good effect at meetings: "The film from Bill Stout took me out of the carpetbagger class," he recalls. "I had a relationship with somebody who gave me this film." Bill Althoff, the first dealer to put down his cash, also buttressed Cotter's credibility. A former president of the Illinois Retail Hardware Association, well-known in the trade, Althoff secured testimonials from manufacturers who knew Cotter and circulated them among many hardware dealers.

Cotter planned a trip to Pittsburgh in November for his most interested dealers, so they could meet Bill Stout and inspect American Hardware's operation firsthand. Eight dealers took a night train from Chicago on Sunday, November 23, spent Monday in Pittsburgh, and arrived back early Tuesday morning. They joined 7 other paid-up dealers at Red Oakes' office that morning and conducted the first stockholders' meeting of Cotter & Company, approving articles of incorporation and appointing a nominating committee. By the end of the year, Cotter had secured his initial 25 paid members and had lined up at least 25 more good prospects. Then his attorney, T. G. McBride, supposedly an authority on cooperative law, noted a defect in the incorporation papers. He instructed Cotter to mail a new copy out to all 25 members for their signatures. Cotter thought to himself:

"Well, hell, if I mail it out I'll never get it back. So I got in the car the day after Christmas and I made the circle of all the stores that week. . .and came in the morning of New Year's Eve. As soon as I was home the Lord dumped the snow basket upside down. From then on we had the damnedest winter."

THE FIRST TEAM
Cotter & Company officially incorporated on January 15, 1948. Twenty-five dealers had each put $1500 in an escrow account at the Harris Trust and Savings Bank for an initial working capital of $37,500. This began a long and mutually beneficial relationship between the new company and the Harris. Don Waterbury, Harris Vice-President, appreciated Cotter's honesty, and Cotter found Waterbury happy to meet the company's credit requirements.

Ed Lanctot resigned from Tru-Test that same day; and he, John Cotter, and a secretary moved into a tiny office they rented from Red Oakes, for $35 a month, at 650 S. Clark Street. Eight dealer-members served with John Cotter on the Board of Directors, which met for the first time on January 29. Cotter insisted on owning the same voting stock as any member and on his election to the Board, so that he could never be asked out of a Stockholders' meeting. Over the years, the directors have contributed their time lavishly to the company and have never been a mere rubber stamp board.

On June 1, 1948, Cotter & Company moved into 5000 sq.ft. of

TABLE 1

TWENTY-FIVE CHARTER MEMBERS OF COTTER & COMPANY

John M. Cotter	Chicago, Ill.
S. A. Staskey	Elgin, Ill. (38,333)*
Joseph O'Neill	Lake Forest, Ill. (6,885)
T. J. Rynbrandt	Byron Center, Mich. (400)
Norman Ludlow	Springport, Mich. (502)
George E. Gilley	Harvey, Ill. (17,878)
Dorsey D. Husenetter	Highland Park, Ill. (14,476)
J. L. Nesley	Oregon, Ill. (2,825)
M. H. Williams	Waverly, Ill. (1,385)
W. P. Christenson	Griffith, Ind. (2,116)
R. A. Beranek	Mt. Vernon, Iowa (1,489)
John C. DePree	Zeeland, Mich. (3,007)
William H. Althoff	West McHenry, Ill. (1,596)
Roy C. Baseman	Elgin, Ill. (38,333)
E. B. Taylor	Winnetka, Ill. (12,430)
H. J. Lampen	Hamilton, Mich. (500)
Fred McGaughey	Russellville, Ind. (380)
Urban Bachmann	Park Ridge, Ill. (12,063)
Carl E. DeMeritt	Adrian, Mich. (14,230)
L. W. Moore	Rochelle, Ill. (4,200)
Burton Baity	El Paso, Ill. (1,621)
Otto Wichmann	Colfax, Ill. (160)
R. F. Peabody	Ionia, Mich. (6,392)
Ray W. Essig	St. Charles, Ill. (5,870)
P. H. Koester	New Holland, Ill. (336)

*Population of town in parenthesis

rented warehouse space in the North Per Terminal on Chicago's downtown lakefront at 365 E. Illinois Street. Bill Stout had suggested a terminal building to Cotter. American Hardware had shipped out of a warehouse terminal in Pittsburgh from the start, and it furnished them maximum flexibility for they could easily rent additional space as their business grew. This proved to be good advice, as Cotter & Company

TABLE 2
FIRST BOARD OF DIRECTORS

William H. Althoff	West McHenry, Ill. (1,596)**
Burton Baity	El Paso, Ill. (1,621)
Roy C. Baseman	Elgin, Ill. (38,333)
R. A. Beranek	Mt. Vernon, Iowa (1,489)
*John M. Cotter	Chicago, Ill.
John C. DePree	Zeeland, Mich. (3,007)
*L. W. Moore	Rochelle, Ill. (4,200)
Joseph O'Neill	Lake Forest, Ill. (6,885)
T. J. Rynbrandt	Byron Center, Mich. (400)

*Still a Board Member
**Population in parenthesis

rapidly expanded into 10,000 sq.ft. of space by September. Cotter dedicated himself to low-cost operations from the start, furnishing the office at North Pier Terminal with a truckload of secondhand desks and office equipment he bought for $50. In an early letter to dealer-members, he boasted that the entire fixed assets of the company, in warehouse and office equipment, amounted to less than $3400 — ''This figure. . . shows that a large percentage of the dealers' money is invested in fast selling hardware inventory.''

After moving to North Pier Terminal, the fledgling wholesale house expanded its staff. Cotter hired Jack Pfeuffer, Oakes' building superintendent at 650 S. Clark, to work in the warehouse; and Jim Eller, a young lad fresh out of St. Philip's High School on the west side, answered a tiny ad in the paper and signed on three months later. Nick Phillips joined Pfeuffer and Eller in the warehouse by the end of the year. Pfeuffer never advanced to higher levels within the company, but he remained with Cotter until retirement and, nostalgically, he always signed the company Christmas card as ''first warehouse employee.'' Eller worked his way up rapidly, and currently manages the Harvard, Illinois distribution center.

Frank Morman joined Cotter and Lanctot in the office immediately after the move to North Pier Terminal. Morman came from a Chicago hardware family. He and his brother had worked in their father's hardware store, but the brothers did not get along, so Frank took a job as a salesman for Rehm Hardware. Cotter hired him away from Rehm for the Tru-Test organization in 1943, then brought him over to his own company as soon as possible. Short, balding, five years older than Cotter, Frank Morman was a disciplined, meticulous "Prussian" with the energy of a tightly coiled spring. "Like the legendary Dutch carpenter, he always measured twice and cut once. Frank Morman could do anything," John Cotter attests emphatically. Jim Eller agrees, "I used to ask myself, 'How can one man know as much as Frank Morman?'"

Morman came down to E. Illinois Street and laid out the first warehouse space for Cotter, fitted linoleum coverings on the old second-hand desks in the office, and took charge of everything mechanical in the company. Morman also devised the first catalogue and price book for dealers to use in writing orders, a crucial contribution to a dealer-owned company. Maintaining, refining, and updating the CPB, as the price book was named, remained his responsibility until he retired in 1971. In his spare time, Morman served as buyer of tools, garden supplies, builders' hardware, paint, electrical supplies, and plumbing equipment. A perfectionist and a stern taskmaster, he made himself indispensable in all aspects of the business, yet he often rubbed against the grain. According to Cotter, Jack Pfeuffer hated Morman's guts; and Morman and Lanctot sometimes went for days without speaking to each other.

John Cotter had instinctively adopted the triple division of labor traditional in wholesaling and added the fourth dimension, advertising — Cotter was the man on the road, Morman the man in the warehouse, and Lanctot the man in the office. Yet something was still missing, a first-class finance man. Ed Lanctot handled a thousand details in the office, he pieced together the first advertising material, and doubled as buyer of housewares, appliances, and sporting goods; but he had little interest in finance. Sam Sorenson, CPA, the accountant at Tru-Test, had first set up the bookkeeping system for the new company, but Cotter could not afford to hire him permanently. Looking around for alternatives, he asked the Christian Brothers at St. George High School in Evanston to recommend one of their business studies graduates, and at their suggestion, he hired Don Grass right out of school. Grass, however, could not handle the financial chaos of an embryonic business; so after about a year, Sam Sorenson mentioned to a friend of his, Harold Ost, that Cotter desperately needed bookkeeping help to get over a hump. Ost went in temporarily at the end of 1949 to clean up the books; he stayed more than 20 years.

A short, quiet, reserved man of German background, Harold Ost was born in Danville, Illinois, attended a business and accounting institute in Fort Wayne, Indiana, and arrived in Chicago just before the stock market crash. He never did qualify as a CPA, and he only survived the Depression because his business course had included typing and shorthand. He finally caught on as an office manager at J & R Motor Supply on the south side, where he met Sorenson, then J & R's accountant. When Spiegel's, a Chicago mail order house, bought out J & R, Ost lost his job; and he was planning to join a relative as partner in a gas station when Sorenson directed him to Cotter & Company.

Ost found a mess in the office on E. Illinois Street; numerous accounts receivable from dealers were past due. Ost cleaned off Grass' desk for him and brought some order out of the chaos. Two weeks later, John Cotter talked him out of the gas station business — "How's a fellow your size going to fix a truck tire anyway?" — and hired him permanently. Grass remained with the company for a few months longer, then left to enlist in the Army after the outbreak of the Korean conflict.

Cotter added people cautiously as the company grew, always careful to keep the overhead down. A few remained only a short while, such as Mark Peters, a buyer from Rehm who left after a year and a half to start a business in Florida. Others stayed until retirement, such as Ted Ekstrom, another buyer from Rehm. When Cotter determined to cut loose his legal counsel, McBride, whom he had never found satisfactory, he retained the firm of Levinson, Becker and Peebles. First Frank Greenberg, then Ron Aronberg, from that firm, have handled Cotter & Company's legal matters ever since.

One early recruit proved to be a key contributor to the company's growth. Herb Haller, another Duluth native, had known John Cotter even longer than Ed Lanctot did. Haller joined Kelley-How-Thomson just a few months before Cotter began his second hitch with that firm, he performed a variety of sales and buying duties, then succeeded Cotter as stove department manager. Haller came to Tru-Test in 1944 as toy and sporting goods buyer, but travelled a good deal to arrange meetings of distributors and dealers. Short and slight of stature, with a corny sense of humor and an outgoing personality, Herb Haller was a born salesman. He could (and claims he did) sell fishing tackle in International Falls, Minn. at 40 below zero. Cotter couldn't afford to hire Haller immediately for his new company, but by 1950 the need for a full time sales manager (to sell the program, not merchandise) had grown acute. Cotter loved to travel as an evangelist of dealer-ownership, but he couldn't be everywhere and a thousand details demanded his attention back in the office. So in December, 1950, he hired Herb Haller to be his eyes, ears, and voice on the road. He still couldn't afford him; Haller took a $3000 cut in pay when he signed on.

John Cotter had finally recruited his first team — Ed Lanctot, buying, merchandising, and advertising; Frank Morman, operations manager; Harold Ost, bookkeeper and office manager; Herb Haller, sales manager. It was an odd assortment of individuals — short and tall, heavy and lean — rough-edged, homespun, not always compatible. None was rich, successful, or college-educated; each was a creature of the Depression, with a survivor's instincts for hard work and dogged determination. Above all, they were straight, dependable, and honest, the sort John Cotter could leave in charge and know they wouldn't rob the company blind.

THE COMPLETE SYSTEM IN EMBRYO

From the earliest days, Cotter tried to offer the dealer-members at least a hint of all the advantages they would derive from a dealer-owned wholesale organization. He had promised them "low-cost distribution and a merchandising program to help move the goods through the hardware store," and he aimed to deliver. At first, of course, before moving into the warehouse at North Pier Terminal, he could only offer direct shipments, from factory to dealer, of some limited merchandise lines available through Tru-Test. He mailed the first merchandise bulletin on January 17, featuring Alladin picnic jugs and vacuum bottles. The minimum order for factory shipment was 30 jugs, but some dealers

ordered two or three hundred. Other early bulletins offered direct shipments of Monark Silver King bicycles, Carlisle bicycle tires, Universal garden sprayers, private brands of rope and flashlight batteries
developed by Tru-Test, and aluminum mail boxes and electric fence
chargers for the rural trade. All of these represented second or third
rate lines of goods, but the dealers got them at an attractive price. Baltimore Brush, a leading manufacturer of paint brushes, was the first
merchandise line Cotter secured on his own, without an Oakes Tru-
Test connection; and Baltimore remains the major supplier of paint
brushes. Cotter is loyal to those who trusted him in the beginning.

In order to stock an inventory after moving to North Pier, Cotter,
Lanctot, Morman, and the other buyers added later, worked doggedly
to overcome the resistance from old line wholesalers and convince
manufacturers to sell them goods. "We flew by the seat of our pants
— we took what lines were offered to us and said 'Thank you,'" Cotter remembers. O'Cedar, Ray-0-Vac, and Rubbermaid were among
the earliest name brands in stock; Ekco, Nesco, and others came in
soon thereafter. Then in August, 1949, Cotter mailed a flash memo
to dealers: "Hold everything! Please don't buy another electric drill,
electric polisher or electric saw . . . because we are working on a deal
which . . . will make available to you through your own wholesaler the
products of the world's largest maker of electric tools. 'Nuff said."
Black & Decker began selling Cotter & Company that month. But only
three months later, they bowed to pressure from other wholesalers and
withdrew the line. For almost a decade, the acquisition (or loss) of a
national brand marked a company milestone.

In accord with the tradition of dealer-owned wholesalers, Cotter &
Company hosted their first merchandise show to display goods and
solicit orders on August 11, 1948. Only 35 manufacturers' representatives displayed their wares at this modest one-day affair in the company's tiny warehouse space; and the dealers in attendance had to grab
lunch at the North Pier cafeteria. But the following January, a second
dealer show boasted more than 100 manufacturers and featured a get-
acquainted dinner in the Sherman Hotel with E. A. "Zeb" Hastings,
finance man for American Hardware, as guest speaker. Thereafter,
the company invariably conducted two dealer shows, or markets, every
year, focusing on seasonal goods. Fall markets featured fishing tackle,

sporting goods, and lawn and garden items for the following summer. Eventually, the early market moved to June and featured fall and winter merchandise, toys, and other Christmas goods.

Ed Lanctot created the first consumer direct-mail advertising, a 32-page, two-color rotogravure catalogue for distribution in the fall of 1948. This first catalogue featured the most attractive lines of merchandise Cotter & Company carried; but, realistically, it also illustrated several national brands—Pyrex, Disston, Mirro — which Cotter couldn't supply but which the dealers obtained from other wholesalers. Building traffic for the retailers was vital; if another wholesaler got a little extra business, that price had to be paid for the time being. Cotter and Lanctot offered the circulars to their dealer-members at $39.50 per thousand plus a cost of $4.50 for imprinting the store's name. To make the most of their printing investment, they also sold the circulars at a higher price to non-member retailers in towns where they didn't yet have a member. 68,000 copies of this first direct-mail brochure went into circulation in the fall of 1948. Sharp dealers, such as Bill Althoff and Lew Moore, found that this form of advertising worked; so they doubled their orders to 3 or 4 thousand copies for the spring catalogue the following year.

Twice a year consumer mailings helped move the seasonal goods dealers had ordered at the semi-annual markets; and, beginning in April, 1949, Cotter & Company supplemented their catalogues with newspaper advertising. The first full page ad ran in the *Chicago Tribune* on Sunday, April 24, 1949, picturing the catalogue and listing the names of all participating dealers. Cotter urged all his members to "get ready and cash in." He happily reported in a weekly letter:

"Saturday, April 23, Frank Morman and the writer made a trip across northern Illinois to Sterling and back. In the course of the trip we stopped at six stores, 5 out of the 6 stores had their windows trimmed with merchandise that appeared in your own catalog, they also had a copy of the Tribune ad posted on the windows..."

In September, 1949, Cotter organized a sales clinic for his dealer-members' employees; 38 people attended. Product-knowledge seminars for dealers and sales meetings for their employees became ongoing responsibilities of Cotter & Company thereafter. "With the accomplishment of this first Retail Sales Personnel Meeting,'' John Cotter wrote his members, ''I believe we have pretty well rounded out the program set down in our original presentations. This dealer-owned organization has brought to its members a recognized, active, low-cost wholesale hardware organization.''

Hardware merchandise at attractive prices, a barebones warehouse operation, semi-annual dealer markets, consumer advertising, and merchandising help for the retailer — all this began within a year and a half of the company's founding. Though some of its features were still embryonic, Cotter had put the essentials of a dealer-owned system in place. Dealers wrote their own orders from Frank Morman's price book and paid their bills every Tuesday. If they didn't pay regularly, John Cotter handed them back their investment and asked them to leave the organization. Ed Lanctot continually expanded the advertising program, and the most active dealers gobbled up all the direct-mail catalogues they could get.

Results came a little slower than expected. Bill Stout had predicted that they could have 100 dealers and $3 million in business the first year. As it turned out, Cotter & Company did not hit the 100 dealer mark until the end of 1949, and sales did not reach $3 million until 1952. But the company showed a profit right from the start and distributed $24,388 in patronage dividends on the first full year's warehouse shipments. John Cotter was pleased and persistent, and he tried to instill some pride of ownership in the dealers. At the end of 1949 he wrote:

> ''Many dealers say 'I have just bought this or that from you,' meaning me, John Cotter. Let me suggest, folks, that you did not buy the material from me but from your own wholesale organization. This is your business—you own it...We should start to refer to this organization as 'our' organization, 'our' wholesaler.''

THE ENTREPRENEUR AND HIS MOMENT

Popular economists have written much romantic nonsense about entrepreneurship in recent years. The pen of George Gilder, for instance, in his popular tract *The Spirit of Enterprise*, transformed a half-dozen case studies of entrepreneurs into an ''Economy of Heroes.'' Chrysler president Lee Iacocca's best-selling autobiography reads like a Superman comic book. In the eyes of such publicists, entrepreneurs are Clint Eastwood-like loners, battling personal demons, long odds, and government regulations to create wealth for themselves and for American society. Gilder, the most fervent of the Standing Tall school, transports economics to the realm of theology: "The achievements of enterprise remained the highest testimony to the mysterious strength of the human spirit. . .a thrust beyond the powers and principalities of the established world to the transcendent sources of creation and truth." Reality, however, has a way of deflating such fables. Certainly, John Cotter's entrepreneurial moment was more complex, and more earthly.

Many well-established characteristics of entrepreneurs do fit John Cotter's life and career remarkably well. A Louis Harris study of "Entrepreneurship in America," reported in *Hardware Retailing*, concluded:

"Money and risk are the major forces that motivate entrepreneurs. These people go into business for themselves because they want to be their own boss, because they want to make more money and provide more security for their families, because they think they can do a better job in their specific field of endeavor than existing competition."

Cotter felt little urge to be his own boss for its own sake — he had enjoyed remarkable freedom of maneuver under both Higgins and Oakes; but the other three motives drove him — to make more money, to provide security for his family, and to prove he had a better way of doing business.

The Gallup organization and the *Wall Street Journal* dug a little deeper into "inner drives, personality quirks, family backgrounds and circumstances" of entrepreneurs. They found "an early inclination toward hard work and achievement that remains undiminished in middle age," an understatement when applied to John Cotter, still a workaholic at age eighty-two. A further finding is also apt: "Nor do entrepreneurs tend to be joiners or team players. They were less likely to have been student leaders or varsity lettermen. . .and, today, comparatively few are country clubbers or Rotarians." Cotter's wife and children emphasize that he has no interests or activities outside his family and his business; he is neither a country-club socializer nor a Little

League father. Cotter repeatedly turns down invitations to sit on corporate or charitable foundation boards of directors. A hard-working loner with a stubborn streak of independence, he concentrates his energies on this dealer-owned business.

Some studies, however, have found that entrepreneurs carry their personal independence to extremes; and here they part company with John Cotter. "The entrepreneur is a misfit," the *Wall Street Journal* wrote, more likely to have been expelled from school, to have been fired one or more times, to have changed jobs frequently. George Gilder highlights personal instability, a history of broken homes or marriages, a "crisis of breaking away" as key entrepreneurial traits. "Breakthroughs spring more often from mental breakdowns than from lucky breaks," he concludes. Nothing could be farther from John Cotter's experience; above all, Cotter's life is remarkably, even boringly, normal and ordinary. He had a happy childhood, lived with his parents for years as a young adult, courted for six years and remained married to the same wife over fifty years, brought his aged mother into his home until she died — no crisis of breaking away, no personal instability here. Certainly, the act of entrepreneurship brought strain. Cotter himself identifies strongly with the deep loneliness Lee Iacocca felt when Henry Ford fired him, for Cotter experienced this same pain after leaving the comfortable world of old-line wholesaling. Constant travel, uncertainty, and belt-tightening tried his family's patience. Still, Cotter's family never wanted for necessities; and his marriage, his health, and his sanity survived robustly.

According to George Gilder, many an entrepreneurial plunge was followed by a splash, or a splat, and "a terrible period of submergence" when losses mounted, friendships crumbled, and doubters gloated. Cotter & Company never took this dive. Though it did not expand as rapidly as Bill Stout initially predicted, the company grew steadily from the start. As early as December, 1948, just six months after full operations commenced, Cotter adopted the slogan "nothing succeeds like success;" and a year later, he first published the company growth chart which has become a distinctive trademark. From the outset, the growth chart has shown a smooth, upward curve — a snowball effect rather than an entrepreneurial splat.

The most noteworthy anomaly in Cotter's entrepreneurial profile

— which probably explains the others as well — is his peculiar mix of caution and daring. In short, John Cotter is a conservative entrepreneur. He took a risk by starting his own company in 1947 and made a definite financial sacrifice. His first management contract provided compensation equal to 1½% of gross sales up to $2 million and 1% over $2 million, with a minimum guarantee of $4800 the first year, rising to $9600 the fifth year. In 1948, the first year of operation, Cotter earned only the minimum $4800, in contrast to his $35,000 salary at Tru-Test. Not until 1952 did his compensation level catch up with his Tru-Test salary.

Yet Cotter didn't gamble recklessly with his own or his family's welfare. Alice Cotter states emphatically, "He's not a bit foolish; he would not take foolish chances on anything at all." Thrifty to the point of penny-pinching all his life, he had amassed substantial savings. When he first moved to Evanston, the real estate salesman and his neighbors thought he belonged to the Mafia, since he paid cash for his house. Furthermore, he earned a considerable income on the side. In the tight postwar market of continuing shortages and allocations, anyone with goods to sell could unload them quickly and profitably. Cotter struck a deal with the Prentiss-Wabers Manufacturing Co. of Wisconsin Rapids to distribute Preway oil heaters. He and his wife incorporated as the AGC (Alice Germain Cotter) Corporation and sold the heaters to wholesalers and retailers by mail and phone. This moonlighting brought in a substantial income which enabled him to support his family and pay his start-up expenses for Cotter & Company. Cotter earned about $17,000 in total income for 1948; his manager's salary accounted for only about a quarter of this.

In business, as in personal finance, Cotter took only calculated risks. He didn't consider dealer-ownership an untried, unproven crap shoot; he had seen it work elsewhere. His first approach to dealers, the 7½ minute letter he mailed in 1947, hammered home this theme — "This is not new—nine other cities have well-established dealer-owned wholesale hardware organizations that have operated successfully—some for as long as 37 years." He thought big, but took action in small chunks, always testing the water first, keeping costs down, proceeding one step at a time.

Cotter didn't act alone and he didn't create something out of nothing.

Tru-Test helped him incubate his company until it was ready to hatch. Red Oakes furnished him with encouragement, contacts, his earliest supplies of merchandise, and most of his key personnel. Bill Stout, Steve Duffy, and other dealer-owned managers served as an instant support group and board of advisors. Illinois hardware dealers were ready to hear Cotter's message, Charlie Gilbert's list of disgruntled dealers proved that. Bill Althoff recalled, years later: "For 3 years several of us in the Hardware Association studied the possibility of organizing a dealer-owned Hardware. Our problem was to find a man to manage such a company. 1947 came along and a fellow by the name of John Cotter." The time was right and the ground had been prepared.

None of this, however, minimizes Cotter's achievement, his daring, or his sense of timing. One of the simplest and most valid maxims in George Gilder's hymn to entrepreneurship comes from Idaho potato magnate, J. R. Simplot: "When the time is right, you got to *do* it." John Cotter would heartily agree. "Nothing will ever be attempted if all possible objections must be first overcome."

The time was right for a dealer-owned hardware wholesaler in Chicago in 1947. Only Ace provided low-cost distribution in the Midwest and they served only a tiny fraction of hardware dealers, with many strings attached. Illinois dealers chafed at the arrogance and high overhead of old-line wholesalers, principally Hibbard's, the king of the territory. Start-up costs were relatively low for a new company, as inflation had not yet galloped out of sight. Cotter & Company began with total capital of $37,500, and John Cotter paid his own way while travelling constantly around the Midwest. He recalls in some amazement: "I stayed at the best hotels. The cost didn't make much difference. I paid my own bills, my own expenses. You couldn't afford to do that starting up today." Still, the moment did not seem perfect to many at the time. Most dealers adopted a "show me" attitude — "the idea looks good but prove it to me first." In an atmosphere of shortage, which persisted after World War II through the Korean War, old-line wholesalers exercised considerable leverage over retailers. They could, and did, threaten to cut off Cotter members from the allocation of scarce goods. Postwar shortages also meant that dealers had no need, in the short run, for lower prices. Cotter admitted the lack of urgency: "Truly enough...we are still in a seller's market...For almost eight years hardware dealers have sold pretty well anything they could get their hands on and at about any price.'' Yet Cotter remained convinced the time was right and he persuaded dealers ''You got to *do* it.''With foresight, he predicted: ''These conditions are bound to change. They may change slowly to a buyer's market, but history has indicated they may change very rapidly . . . so why not be prepared? Why not be assured of a continuous dependable source of supply — your own — owned by you and other dealers like yourself.''

A stable, well-adjusted person, with both feet on the ground, a cautious businessman, avoiding reckless gambles, John Cotter, nonetheless, recognized an entrepreneurial moment and seized it. Nor has he changed his opinion of that moment after all these years, ''You have to be there. Opportunist. You have to keep your basket ready to catch the apples when they fall off the tree.'' Above all, he passed the ultimate test of entrepreneurship — he convinced others he was right. In building a cooperative enterprise, no other personal trait served him better than his magnetic ability to persuade.

CHAPTER FIVE
BUILDING
THE
COMPANY

"I watched them tearing a building down—
   a gang of men in a busy town.
With a heave ho ho and a lusty yell,
   they swung a beam and the side wall fell.
I asked the foreman, 'Are these men skilled
   as the men you would hire if you had to build?'
He laughed and said, 'No indeed,
   just common labor is all I need.
I can easily wreck in a day or two
   what builders have taken a year to do.'
I asked myself as I went away,
   'Which of these roles have I tried to play?
Am I a builder who works with care,
   measuring life by the rule and square?
Or am I a wrecker who walks the town
   content with the labor of tearing down?'"
—Anonymous,
   quoted in *Weekly Letter*
   November 11, 1949

While building his company in its early years, John Cotter confronted a rapidly changing consumer economy. Depression gloom and wartime scarcity yielded to expansion and boom in the 1950s, but only after a few false starts. Cotter thought, as early as January, 1949, "We are getting into a buyers' market much faster than most of us realize. We here in Chicago see things happening every day that have not happened since way back in 1939 or 40. The customer is again a king." But the Korean War choked off this optimism and reimposed a sellers' economy of scarcity and allocations. As that war ground down to a stalemate in 1952 and '53, the long-expected buyers' market finally arrived. A *Hardware Age* editorial in January, 1953 announced it:

"Employment is at an all time high; spendable income is setting records; savings are high; credit is available in ample supply; industrial production shows no signs of slackening. But there is one important element present that has not been present for some time... There are no shortages to spur artificial demands. It's a buyers' market now... Hard selling is not something new to us. It's just that we're a little rusty."

THE PHENOMENAL FIFTIES AND THE SOARING SIXTIES

Hard selling, indeed, and new techniques would prove necessary; for with the return of "normalcy," competitive trends that first appeared earlier in the century blossomed into full bloom. Discount houses sprang up, threatening to snatch away business from traditional retailers, just as mail order catalogues and chain stores had done earlier. Americans climbed into automobiles in record numbers and began shopping for bargains in the new shopping centers out in the exploding suburbs. Suddenly everyone was selling hardware; not just mass merchandisers such as Sears, Ward's, and the new upstarts like K-Mart, but everyone. Specialty appliance and sporting goods stores opened, to satisfy long-pent up demand for those goods; auto supply chains proliferated as Interstate highways unrolled ribbons of concrete; drug and variety stores expanded, remodeled, and transformed themselves into one-stop shopping centers. Even supermarkets sold hardware and housewares, and a host of specialized, short-line "rack jobbers" jumped in to fill the supermarket racks with merchandise.

The discount phenomenon dominated retailers' thoughts. Cut-price specials and bargain basements were nothing new, of course; but in the post-World War II scramble discounting became a way of life. Pioneered in New York and New England, huge discount department stores surrounded by acres of parking spread across the country, especially in suburban shopping centers. Traditional retailers struggled to define the phenomenon and pinpoint the secret of its success. "Do you know what discounting is?" one department store executive growled. "It's nothing more than selling inferior merchandise on Sundays." A less colorful but more accurate definition of a discount house is "a store that sells at a lower average markup than conventional stores selling the same type of merchandise." Low margins, high turnover, self-service, and extended evening and weekend hours distinguished the discount emporiums from older department stores. Discounters kept their capital investment and their overhead low, and by turning over their money and their stock rapidly they produced a high return on net worth (11.8% in 1962 compared with 4.9% for department stores and 4.2% for hardware stores, according to a Dun & Bradstreet report). Low overhead and high return, then, marked the discounters' balance sheets; but from the consumer's point of view, it all meant lower prices.

The discount onslaught buried Fair Trade and the idea of a fixed minimum price. A 1951 Supreme Court decision held that Fair Trade agreements between manufacturers and retailers were constitutional but that they couldn't be enforced against non-signers. This freed the discounters to sell at any price they wished so long as they didn't sign price maintenance contracts. New laws were passed in an attempt to plug the gaping holes in price maintenance, but by the end of the decade, Fair Trade was largely a dead issue. One of the earliest discounters, Steve Masters, summed up the popular attitude well: "Fair trade is unpopular, unrealistic, socially backward and repulsive to the housewife, the wage earner, and the public generally. Competition is the sparkplug of America. It is the enemy of monopoly, cartels, and dictatorship." Traditionalists saw it differently. The president of Sunbeam, whose home appliances were subject to unusually heavy discounting, predicted gloomily: "Through incessant price wars the capital of thousands of regular stores will be eaten away leaving a handful of monopolistic parasites plus a fringe of hole-in-the-wall stores of the lowest type."

Hardware retailers responded to the discount competition by shedding their ''hole-in-the-wall'' store image. Many moved into the new suburban shopping malls, and some of them found that a location right next to Sears or a discounter actually benefitted them. The mass merchandiser drew traffic which spilled over to them as well. Others heeded the gospel of store modernization preached by the hardware trade press and remodeled their old Main Street stores. *Hardware Age* reported, for example, that the owner of a 29 × 80 ft. store in Mt. Horeb, Wisconsin removed the bulky center pillars, replacing them with steel girders in the sidewalls, and also extended the length of the store to 105 ft. The owner of a 20 × 80 ft. store in Urbana, Illinois leased the neighboring storefront, broke through the wall, and doubled his selling space. Joe O'Neill in Lake Forest, one of Cotter's charter members, installed fluorescent lighting and concluded: ''We look upon the lighting of our store as an advertising investment. . . . It encourages people to step into every area of the store.'' All-glass storefronts, without traditional window displays but with brilliant lighting inside, transformed the entire store into an advertisement.

Hardware retailers also expanded their product mix and introduced self-service to encourage impulse buying among browsing customers. Though hardware stores had always sold pots and pans, the labor-saving appliances and brightly colored housewares available in the 1950s opened a whole new market among women customers. Already by 1953 housewares were accounting for 30% of the volume of large hardware stores. As more women were attracted to these formerly male bastions, the urgency of cleaning up, lighting up, and modernizing the stores increased. The baby boom also opened up opportunities for growing sales of toys, sporting goods, and outdoor recreational items. *Hardware Age* predicted that the 1300 children per hardware store of 1950 would grow to 1900 per store by 1962. Some store owners went after these children and their parents, attempting to draw in the whole family as Sears did. Self-service, as well as new forms of packaging and displaying goods, became a necessity to accommodate browsing families. Rather than selling screws and nails in bulk, manufacturers now packaged small quantities on brightly colored cards encased in plastic, ready for display on hardware store racks. Customers could locate what they wanted, then head straight for a checkout counter, just like in a supermarket.

Some stores attempted to meet discount competition with special promotions and gimmicks like trading stamps. Many found that giftware increased female traffic. One wag has defined giftware this way:

"It isn't something like a fishing rod, a set of golf clubs, or anything else you wish someone would give you. Rather, it is something like a pewter figurine of a scuba diver, a tiny panda sculpted from 'hydrostone,' a pencil sharpener in the shape of a monkey standing in a shoe, or a ball point pen packaged with a color-coordinated lady's bow tie. It is, in brief, a thing that is generally thrown away shortly after it is received."

However silly, gift departments attracted customers in the affluent post-war years.

Despite the flurry of store modernizations, however, hardware stores barely held their own against mass merchandisers. Few stores went broke; hardware stores consistently enjoyed a lower bankruptcy rate than trendy specialty stores or discounters. Yet they didn't expand in proportion to the population and the volume of business. The number of retail hardware stores increased only ½ of 1% from 1948 to 1954; their sales rose only 8% compared to a 30% increase in all retail trade. In short, as one business analyst remarked, "It means that other types of outlets have been getting the business." To avoid stagnation or decline, hardwaremen had to do more than paint up or fix up their stores; they needed competitive prices and expert advertising. They needed a source of supply who could get them the right goods, at the right price, at the right time.

John Cotter tried to persuade independent hardware dealers he was that supplier. He spent nearly all of the 1950s selling — selling his Value & Service program, as it was then called, to retailers; and selling his company's prospects to manufacturers, convincing them to let him distribute their products. The two selling efforts complemented and reinforced each other; for the more dealers he had, the more potential sales volume he could offer manufacturers, and the more product lines he carried, the more ammunition this gave him to persuade dealers with. After ten years in business, he had established a firm beachhead as a Midwestern wholesaler and had begun to earn some grudging recognition.

SELLING THE PROGRAM

As soon as he was authorized to sell stock in the five states surrounding Chicago, Cotter set out to increase his group of members in order to get the sales volume he needed to lower costs further. He enlisted his charter members to help him, soliciting testimonial letters from them and urging them to talk up his program with non-competing retailers in neighboring towns. At Christmastime in 1948 he offered a $15 Stetson hat and a five lb. box of candy to any of his 68 dealer-members who signed up an additional member. He made becoming a member as easy as possible, offering, for example, a six month trial membership plan with no initial investment. When a dealer did decide to join permanently, Cotter allowed payment of the $1500 stock subscription on just about any terms the dealer requested, accepting as little as $50 down payment and taking the rest out of year-end patronage dividends.

Cotter never felt happier than when he was selling the program, but it soon became evident he needed help. So he started to hire field men to beat the bushes for dealer prospects, paying them a commission of $200 for each dealer signed up plus 1% of the new dealer's purchases in the first year. His first field men were a rather motley crew of castoffs and moonlighters. Herb Brown, hired on January 1, 1950 was a temperamental curmudgeon, with the travelling salesman's usual weakness for the bottle. He had knocked around from Our Own, to Hibbard's, and now to Cotter. Brown knew hardware and acquired some good dealers, but he was no diplomat. When he signed a Michigan dealer named Rosenberg, for instance, he scrawled right on the contract, "Not Jewish." Jim Herron, the second field man hired, could not support his family on Cotter's commissions, so he also ran a donut shop on Sheridan Road in Chicago. The beat-up old car he rattled around in reeked with the mingled odors of cigars and fried dough. Then there was Art Janz, the eager-beaver of the lot, picked up by Cotter after Westclox had laid him off. Usually it's necessary to spark a salesman, to get him enthused, but Janz needed to be reined in. "He was telling people we were going to be bigger than Sears. The hell of it is he believed it."

Herb Haller came aboard at the end of 1950 and began to ride herd on these field men. As the staff expanded, he was formally named sales manager in February, 1953. He found that he had to re-train himself and the other salesmen, since selling a program was so different from selling hardware. He told the men, "Don't BS, don't be a big shot, but talk retail, talk to the man about his store, ask him questions about his business, even if you know the answers. And never tell him he's going to go broke without you."

Haller and his field men would go anywhere to buttonhole dealers. They organized evening meetings across the territory, as John Cotter had done from Sycamore onward. They attended all the state hardware association conventions in the Midwest, arranging informal breakfasts and lunches for dealers and their families. Haller remembers signing up one dealer in a bowling alley, the only place he could get a few minutes of his time; and he once had to follow a widow all over her back yard, contract in hand, tripping over ducks and geese, while she took in the laundry. Whenever possible, however, Haller made appointments with dealers at home in the evenings, for it took about 1½ hours of uninterrupted time to make a full presentation. "If you could get 2 hours with a dealer, you usually got four," because of all the questions. Still, unexpected events could upset the most carefully laid plans. Haller recalls one time in Rockford, he visited a couple at home so their two sons could listen in. No sooner had he sat down at the kitchen table and pulled out his catalogue and price book, when a siren blared and the two boys went racing off with the volunteer fire brigade. Even the catalogue itself could pose a problem. One family spent so much time inspecting the illustrations that it took Haller all day to make his pitch. Despite the frustrations, Haller found selling the Cotter program a uniquely gratifying experience: "I enjoyed selling goods but I enjoyed selling the program more, because I was really selling a way of life, a set of principles, something bigger than an order of steel goods. We have been a factor in the perpetuation of hardware stores as a family business."

If Haller or the other field representatives could get enough time for a decent presentation, they usually found the dealers receptive. They explained the important responsibilities a dealer assumed in a cooperative organization — writing his orders, concentrating his purchases, and paying his bills weekly. "The program is the best in the industry but it's no better than the individual dealer in the store." Then they emphasized the benefits of "dealers doing collectively what they couldn't do individually'' — concentrated buying and advertising power. The better-rated hardware dealers, the kind they were trying to recruit, knew very well what their problems were and recognized the need for lower distribution costs; so, to some extent, the program sold itself.

Inadvertently, Cotter's major low-cost competitor, Ace Hardware, made the task of recruiting dealers easier. Richard Hesse ran Ace with an iron hand, demanding of dealers 100% loyalty and rigid adherence to company rules. Any dealer who joined Ace had to take his own name off the store sign and put up the red and white Ace logo, he had to drop his other paint lines and sell Ace's private brand, he had to sign a contract promising to buy all his merchandise from Ace. Ace's dealer conventions proceeded in lock-step, quasi-military fashion, complete with martial music and Patton-like harangues from Hesse. This ''Little Caesar'' attitude at Ace opened the door to a softer sell by Cotter, Haller, and their associates. They didn't insist on changing the store signs or the paint lines; they cajoled the dealers to concentrate their purchases with Cotter & Company but they didn't demand exclusivity. A Cotter brochure mailed out to 700 dealers in 1951 emphasized ''Cotter & Company dealers are not members of a chain gang.''

"TREAT ALL THE MEMBERS ALIKE, AND KEEP THE OVERHEAD DOWN"

Cotter wanted dealer loyalty, for he knew that ultimately it was the only way a cooperative organization could succeed; but he set out to earn it rather than demand it. He offered a complete program of store merchandising aids, beginning with the Value & Service store identification. He had devised this trademark in order to emphasize the two leading qualities of an independent hardware store. In order to distinguish his program from Hesse's, he didn't push the dealers to change their signs to V & S, but he did emphasize its advantages for advertising tie-ins. Sampson Hardware in Spencer, Wisconsin, was the first Cotter dealer to hang out a V & S sign, in September, 1951. Others changed over gradually. Cotter usually urged the dealers to adopt a middle course with their store signs, identifying themselves as Sampson's V & S or Smith & Jones V & S Hardware, thus enjoying the dual advantage of a local reputation and a regional chain identification. Cotter supported the trend to store modernization vigorously, boasting proudly in 1952 that 8 of the 24 stores refitted by the Illinois Retail Hardware Association were Cotter members. He urged dealers to campaign for more off-street parking "across the alley from Main Street," and he cautiously endorsed self-service wherever appropriate in hardware stores, so long as knowledgeable personnel remained available to assist customers.

There was nothing very remarkable about Cotter's dealer services. In the 1950s everyone was offering merchandising assistance to retailers, from the National Retail Hardware Association and its state affiliates to the most backward old-line wholesaler. Frankly, merchandising aids were a dime a dozen. Actually, Cotter sold his program most effectively by the way he ran his program. If nothing succeeds like success, nothing sells like the testimony of satisfied patrons. Cotter kept his patrons (the dealer-members) satisfied by adhering to two primary principles: Treat All the Members Alike, and Keep the Overhead Down. In the final analysis, these two maxims provide a key to Cotter & Company's continuing success.

Since each member of the dealer-owned company purchased the same number of voting shares and enjoyed an equal voice in company affairs, Cotter went out of his way to highlight this equality. He didn't form an executive committee of directors, he never set a head table at banquets, he didn't grant insider price deals or special services to selected members. Nor did he stock a hospitality suite or private bar for fair-haired members. At first, dealers close to Chicago would occasionally drop into the warehouse to fill their own orders; Bill Althoff's son Jim came in with a truck nearly every week. This disrupted the warehouse routine, lowered efficiency, and raised costs. So to prevent all dealers from paying for the convenience of a few, Cotter put a stop to this practice. Likewise, if a dealer did not pay his bills on time, Cotter charged him sufficient interest to cover the costs of processing his account and to build up a reserve for bad debts. To this day Cotter & Company doesn't even have a credit department, only an accounts receivable department. Dealer equality meant pay as you go and no special favors. "You got to be psychologically right," Cotter emphasizes.

Above all, however, Cotter had to deliver lower prices to justify his operation. "First of all, they wanted to buy merchandise for less and if you really want to know the truth, that's the only reason they're with us today, most of them.'' Cotter passed on lower prices to his dealers by securing quantity discounts and by keeping the overhead down. He eliminated the costs of travelling a full sales force, eliminated credit costs, and kept the inventory lean and the warehouse clean. He offered merchandise to dealers in three basic ways: direct shipments, pool or relay orders, and regular warehouse shipments. Whenever a dealer could handle a large enough order to qualify for direct transportation from the factory, Cotter would arrange the shipment at cost plus 2%, or sometimes less. When dealers didn't order large enough quantities to utilize direct shipments, they still could take advantage of a pool or relay order. Cotter accumulated orders for seasonal goods at the semi-annual markets, and by mail at other times, ''pooled'' them and ordered truckloads from the factory. When delivered at the warehouse, they would be repacked and ''relayed'' to individual dealers. This method required more costly handling than direct shipments, but less than warehousing; so Cotter billed dealers at cost plus 6%. Dealers enjoyed an additional advantage on relays, since manufacturers usually granted extended ''dating'' or credit terms on these orders. Finally, Cotter & Company carried a lean but adequate inventory to fill the dealers' weekly orders for smaller quantities of goods. Cotter worked hard to reduce warehouse overhead, and as a result, dealer prices averaged about 10% above cost on warehoused items. Cotter aimed for a ⅓-⅓-⅓ mix of direct, relay, and warehouse orders, but he never actually attained this goal. Generally, dealer orders broke down to about 40% warehouse, 40% direct, and 20% relay.

John Cotter supported Fair Trade whenever manufacturers insisted on it; he couldn't do otherwise if he wanted to market their products. To simplify matters, he secured power of attorney to sign Fair Trade contracts in his members' names and he required dealers to adhere to Fair Trade retail prices on all items covered by contracts. Yet Fair Trade was crumbling under the discount onslaught, and many manufacturers sold goods to anyone who would take them, winking at any price-cutting. Cotter, therefore, tried to drive his wholesale price low enough on competitive goods so that his members could meet the price of Sears, K-Mart, or others.

To illustrate how this all worked to the dealer's advantage, Cotter used Harry Debo of Peru, Illinois, the first high volume dealer in his program, as an example in a 1951 dealer-recruitment letter. Debo purchased $60,610 worth of goods from Cotter in 1950. He saved, on the average, about 6% on the billing price in comparison with his other major supplier, Hibbard's, for a saving of $3636. In addition he earned a 3.54% patronage rebate from Cotter's profits, totalling $2147. In just one year, therefore, Debo gained $5784 on his initial $1500 investment in Cotter & Company.

The cost savings on goods were real and tangible benefits, allowing the dealer a choice of lowering his retail price to meet competition or else maintaining his regular selling price to earn a hefty profit. Cotter's price book contained a suggested retail price, but John Cotter always emphasized that the dealer had to engage in "noodle pricing," making up his own mind on final retail prices, for he knew his own business best. Patronage rebates represented less tangible benefits, for Cotter didn't pay them all in cash but in five-year notes and nonvoting stock. The discipline of dealer-ownership required dealers to view their rebates not as cash flow but as a long-term investment. Cotter explained to the dealers the importance of reinvestment with this 1952 cost illustration:

> "The value of Your Own Wholesaler's inventory is now $480,000. This money has come from the following sources:

Dealers' initial investment $1500 each	$200,000
Dealers reinvestment of earnings	$180,000
Seasonal bank loans on straight 90 day notes	$100,000
	$480,000"

In brief, the dealers' stock subscription got the company going, reinvestment of rebates kept it growing, and short term borrowing eased it over cash flow humps.

In the mid-1950s, Cotter dramatically demonstrated his dedication to low overhead, and proved again his instinct for the psychologically appropriate gesture, by reducing his own salary. His initial contract terms of 1½% of sales up to $2 million and 1% over $2 million had dropped to a flat 1% of sales in 1953, but this was beginning to provide a healthy income which promised to rise sharply as the business grew. His mentor, Bill Stout in Pittsburgh, had refused to reduce his 1% of sales agreement when dealers grumbled about the size of his salary, so in 1953 American Hardware's board of directors called in Bill Phair, the respected editor of *Hardware Age,* to mediate informally. Phair talked to John Cotter on the phone and Cotter told him: "Stout is out of his mind. He can't go on like this. Bill, try to change his mind." Stout remained adamant, however, and American's directors forced his resignation. Cotter heeded the message of this incident and voluntarily altered his own contract, effective January 1, 1954. He devised a complicated sliding scale of percentages, beginning with 9/10 of 1 per cent up to $2 million in sales and gradually declining to 45/100 of 1 per cent on sales over $10 million. In return for this voluntary reduction, Cotter asked for and received an 18 year contract, which would carry him past the retirement age of 65. Cotter thus gained security of tenure and a psychological advantage by not being greedy.

Throughout the early years of his company's growth, while selling his program and seeking dealer loyalty, John Cotter performed a careful balancing act, alternately babying and bullying the dealers. He used the soft sell and a velvet glove to undercut Dick Hesse at Ace, but he he acted decisively in treating all members alike and insisting they fulfill their cooperative responsibilities. He soft-pedalled store identification and paint lines, but insisted on weekly payment of bills.

In enforcing one company regulation, however, he proved as vehement and authoritarian as Hesse. The standard dealer contract included a pledge "that all information furnished me from week to week such as bulletins, check lists, price lists, price services, illustrated catalogs, etc., is confidential." Every order form and price page had imprinted at the bottom, "This information is confidential—for your use only." Cotter harped on the theme of confidentiality repeatedly in his weekly letters, and cancelled dealers' contracts if he discovered they had leaked price information to competitors' salesmen. He became so incensed at price leaks late in 1953 that he required every dealer to sign a "loyalty oath," reaffirming his adherence to the security provisions of the basic contract. Cotter explained his extraordinary concern for secrecy in dollars and cents terms:

"Loose Talk Costs Money. Loose talk with competing wholesale salesmen costs you, the dealer, money... Now, in general, we follow the suggested retail price of the manufacturers. We do not try to upset the market. However, there are certain items on which it is necessary for the dealers to receive a lower price in order to put them in a position to meet other forms of retail competition. When these prices get back to competing wholesalers, there is an immediate howl set up to get us to raise our price which automatically puts you in an unfavorable position as far as meeting the chain and mail order competition is concerned.''

When I asked John Cotter about this secrecy obsession, he shrugged it off and said he ''had to tie himself to something,'' had ''to have something to holler about'' when preaching dealer loyalty. Yet, it's easy to understand his concern and frustration at price leaks when you realize what enormous efforts he made to secure manufacturers' lines in the first place and to get favorable price deals. Throughout the 1950s, Cotter engaged in a continual struggle for recognition by manufacturers.

THE STRUGGLE FOR MANUFACTURER RECOGNITION

It may seem strange that some manufacturers of hardware refused to sell their goods to Cotter & Company — weren't they in business to move their products? But many of them felt they had compelling reasons. First of all, they invoked the bogey of postwar scarcity and allocations, claiming their production quotas barely satisfied their long-established customers, so they certainly couldn't take on any new ones. This argument had validity in some cases, for a time; but it was far from the whole story. More importantly, hardware manufacturers wanted to protect their reputations by keeping their products out of the hands of discounters and price-cutters. As Shakespeare wrote in *Othello,* ''Who steals my purse, steals trash . . . , but he that filches from me my good name . . . makes me poor indeed.'' Discount houses regularly used national brand items as ''footballs,'' i.e., they bounced the price up and down frequently in special sales. ''Footballing'' of an item eroded consumer confidence in it. If, for example, an appliance sold for $5 one week, $10 the next, and $4.50 the week after, nobody knew what it was really worth. In order to protect their reputations, then, some manufacturers would actually turn down business — if they thought a wholesaler was selling to discount outlets or cutting prices himself.

The decisive reason for manufacturers withholding their lines from dealer-owned and other low-cost distributors, however, was pressure

An old-fashioned hardware store from around the turn of the century. Goodenough Hardware, Chicago, Illinois.

A Mister Oswald cartoon spoofing the old fashioned hardware store. Russ Johnson, who has drawn Mr. Oswald for *Hardware Retailer* magazine since 1925, was a Cotter & Company member in the early years of the company.

John M. Cotter at about age four.

The corner of 7th and Fauquier, St. Paul, Minnesota, around the turn of the century. The hardware store at the far left later was named Dayton's Bluff Hardware. John Cotter began his 70 years of hardware in this store in 1916.

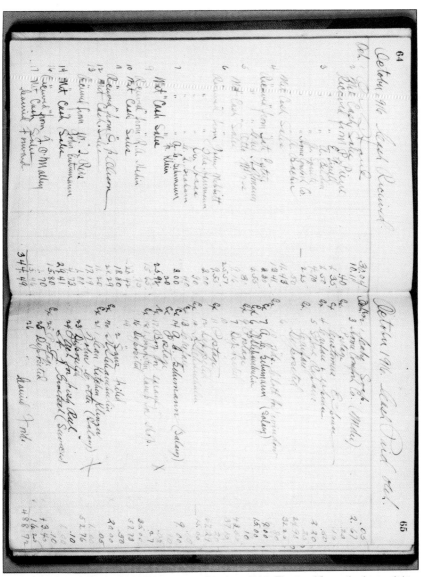

Ledger page from Dayton's Bluff Hardware, October, 1916. The two X's on the lower right mark John Cotter's hiring on October 17 and his first weekly earnings of $1.00 on October 21.

The 3-M company factory in St. Paul, Minnesota. The house John Cotter was born in once stood on this site.

Kelley-How-Thomson's second Hardware Train of Progress, January, 1935. John Cotter is the third from the right, standing on the engine.

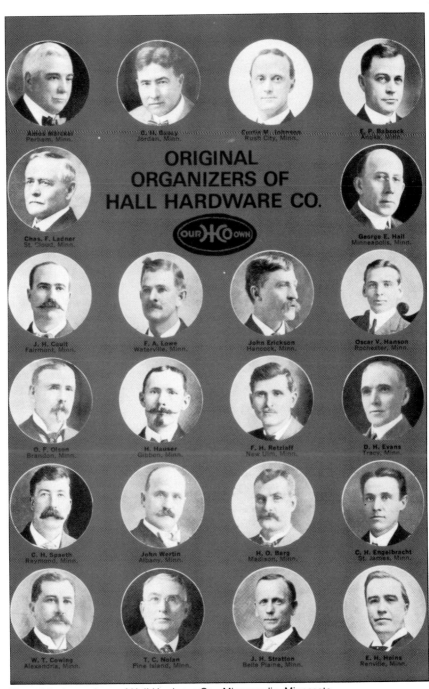

The original organizers of Hall Hardware Co., Minneapolis, Minnesota.

Edward E. Lanctot at about age 25, Oakes & Co., Chicago.

John Cotter at about age forty, Oakes & Co., Chicago.

John Cotter and Ed Lanctot in Cotter & Company's first office, 1948.

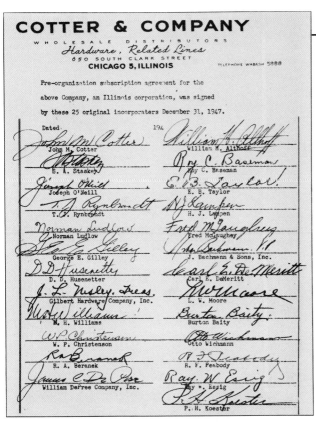

Signatures of Cotter & Company's 25 charter members, 1948.

John Cotter's first pay check at Cotter & Company, March, 1948.

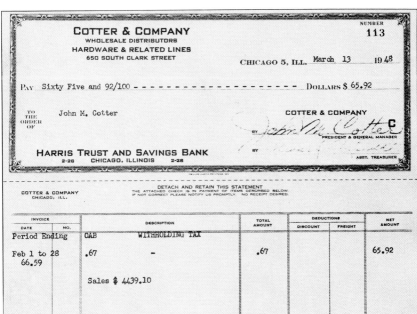

Six original employees of Cotter & Company: (l. to r.) John Cotter, James Eller, Nick Phillips, Frank Morman, Jack Pfeuffer, Edward Lanctot.

Early department managers of Cotter & Company: (Clockwise from top left) Frank Morman, Herbert "Red" Lynes, Herb Haller, Harold Ost.

First Cotter & Company full-page newspaper advertisement, *Chicago Tribune,* April, 1949.

John Leith the printing salesman who set the pattern for the early Direct Mail Catalog and Circulars.

First Cotter & Company direct-mail consumer catalog, Fall, 1948.

Donald M. Cheperka, who produced the first 32 page Direct Mail Catalog in 1948 and is still active in the Art Department.

Cotter & Company's first warehouse space was located in this building, North Pier Terminal, Chicago.

An early Cotter & Company market at North Pier Terminal, January, 1950.

Cotter & Company's warehouse and office on Clybourn Avenue, Chicago, in 1959.

Cotter & Company's General Offices Today.

Hibbard, Spencer, Bartlett's various warehouses over a century of wholesaling. Their last warehouse, built in Evanston, Illinois, in 1948, is at the bottom.

Two key employees acquired from Hibbard, Spencer, Bartlett: (l. to r.) George McIntyre, Edmund S. Kantowicz.

An unusually convivial meeting of three archrivals. (From left) Orville W. Ahl, Hibbard, Spencer, Bartlett; Richard Hesse, Ace Hardware; John Cotter. With Harry Levy, Block & Co. (far right). Corning Glass Century Club Dinner, 1959.

True Value dealers waiting to sign up with Cotter & Company after the Hibbard takeover, 1963. John and Dan Cotter, standing in far corner.

John Cotter and Lawrence L. "Red" Oakes, at the anniversary dinner for John Cotter's fiftieth year in hardware, 1966.

(Right to left) Red Oakes, John Cotter, Bill Stout, and Ben Levy, at fiftieth anniversary dinner.

A paint merchandise committee meeting, 1965.

Occasionally something goes wrong at even the best run companies. Run-away boxcar, Philadelphia distribution center, 1973.

A recent Cotter & Company market.

Outstanding achievement award presented to John Cotter by the National Wholesale Hardware Association, 1981. Much crow was eaten at NWHA on this occasion.

John Cotter and Paul Fee in front of the wall of plaques.

Dan Cotter, president, and Paul Fee, executive vice-president. (l. to r.)

from established, old-line wholesalers. The National Wholesale Hardware Association, shortly after its formation in 1895, had compiled an "approved list" of regular wholesalers, and it constantly reminded manufacturers to maintain this list. Most hardware manufacturers were relatively small and produced only a handful of products, so they were vulnerable to pressure from large wholesale accounts. If a dominant regional wholesaler, such as Hibbard's in Chicago, wanted to strangle an upstart competitor by denying him access to goods, he enjoyed considerable leverage. A manufacturer would think twice about exchanging Hibbard's large volume for the uncertain prospects of a new company. Overt pressure, of course, constituted a "conspiracy in restraint of trade" and could be prosecuted under the anti-trust laws; but such prosecution always proved difficult as wholesalers acted through hints and innuendoes rather than outright threats. They spread gossip around the industry alleging that Cotter & Company was a "fly by night" operation with practically no inventory, that it wouldn't last, and that it couldn't pay its bills. Under the circumstances, it's surprising how many manufacturers ignored this nonsense and did business with Cotter. Perhaps two or three dozen major companies out of hundreds in the industry, persisted in "blacklisting" them beyond a year or two.

John Cotter pursued these manufacturing hold-outs with a variety of techniques, but mainly he wore them down with his persistence. A favorite Cotter phrase sums up his methods: "A Christian endeavor and a frantic effort." He devised a basic form letter, changing it every year or so, and sent it out repeatedly to manufacturers' sales managers. He began each letter in friendly, disarming fashion. The 1949 letter, for example, started out: "You know how it is in business, there are probably a few people that you would like to sell to that don't buy from you and then there are people like ourselves that would like to buy from you that don't seem to arouse your interest." He then went on to relate his company's growing volume of business and describe its aggressive merchandising tactics. He enclosed copies of his company growth chart, various consumer advertising catalogues, testimonials from manufacturers who did sell him goods, and letters from dealers.

Cotter followed these letters up tenaciously, with phone calls and personal visits. Bill Stout advised him, "I don't think it will do any harm for you either to write or call (a sales manager) occasionally, say every 60 days.'' Cotter wasn't too shy to heed this advice. He showed up at Stanley Tools in New Britain, Conn. one day in 1952, and camped outside the office of the executive v-p, Rod Chamberlain. ''How long are you going to be in town?'' Chamberlain asked him. ''I have a comfortable room at the hotel,'' Cotter said. ''I'm going to stay here until I get the line.'' Chamberlain decided to sell him that day before lunch. When Cotter struck an agreement with Revere Copper in 1953 to market their cooking utensils, he pencilled on the final correspondence: ''16 letters, 1 trip to Rome, N.Y., 7 or 9 dealer letters, 8 or 10 phone calls, several meetings, etc.'' He overcame the usual threats from Hibbard's to drop the Revere line by convincing Revere to sell to both Ace and Cotter, thus picking up enough new volume to neutralize Hibbard's threat. After he secured the Master Lock line, Master's sales manager, Earl Tower, wrote Cotter's tool buyer:

''You don't know what a pleasure it is to see a Cotter letterhead sticking out from under the corner of a pile of mail, and know that it is going to be on a subject that we can join with you! For years we used to duck instinctively as we wondered what on earth we were going to say to that man this time. John was never anything but properly persistent, but he sure could think up a lot of questions that were hard for us to answer.''

One question Cotter asked frequently was, ''Who's in charge?'' He discovered in the Master Lock case, after repeated conversations with the sales manager, that Tower lacked the authority to take on new accounts. Only a personal interview with Sam Soref, one of the owners, finally broke the ice. Cotter also discovered that the manufacturer's bottom line furnished him the ultimate weapon. If V & S dealers bought ''blacklisted'' lines, such as Pyrex ware, from old-line wholesalers and sold them in their stores, Pyrex lost nothing by continuing to blacklist Cotter. So Cotter, on occasion, urged his dealers to drop the blacklisted line, market aggressively a competing product purchased from their own wholesaler, and then write the offending manufacturer to tell him about it. Whenever enough dealers cooperated, this tactic invariably worked. Occasionally, too, some sleight of hand proved necessary. Many manufacturers performed a hypocritical little dance around Fair Trade. They insisted that dealers maintain the standard retail price, but they winked at Cotter if he cut his wholesale price and granted the dealers some extra profit. This had to be done secretly to keep the old-line wholesalers from complaining, so many agreements between Cotter & Company and a manufacturer contained the following opaque sentence: "We have agreed that we will exclude from our accounting procedure the distribution margins on your products so that you can assure any wholesaler that our dealers are buying your products here on exactly the same basis as they are from any other wholesaler." What this meant, in plain English, is that Cotter invoiced his dealer at the standard wholesale price, but at month's end he would pass on a discount under the guise of a "freight allowance." No wonder he grew so agitated at price leaks!

Through persistence, dealer pressure, and occasional subterfuges, Cotter gradually convinced the leading hardware and housewares manufacturers to recognize his company as a legitimate wholesaler of their products. The 18 months from Christmas, 1952 to May, 1954 proved decisive in breaking the logjam. Cotter acquired 21 famous name brands during this period, including Stanley and Defiance tools, Mirro, Revere, and Cosco housewares, Westclox clocks and watches, Master padlocks, and General Electric small appliances. A few major lines signed up later, notably Sunbeam, in May, 1955; and a few, such as Black & Decker who sold Cotter briefly in 1949 only to drop him a few months later under pressure from Hibbard's, continued to hold out. Yet by July, 1956, when Cotter acquired the Plumb line of hammers and hatchets, he wrote Plumb's sales manager: "Now there is not one single line which we need, with the exception of Guns and Ammunition, and we are in no hurry to add these." This statement was largely true, except for one further exception Cotter didn't mention — Fisher-Price toys. The great toy controversy is worth recounting from the beginning, as it illustrates well the difficulties Cotter faced in gaining manufacturer recognition and completing his inventory as a full-line wholesaler.

THE TOY CONTROVERSY

Back in 1949, Cotter & Company was just getting established in general hardware and housewares, but it had not yet acquired many toy or sporting goods lines. Hardware stores traditionally sold toys, primarily at Christmas time; but some retail dealers and old-line wholesalers had begun to back away from them due to sharp competition from mass merchandisers. John Cotter didn't intend to abandon toys to the competition, and many members believed that toys could be successfully marketed year-round as a means of drawing more families into hardware stores; so he made plans to go into the toy business. He talked to Walter Scott, an Evanston friend and neighbor who had been toy and cutlery buyer at Shapleigh and Hibbard's before joining Red Oakes at Tru-Test. Cotter asked Scott to take Ed Lanctot by the hand at the March, 1950 New York Toy Fair, an annual merchandise show conducted by the toy manufacturers, and introduce him to the top toy men.

In the meantime, he had surveyed his members and found enough interest in toys that he decided to proceed with a toy show of his own in June to display the goods Lanctot and Scott lined up. Herb Haller had not yet joined Cotter & Company, but his wife, Margaret, was available and willing to help, so Cotter hired her part-time to organize the first toy show. She made the warehouse space at North Pier Terminal as attractive as possible, set up displays as the toys arrived from the manufacturers, and employed her daughter, Geri, and Dan Cotter, to run errands for her. On opening day, Ed Lanctot blew up a gigantic inflatable Santa to greet the dealers and took endless ribbing from his colleagues who avowed they couldn't tell which was Lanctot and which Santa. This first toy show proved successful and Cotter & Company was launched in the toy business. Because of the system of direct and pool orders, Cotter could offer a wide selection of toys, even though he didn't stock very many in the warehouse. Cotter offered width of selection in contrast to the old-line wholesaler's depth of stock.

Then at the 1952 Toy Fair in New York the established wholesalers struck back. Ed Schutz, the toy buyer for A. C. McClurg & Co., a leading wholesaler of toys, stationery, and giftwares in Chicago, spearheaded a campaign among the toy manufacturers to stop selling Cotter. Schutz freely dropped the names of other toy buyers and merchandise managers, including Ed Kantowicz from Hibbard's, and created the illusion that all the established wholesalers backed him. When Kantowicz confronted him about the unauthorized use of his name, Schutz shrugged and said, ''We got to stick together on this.'' Ed Lanctot, in a panic at the seeming conspiracy, called John Cotter back in Chicago early Sunday morning and Cotter told him, ''Put your necktie in your suitcase and come home.'' Lanctot decided to stay on, however, and perform some damage control; and in the end, only about 6 or 8 manufacturers withdrew their lines. The leading line which they lost was Fisher-Price.

Herman Fisher, president and founder of Fisher-Price, was a fishing and drinking buddy of Ed Schutz. He could afford to do Schutz a favor since Fisher-Price enjoyed all the business they needed. Then, as now, F-P manufactured high quality, fairly priced, preschool toys which were nearly indestructible. It was one of the few toy lines that sold year-round. Fisher ran his company very conservatively and usually produced just enough goods to leave a little scarcity at the end of the year. His products were in constant demand, and he felt no need to cultivate the business of new and untried wholesalers like Cotter & Company. So he readily agreed when Schutz asked him to drop Cotter in 1952.

After Lanctot returned from New York, John Cotter got on the phone and called all the manufacturers who had dropped his company. His usual persistence paid off and most of them reinstated his account in short order. But every time he called Fisher-Price in East Aurora, N.Y. Mr. Fisher was always ''in a meeting.'' Finally, one morning he got so frustrated he told Fisher's secretary, ''Hell, you get him out of the meeting or else I'll sue him.'' Fisher came on the line, and Cotter claims they had a long heated discussion. It must have been a hell of an argument, for Fisher remained adamant until 1961.

Cotter then pursued legal action. His lawyer, Frank Greenberg, filed a brief with the Anti-Trust Division of the Justice Department alleging ''discriminatory tactics'' and ''restraint of trade'' on the part of certain wholesalers and manufacturers. The brief rehearsed the old story of Black & Decker ceasing to deal with them in 1949 as well as the recent events concerning Schutz and Fisher. W.J. Montgomery, sales manager for the Dowst Manufacturing Co., maker of Tootsie Toys, appears to have been Cotter's main source of information on the Schutz campaign. Montgomery ''admitted that Mr. E. Schutz and Mr. Elmer Johnson of A. C. McClurg & Co. . . had cornered him at the Toy Fair in New York and given him strict instructions not to sell to Cotter & Company unless he was willing to have McClurg discontinue Tootsie Toys all together.'' The government investigated Cotter's charges thoroughly and apparently FBI agents looked through some toy manufacturers' files, but eventually the Justice Department declined prosecution.

Cotter needed Fisher-Price Toys to build a year-round toy program for his V & S dealers. He tried all his usual tactics on Fisher and his sales manager, Chuck Kelsey, pointing out the large toy volume his dealers sold, urging the dealers not to buy F-P toys from other wholesalers — all to no avail. In 1960 Cotter even apologized to Fisher:

"When one is suddenly confronted with a combination of circumstances that are both abnormal and damaging, a person is likely to act impulsively and in a manner that may not be in the best interests of all concerned. This was exactly the situation in 1952 and resulted in our phone conversation which, in retrospect, was perhaps unnecessary and uncalled for on my part."

Fisher replied coolly, "It is hard to turn down good business, but our overall policy. . .has not changed. . .I am sorry." Finally, a year later, the bottom line overcame Fisher's pride and anger and in June, 1961, Cotter & Company again became a distributor of Fisher-Price Toys.

One might think that men who market happiness to small children would have more pleasing dispositions, but the toy controversy illustrates the panic which old-line wholesalers felt at the rise of new distribution methods. Fisher-Price enjoyed a strong position and was in no danger from anyone, but Schutz and his wholesaler allies feared Cotter and the other low-cost distributors and tried to use Fisher's strength against them. Cotter was trying to build a company but others were intent on tearing it down. The wreckers caused Cotter and Lanctot some aggravation, but they didn't stop them. After a decade in business, Cotter & Company had succeeded in acquiring most of the major hardware-housewares lines and had built a wide dealer base to market the goods. The company not only survived its early tests, it was flourishing.

A TEN-YEAR BALANCE SHEET

In 1958, its tenth full year of operation, Cotter & Company shipped $13 million worth of goods to approximately 460 members. 1958 was not a good year for the American economy; indeed, the worst recession since World War II had temporarily slowed the boom of the phenomenal fifties. It was a year of increasing attrition among traditional hardware wholesalers, as we shall see in a later chapter; but Cotter & Company recorded a 24% increase in sales over the previous year.

The company had established itself firmly as a regional, Midwestern wholesaler, with 39% of its dealer-members in Illinois, 18% in Wisconsin, 16% in Michigan, 7% in Indiana, and 7% in Iowa. Eight other states counted a handful of V & S dealers, ranging from 1 in Alabama to 3 in South Dakota. Dealerships were no longer limited to small towns, as they had been originally, but showed a good mix of city, suburban, and small town locations. In Illinois, for instance, Cotter recorded 184 dealers: 32 in Chicago, 59 in the suburbs, and 93 downstate.

Not all of these dealers contributed equally to the success of their own hardware wholesaler. Too many of them bought minuscule amounts of goods from Cotter & Company, and some tried to play both sides of the street by participating in a stores program from an old-line wholesaler or another dealer-owned organization. Cotter, Lanctot, Haller, and their associates constantly exhorted the dealers to concentrate their purchases, and they instituted various deterrent fees to discourage small, infrequent orders. For a variety of reasons, the company experienced about a 5% annual turnover of dealers, as some members dropped out voluntarily and others were asked to leave.

In February, 1949, Cotter had begun circulating a list of "Ten High Dealers," a monthly tally of the leading dealers, the volume of their purchases, and the population of their towns or trading areas. This regular monthly box score (which expanded to 20 High, 50 High, and 100 High as the company grew) served as a subtle psychological goad to laggard dealers, prodding many to reexamine their operations. "If Joe Smith in a town of 3000 can purchase $100,000 worth of goods, why can't I in a town of 10,000?" These lists reveal that a comparative handful of dealers carried the company in its early days. In 1952, the first 20 dealers (out of 200 total) accounted for 31% of Cotter's business; the first 100 (about half the dealers) recorded 92% of the purchases. These percentages decreased, as Cotter weeded out inactive dealers and more members concentrated their purchases; but in 1958 the first 50 (out of 460) still did 31% of the business; the first 100, 48%.

Figure 1

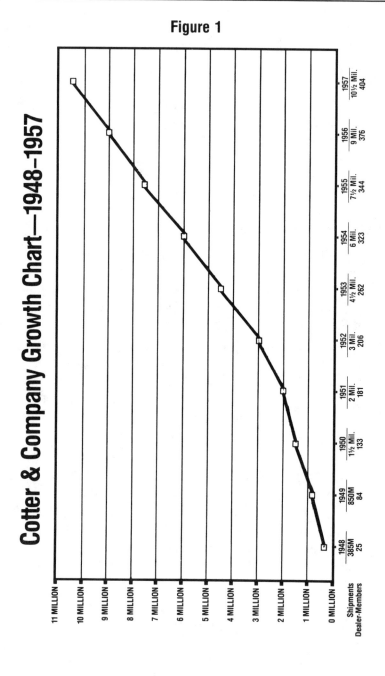

Cotter & Company Growth Chart—1948–1957

TABLE 3
TOP TEN DEALERS — FIRST TEN YEARS

Name	Dealer #	Location & Population	No. of Years Affiliated	No. of Years In Top 10	Total Purchases	Yearly Average
Harry Debo & Son	45	Peru, Ill. 8900	10	10	$1,012,000	$101,200
Gurnee Hardware	42	Gurnee, Ill. 1000	10	10	$ 980,000	$ 98,000
Gus Book's Hardware	21	Lansing, Ill. 15,000	10	10	$ 937,000	$ 93,700
Bowen Hardware	215	Arlington Hts., Ill. 19,000	6	6	$ 895,000	$149,000
Moore Bros. Hardware	19	Rochelle, Ill. 5,000	10	9	$ 671,000	$ 67,100
Christenson's	41	Griffith, Ind. 4,000	10	6	$ 656,000	$ 65,600
Rosenthal Lumber & Fuel	106	Crystal Lake, Ill. 4,000	8	7	$ 650,000	$ 81,250
Wm. DePree Co.	32	Zeeland, Mich. 3,000	10	5	$ 625,000	$ 62,500
⁚. Bachmann & Sons	15	Park Ridge, Ill. 27,000	10	7	$ 617,000	$ 61,700
E. B. Taylor & Co.*	7	Winnetka, Ill. 13,000	10	4	$ 576,000	$ 57,600
Schanck Hardware*	200	Libertyville, Ill. 6,000	6	4	$ 576,000	$ 92,600

*Tied for tenth place
Figures based on "Fifty High" Reports, 1949-1958

Table #3 illustrates the heavy debt John Cotter owed to his leading dealers during the company's crucial first decade. Harry Debo alone purchased over $1 million worth of goods in ten years, and the eleven dealers listed accounted for 14% of Cotter's business over the ten year span. The table also reveals that eight of the eleven leading dealers were located in suburbs of Chicago. Obviously, V & S Hardware was well positioned to capitalize on the postwar suburban building boom.

John Cotter marked every milestone of growth in order to create a snowball effect and encourage even greater growth. The company recorded its first million dollar month in March, 1956, "quite a contrast," Cotter remarked to his members, "with March '48 — the second month in operation — with shipments of $14,351." Then in 1958, Cotter & Compnay earned the first of many manufacturers' awards which now line the walls of company headquarters. Ekco Products of Chicago awarded Cotter its Century Club trophy to mark $100,000 worth of purchases in 1958; Rubbermaid of Wooster, Ohio made a similar presentation. These two manufacturers had sold merchandise to Cotter almost from the beginning; but before long, Cotter would be earning awards from manufacturers who refused to sell to him just a few years previously.

Probably the most important sign of the company's growing maturity was the purchase of its own warehouse on Clybourn Avenue in 1958. North Pier Terminal had served the fledgling company well, allowing it to expand its rented space rapidly as it acquired new manufacturers' lines. Frank Morman used to say, "We never moved into an addition, we exploded into it." Yet the terminal building presented several disadvantages. Not all of Cotter's rented space was contiguous, rather it was scattered over five floors and several sections of the building. Furthermore, there was no point in installing the latest conveyor belts and other equipment in a rented facility. Cotter's lease at North Pier ran until April 30, 1955, but he began looking for new facilities in early 1954. He put in a bid on a warehouse building at 1030-50 W. North Ave., in the old Goose Island industrial district along the north branch of the Chicago river; but he was unable to arrange financing for the mortgage so the deal fell through. Industrial mortgage lenders considered Cotter & Company too young and under-capitalized for a large loan. Cotter did get something out of this abortive purchase, however. He had reported the purchase negotiations to his current landlord, Bill Huggett, president of North Pier Terminal, and Huggett immediately tried to induce him to stay put. Eventually Cotter and Huggett re-negotiated a five year lease extension, with a 20% reduction in rent; and Huggett agreed to consolidate Cotter's warehouse space into adjoining sections, even if he had to move other tenants at his expense.

Despite the favorable terms, Cotter began looking around again in 1957, and he finally discovered that his landlord owned just what he wanted. Besides its main terminal buildings downtown, North Pier Terminal Co. owned a few other warehouses around the city, including a building at 2740 N. Clybourn Ave. This five-story warehouse, originally built by International Harvester in 1907, contained 200,000 sq. ft. of space and was in relatively good repair and sprinklered throughout. Huggett offered it for $650,000 on a land contract. A contract purchase poses more risks than conventional mortgage financing, for the buyer builds up no equity in the building and does not gain legal title to it until the final payment is made; but in this case, it provided a way around the reluctance of mortgage lenders.

In fact, the Clybourn Avenue purchase turned out very favorably. Cotter & Company made a $100,000 down payment in 1958, raised by a subscription drive among the members, then owed the balance in annual installments of $50,000 plus 5½% interest. Total annual payments amounted to less than the rental fees at North Pier. The contract also allowed pre-payment without penalty and offered a $25,000 discount if the total price was paid off before December 31, 1964. Cotter exercised this option, making his final payment and taking title to the building on August 11, 1961.

Ben Maze, Marty Seplak, Frank Morman, and Jim Eller began laying out the warehouse at 2740 N. Clybourn in November, 1958; some merchandise was moved over in January, 1959, and for two chaotic months the company shipped goods from two separate locations. The move was finally completed in March. Cotter immediately negotiated with the owner of a smaller warehouse building next door at 2752 N. Clybourn, buying it through a trust for $260,000 in June, 1959. Though close together, the two buildings were not connected, so Cotter built a one-story connector which doubled as a loading dock. Altogether the company headquarters acquired in 1959 added up to 288,000 sq.ft. of floor space. The total price for purchase and renovations approached a million dollars.

Ownership of its own ample warehouse gave Cotter & Company legitimacy in the hardware industry. Old-line wholesalers frequently charged that Ace and the dealer-owned firms were mere brokers, not true wholesalers, since they primarily arranged direct shipments from the factory and stocked little or no inventory themselves. When John Stiles, the head of Morley-Murphey Co. in Green Bay, Wisconsin, was elected President of the National Wholesale Hardware Association in 1957, he referred to such firms as ''pseudo-wholesalers.'' Such charges, true in Cotter's case only for the first six months, now appeared totally ridiculous. Cotter & Company, in one hectic decade, had arrived. Not yet a national firm, the dealer-owned V & S organization had shown that hardware dealers could meet mass merchandisers on their own terms, with competitive prices and aggressive advertising. The company headquarters on Clybourn Avenue — a converted warehouse in a grimy industrial district, with painted brick walls in the executive offices — aptly symbolized the commitment to low costs. From this bastion, Cotter took over leadership of the still-controversial dealer-owned cooperative movement.

CHAPTER SIX
THE DEALER-OWNED MANAGERS' CAUCUS

"The ultimate aim of dealer-owned wholesalers is not to eliminate the recognized and needed wholesaler function but to keep independent retail hardware merchants in business. . . . The degree to which we succeed in this endeavor will, to a large extent, determine the future of the entire hardware industry as we know it today."

—Arnold E. Poole, general manager of
  Western Hardware, in *Hardware Retailer,* May, 1960

The managers of dealer-owned hardware wholesalers, though primarily hard-headed businessmen, sometimes expressed a sense of mission. They considered themselves men of the future, the best hope for saving independent retailers in the hardware industry. For more than twenty years, they maintained a little-known and unusual institution to express their common loyalty to shared goals — the dealer-owned managers' caucus. Beginning in 1935, at George Hall's initiative, the managers met informally one day a year to exchange information and ideas — usually in conjunction with larger hardware meetings, such as the retail or wholesale hardware association conventions. Since the early dealer-owned firms were all regional in scope and did not directly compete with each other, they could afford to share some business secrets. Still, they were all potential competitors in the same industry, so their exchanges were often marked by wariness and controversy. Nevertheless, their caucus expressed a unique sense of solidarity, most unusual in business; for they were "drawn together by a common struggle for legitimacy." They believed that their real competitors were not each other, but the mail order houses, mass merchandising chains, and discounters who threatened all hardware wholesalers and retailers.

John Cotter attended his first managers' caucus shortly after his company opened for business in 1948. He welcomed the support it offered him and learned a lot at these annual meetings; before long, he started to repay the debt by helping out other managers. Yet, after a decade or so, the managers' caucus began to break up, partly due to the success of Cotter & Company. As Cotter's firm pushed beyond its initial regional borders, the latent competition, suspicion and jealousy in the caucus boiled over and dissolved the sense of solidarity. Dealer-owned hardware companies never replaced the fragile unity of the caucus with a more durable institution, such as a national wholesalers' federation.

THE MANAGERS' CAUCUS

Bill Stout recommended John Cotter to the caucus in 1948; and Tom Willis of Northern Hardware, who was hosting that year's gathering, invited him to the meeting on July 22 and 23 in Portland, Oregon. Though he was just getting his company off the ground, Cotter considered the meeting important enough to travel half way across the continent to attend. He found the free exchange of information invaluable and took notes on everything, from the number of field men employed by each firm to the style of order forms they used. Le Herron, Sr., who had not made the trip West, dismissed the caucus meetings as merely social gatherings; but Cotter disagreed with him: "I must say that the benefit I received from it was immeasurable." He shrewdly recognized a chance to pick the brains of more experienced managers as a rare opportunity. At one meeting, George Allen, from the Walter H. Allen Co. didn't say a word, claiming he had just come to listen. Cotter commented, "If everybody just came to listen, we'd have a mighty informative meeting!"

About a dozen dealer-owned hardware wholesalers kept in touch with each other during the 1950s, as indicated in Table 4. Our Own Hardware and American hardware remained the leaders, with 1949 sales of $15 million and $9 million, respectively, about ⅔ of the sales volume of the whole group. John Cotter's relations with Steve Duffy, the manager of Our Own, were correct but not particularly close. Cotter had a high regard for Duffy's abilities but the two stubborn Irishmen from the Twin Cities seemed to rub each other the wrong way. Once, when he was still working at Tru-Test, Cotter had told Duffy that Coast-to-Coast stores were "eating Our Own's lunch" in many towns and that the Melamed brothers were soft-soaping him at the country club so he didn't notice it. Duffy fumed and sputtered that Our Own remained No. 1 in its area. Cotter quickly forgot the incident, but Duffy did not. He interrogated his field men and found that Coast-to-Coast was indeed making aggressive inroads. Relations between the two stayed prickly after Cotter started his dealer-owned firm, but Our Own's buyers did give Cotter some help in acquiring manufacturers' lines and Duffy and Cotter did exchange financial information.

Ties between American Hardware and Cotter & Company were much closer, as we have seen. Bill Stout helped Cotter every step of the way in the organization of his own firm and the two men liked each other personally. Stout wrote to Cotter at one point, "It goes without saying you are welcome here any time. I enjoy your company. I enjoy your conversation. . . ." Even after Stout's resignation in 1953, the top men in Pittsburgh and Chicago communicated regularly. Zeb Hastings, Stout's successor, examined Cotter's balance sheets with his accountant's eye and continually warned him he was expanding too

TABLE 4

THE DEALER-OWNED HARDWARE "CAUCUS" IN THE 1950S

NAME	LOCATION	DATE FOUNDED	GENERAL MANAGER	COMMENTS
Walter H. Allen	Dallas, Texas	1934	Walter H. Allen	Taken over by Cotter & Company, 1965
American Hardware	Pittsburgh, Pa.	1910	Wm. Stout, E. A. Hastings, F. Leon Herron, Jr.	Bill Stout a major mentor of John Cotter
Cotter & Company	Chicago, Ill.	1948	John M. Cotter	
Franklin Hardware	Philadelphia, Pa.	1939	F. Leon Herron, Sr.	Taken over by American, 1962
Hardware Wholesalers, Inc.	Fort Wayne, Ind.	1945	Arnold Gerberding	
Northern Hardware	Portland, Ore.	1923	Thomas Willis, Don Foss	Taken over by Cotter & Company, 1970
Our Own Hardware	Minneapolis, Minn.	1913	Steve Duffy	Immediate model for Cotter & Company
Southwest Hardware	Los Angeles, Ca.	1912	Harry Izenour, Arne Kammeier	Merged with Western Hardware in 1961 to form Great Western. Taken over by Cotter & Company, 1968
Southwestern Hardware	Oklahoma City, Ok.	1944	Robert Arnold	Taken over by Oklahoma Hardware, 1956
United Hardware	Kansas City, Mo.	1947	Russell Cook	Liquidated in 1956
United Hardware	Minneapolis, Minn.	1957	Newcomb Diehl	
Western Hardware	Phoenix, Ariz.	1955	Arnold Poole	Merged with Southwest Hardware in 1961 to form Great Western. Taken over by Cotter & Company, 1968
Wisco Hardware	Madison, Wis.	1925	John A. Fitschen	Liquidated in 1975

fast. "I don't know why I worry about you and your operations, but I do," Hastings wrote Cotter.

Northern Hardware in Portland, Oregon, and the Walter H. Allen Co. of Dallas, Texas, had both established themselves as moderately successful, small wholesalers in their own regions. Thomas L. Willis, a soft-spoken civil engineer, had guided Northern from its beginnings in 1923 until his retirement in 1953. Hedley Dingle, an aggressive member in Coeur d'Alene, Idaho was elected president of Northern in 1953 and Don Foss moved up from sales manager to take Willis' place as general manager. Immediately upon taking the helm at Northern, Foss and Dingle introduced and promoted the "Home Town Hardware" name for store identification and advertising purposes. Northern averaged about $5 million in sales per year, good enough for third place among the dealer-owneds until Cotter displaced it in the mid-fifties. Walter H. Allen, formerly a travelling salesman for Simmons Hardware, had founded a dealer-owned firm in Dallas in 1934. He and his brother, George, had run the firm since then, splitting the usual manager's salary, 1% of sales, between them. They did about $3 million in sales in 1955, so their compensation was not princely.

Cotter & Company, Hardware Wholesalers Inc. (HWI), and United of Kansas City all started out at virtually the same time, right after World War II; but they experienced drastically different fates. Arnold H. Gerberding, an experienced hardware man from Indiana, had founded HWI in Fort Wayne in 1945. The "H" in its title was somewhat misleading since HWI sold as much lumber and building material as it did hardware. Indeed, Gerberding recalled, "The first eight dealers I signed were lumber dealers." Serving largely a small town market from Fort Wayne, HWI grew steadily but at only half the rate of Cotter & Company. By 1955, Cotter recorded over $7 million in sales and HWI only $3 million. United in Kansas City, on the other hand, did not even reach ½ million dollars in sales volume, and in 1956 the company was liquidated. Russ Cook, another Oakes protege, had formed United at the same time Cotter was starting out; but Cook's former employers, Townley Hardware in Kansas City, fought him head to head and prevented him from getting a foothold.

All the other dealer-owned wholesalers were struggling during the

1950s. Wisco in Madison, Southwestern in Oklahoma City, and Western in Phoenix each suffered from a restricted market area. Franklin in Philadelphia was flying in the face of ruthless competition from old-line wholesalers and modern discounters. Southwest in Los Angeles, the second-oldest dealer-owned firm, had a turbulent history of dealer independence. Harry Izenour had kept the firm financially solvent but had let the dealers go their own way. Arne Kammeier, a former executive secretary of the Pacific Southwest Hardware Association, succeeded Izenour in 1953 and lost control completely. By the time Southwest merged with Western Hardware of Phoenix in 1961, it was running a deficit since the dealers insisted on expensive services, such as will calls and phone orders, and refused to pay service charges for these privileges.

It should be pointed out that Table 4 does not include all the dealer-owned hardware wholesalers in the country, but only those who communicated with each other as members of the "caucus."* Since the caucus was entirely informal, with no charter or by-laws, membership requirements were somewhat nebulous. Cotter's letter of invitation implied several criteria: "dealer-owned wholesalers who are set up along the lines of the Hall Hardware Company of Minneapolis, and who are meeting the requirements of the manufacturers' and fair trade laws." In addition, the managers insisted that a firm be 100% dealer-owned, with no outside stockholders, and that it sell primarily to hardware stores. General Mercantile of St. Louis, for instance, was never welcomed into the fold because a small group of officers and directors owned 90% of its stock, leaving the general dealership only 10%. United of Minneapolis was not admitted until

---

*In 1963, Eugene F. Grape, an economics professor, identified the following dealer-owned hardware wholesalers who did not belong to the informal caucus: Bay Cities Hardware, Burlingame, Ca.; Connecticut Hardware, Cromwell, Conn.; Coin Hardware, Iselin, N.J.; Dash Sales, Long Island, N.Y.; General Mercantile, St. Louis, Mo.; Harlem Valley Supply, Bedford Hills, N.Y.; Inland Hardware, Turlock, Ca.; Keystone Hardware, Cincinnati, Oh.; Master Hardware, Somerville, Mass.; Standard Hardware, Nashua, N.H.; Twin County Supply, Long Island, N.Y.; Western Wholesale Hardware, Oakland, Ca.

1957 when the dealers bought out the Eugene Koblas family's controlling interest, stopped selling to non-member stores, and dropped a furniture business sideline. In some cases, though, there is no obvious reason why a particular dealer-owned firm didn't belong to the caucus. Probably, the managers simply didn't know, or didn't like, each other.

The managers who did meet informally with each other ranged over a great variety of issues — manufacturers' blacklists, techniques of acquiring dealers, direct-mail advertising, ways and means of reducing costs. At meetings in Minneapolis in 1949 and Pittsburgh in 1950, controversy developed over the exchange of operating statistics. John Fitschen of Wisco was reluctant to release his own figures; and when he did, he merged the statistics from his lumber sales into the hardware sales total. This artificially lowered his expense percentages, since lumber requires a much lower overhead, and rendered his figures useless for comparative purposes. Cotter began complaining about this before the 1950 meeting, writing to Stout, "I am against discussing our figures with a Manager present who has not come to the meeting with an accurate set of figures." Fitschen didn't change his ways, so Cotter stopped attending the caucus for three years. He even avoided the 1954 conclave in Chicago, where he would have been the logical candidate for host; Arnold Gerberding from Fort Wayne convened the gathering instead.

Other problems cropped up in the caucus, besides the absence of accurate figures from Wisco. Several of the general managers found it inconvenient to attend personally and sent assistants instead. In addition, curious dealers appeared from time to time, distracting further from the manager-to-manager format. In 1955, Cotter returned to the caucus and tried to get it back on track. He wrote to Arne Kammeier, who had the longest distance to travel, "Please try and be on hand for the managers' meeting. I urge you not to let anything interfere with your visit as Steve Duffy wrote me today that he will be on hand. In diplomatic circles they would call it a top level conference — so if the larger ones are going to be there, all of the rest of us surely should show up." All the general managers, except Fitschen, did show up that year, and they adopted a standardized format for reporting business statistics. These figures were not circulated to any manager who failed to submit his own.

The 1955 statistics, in Table 5, reveal some interesting differences among the dealer-owned firms. Our Own and American remained in the lead, both in sales and number of dealers, but Cotter was coming up rapidly in third place. American paid a much larger rebate to its dealers than Our Own did, primarily because its expenses were lower. Steve Duffy took some criticism for the relatively high expense level but he defended it as a consequence of the high caliber of services Our Own dealers had come to expect. Cotter & Company recorded the lowest expense percentage of any dealer-owned wholesaler in 1955, just over 10%. Cotter made the further reduction of that figure his top priority, driving it below 10% in 1956 and down to 8% by 1962. Perhaps the primary reason for Cotter's low expenses can be found in the high percentage of direct shipments his dealers utilized. Of all the dealer-owneds, only Cotter, Walter Allen, and HWI used direct shipments extensively (27%, 25%, and 21.3%, respectively); and this showed up on the balance sheets in a relatively leaner inventory and a lower expense ratio.

The managers' caucus lurched along uncertainly for a few more years. John Cotter hosted a gathering at New York's hardware show in October, 1956; and Walter Allen convened the group in July, 1957 when the NRHA met in Dallas. It is not clear whether or not the caucus met again in the 1950s. Arnold Poole made another attempt to revive the annual meetings in 1961; but a gathering in Phoenix in March, 1962 appears to be the final time the caucus met.

AN ODD COUPLE — COTTER AND POOLE

John Cotter continued to support the managers' caucus long after it had outlived its usefulness to him, primarily because he felt a sense of responsibility to the dealer-owned cooperative movement. George Hall's example and Bill Stout's counsel had started him in business and he felt an obligation to pay them back. He satisfied this debt in a variety of ways. Even while he was boycotting the managers' meetings in the early 50s, he still exchanged balance sheets with most of the other managers on a bilateral basis. When Arne Kammeier, shortly after taking over at Southwest Hardware, wrote that he would be passing through Chicago, Cotter urged him to stop in and assured him he would give him all

TABLE 5

COMPARATIVE STATISTICS FOR DEALER-OWNED WHOLESALERS, 1955

COMPANY	GROSS SALES	No. of DEALERS	AVERAGE INVENTORY	EXPENSES % OF SALES	REBATES % OF SALES	DIRECT SHIPMENTS % OF SALES
Our Own	$16,342,613	563	$3,345,856	14.00%	4.19%	4.96%
American	$13,716,000	427	$2,700,000	11.99%	6.37%	9.00%
Cotter	$ 7,564,188	340	$1,251,324	10.27%	4.87%	27.00%
Northern	$ 5,197,506	305	$1,173,826	13.87%	3.29%	8.00%
Walter Allen	$ 3,562,069	220	$ 708,084	10.50%	4.70%	25.00%
HWI	$ 3,197,506	198	$ 491,647	10.41%	5.93%	21.31%
Southwest	$ 2,171,810	115	$ 480,000	15.65%	3.40%	7.20%
Franklin	$ 1,767,674	146	$ 414,769	13.80%	2.00%	3.10%

the time he could. Much later, in 1963, a young economics professor, writing a Ph.D. dissertation on dealer-owned hardware wholesalers at Ohio State University asked him for an interview. Cotter encouraged him in his work, gave him permission to survey his dealer-members, contributed to the financing of the survey, and even proofread a draft of the completed dissertation. Largely due to Cotter's assistance, Eugene F. Grape completed his dissertation, entitled "Retailer-owned Cooperative Wholesaling in the Hardware Trade," and received his Ph.D. in 1966. Grape's work remains the only full-scale study of the subject to this day.

John Cotter's odd relationship with Arnold Poole of Western Hardware, however, illustrates in more striking fashion his sense of obligation to the movement. Arnold E. Poole, 10 years Cotter's junior, was born in Pittsburgh in 1914, became Sears, Roebuck's youngest store manager in 1940, then opened his own retail hardware store in upstate New York. Moving West after the war, he settled in Phoenix because someone told him "there was more sunshine in Phoenix than any other place in the U.S." Working as sales manager for the 0. S. Stapley Co. in Phoenix, he conceived the idea of starting a dealer-owned hardware wholesale organization. He called on John Cotter one day in March, 1954 for advice.

Poole was a somewhat eccentric individual, at least he seemed so in the "real-men-don't-eat-quiche" world of hardware. He was a dapper man with a pencil-thin mustache, a fancy dresser, and an amateur magician. When Cotter offered him a tour of his warehouse, he showed up the next day in pink shoes, a cause of undisguised mirth on the part of the warehousemen. Cotter actually tried to discourage Poole from opening up in Phoenix, pointing out accurately that the number of hardware dealers in Arizona was too small to provide adequate volume. Yet when Poole went ahead anyway and organized the Western Hardware Co. on April 12, 1955 in Phoenix, Cotter generously offered him his full and frank advice and assistance.

Poole consciously attempted to model his company on Cotter's as exactly as possible. He began by combing the Dun & Bradstreet listings for dependable dealers, conducted a few pre-organization meetings, then incorporated with 24 charter members. He sent John Cotter a long list of specific questions about his company. Cotter's reply on

April 25, 1955 expresses more completely than any other document his philosophy of management in a dealer-owned company.

He began the letter with an ironic greeting: "May I take this opportunity to extend to you my sincerest sympathy. You are embarking on a program that is very noble and necessary but nevertheless, I believe, one that will require most skillful handling. The reward is great but the effort required is probably just as great." He then went on to assure Poole of his willingness to help: "Arnold, I want to say that in answering your questions if I do not make myself clear, do not hesitate to call on us again and again if necessary until you get a clear picture in your mind." Cotter answered over a dozen specific questions, for example:

Q. Did you use bank financing during the first year?

A. No — but I personally loaned the company substantially from time to time.

Q. What method did you use to get dealers into your company?

A. Both meetings and individual contacts plus a continued barrage of mailings — mail something to your prospective dealers every two weeks — don't let up ever.

Q. If you were just starting to organize now, what basic changes would you make in your plans or policy?

A. *None*"

Poole was planning to offer a flat 6% cash discount to dealers on all goods sold them and asked Cotter, "Do you see anything which might cause trouble under such a plan?" Cotter answered vehemently, and at great length: "Yes — I see everything to cause trouble in this — don't do it... You will not be able to get the good lines and hold them on this basis." Cotter's bitter struggle with the manufacturers had taught him the folly of acquiring a discounter's reputation. "I am going back to the 6% cash discount again — if you insist on this program you are committing suicide before you get started." Cotter got so agitated on this subject he called up Walter Allen and asked him to confirm his advice. Allen wrote Poole immediately, "I am in thorough accord with all the answers John gave you and I would like to — unsolicited — add my comments... For you to agree to give the dealers 6% cash discount on everything you sell them would, in my opinion, be suicide."

Cotter sent Poole copies of stock statements, dealer contracts, balance sheets, and every other piece of paper used in his business, but made it clear why he was feeding him so much information:

"All of this material forwarded to you is on the basis that your organization will be completely dealer-owned . . . All of the material will be kept and used for the development of a 100% dealer-owned organization. If not, I would appreciate your returning all of this material."

Poole admired Cotter extravagantly, looked up to him as a mentor and something of a father-figure, and never stopped using him as a model for his business. It was a somewhat one-sided relationship, for Cotter held no particularly warm personal feelings for Poole and he did not expect Western Hardware to succeed. He did respect Poole's skill with words, however. Western Hardware's weekly dealer bulletin, *The Branding Iron,* was a lively and witty sheet, which Cotter quoted frequently. Poole may have spent too much time laboring over his literary endeavors to the detriment of his company's basic nuts and bolts.

Cotter continued to offer detailed and frequent letters of advice to Poole, but his initial prediction that the Arizona market was too restricted proved true. Poole tried to rectify his initial error by widening his geographic reach. In June of 1961 he merged his firm with the struggling Southwest Hardware of California, calling the new company Great Western Hardware (Great Western International, to be sure. He had several dealers in Tijuana.) Despite the larger dealer base, red ink persisted. Poole wrote despondently to Cotter: "I may be a lousy manager, an idealist who has no business trying to run a wholesale or retail company, but I at least know that everything I have ever done was done to further a cause I believe in to the bottom of my soul . . . You have been able to put these ideas across and turn them into profits so they must be right. Somewhere I have missed the boat. . . ."

Poole remained John Cotter's greatest fan, right up to the day when Cotter finally took over his company (as we shall see later). Poole virtually shouted Cotter's praises from the rooftops: "We have copied, imitated, cribbed, or stole everything we have done from you and I don't care who knows it. I take credit for the fact that I was smart enough to know who to follow, even before he became the leader . . ." Cotter replied, "Somebody said 'Protect me from my flattering friends and I can take care of my enemies,' but flattery sure sounds nice."

Cotter didn't answer every inquiry about dealer-ownership as fully as he did Poole's. When someone he didn't know dropped a letter or a questionnaire in his mail box, he usually answered it perfunctorily and suggested the subject was too complicated to cover by correspondence. Then, too, he frequently turned down men he knew well, such as Don Foss and Walter Allen, when they wanted him to speak at their conventions. But Arnold Poole's sincerity and dedication were so apparent, his capacity for hard work so evident, and his need of assistance so desperate, that Cotter went out of his way to help. Just as Bill Stout had fostered Cotter's enterprise, so Cotter passed on what he knew to a younger colleague.

COTTER'S RISE

By the time Poole chose Cotter as his model and mentor, the rapid growth of Cotter & Company had made some of the other dealer-owned managers nervous. Potential for conflict existed from the start. Some of the dealers who received Cotter's original mailing in 1947 already belonged to Wisco or HWI. Arnold Gerberding immediately complained to Bill Stout, for he knew Stout was assisting Cotter. When Stout admonished Cotter, he readily agreed to avoid open competition for dealers. Yet the Midwest was too small for Cotter & Company, Wisco, and HWI to remain noncompetitive indefinitely, since Madison and Fort Wayne are each less than 200 miles from Chicago. In a very short time, Cotter had clearly outdistanced the other two in sales volume; and before long, he was approaching the leaders in the field as well. After only ten years in business, Cotter & Company's sales volume equalled American's; in two more years, it had passed Our Own's. (See figure 2)

Cotter's spectacular growth eroded the sense of solidarity in the dealer-owned fraternity. Steve Duffy refused to attend the revived caucus meeting in 1961, implying that Cotter used the exchange of information to steal dealers. Cotter wrote Duffy a blunt reply:

"Now, when it comes to competition in the field, let's look at the facts. Wisco, when I was trying to get started, came in and used their advantages to take dealers away from us after I had signed them up... Hardware Wholesalers of Fort Wayne did the same thing... We have lost an occasional member here or there to you,

Figure 2

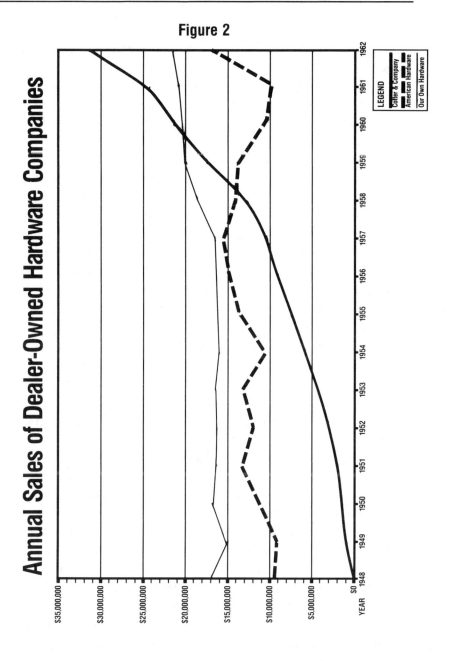

to Ace, to Hibbard, and we have taken our share too, so there has been some jockeying all around . . . Based on the actions of other dealer-owned organizations, it seems I have as many reasons to holler as anybody else. This competitive situation, however, is as it should be. I have never let what any fieldman of any organization said get under my skin, because this is the true competitive spirit — in other words, a survival of the fittest.''

Easy to say when you have already proven yourself fittest.

Actually, Steve Duffy had little to complain about, for Cotter did not directly encroach on his territory; but in 1960, Cotter & Company did begin to expand in American's direction. Often there was more than one progressive hardware dealer in each town; Cotter wanted to offer his program to American's competitors. Cotter recalls the decision to push beyond his original five-state base:

"Red Lynes and I were on the Broadway Limited going to Philadelphia to the National Retail Hardware Association convention in July (1960). It was the early part of July so the days were long, and we sat there going through those towns one after another in Ohio, and we said, here's Ohio, with 12 million people, an empire in itself. And as the train rattled along, we talked and talked and talked some more about what we could do to invade Ohio . . . and we came to the conclusion we would have to get a distribution center down there.''

To this day, Cotter's employees shudder when he goes on a trip and has time to think, since he often comes up with his wildest ideas then.

An opportunity to put this particular "wild" idea to work by "invading" Ohio came up later in 1960. Ben Yankin, owner of the Majestic Paint Co., told Cotter that a small, struggling dealer-owned company in Zanesville, Ohio, called Wholesale Hardware Sales (not to be confused with Hardware Wholesalers Inc. of Ft. Wayne) might be ready to sell out. With Yankin's help, Cotter and Lynes convinced the eighty Zanesville dealers that Cotter & Company offered them a better program; but the process of working out a merger was protracted.

First, Lynes secured authorization from Ohio authorities to sell stock in the state. Then, he had to head off an attempt by Ace Hardware to "horn in on the deal." Finally, he and Cotter had to convince the six members of WHS's board of directors to endorse the merger. David

Farley was the key board member who engineered the replacement of two dissenting directors with more agreeable dealers. All this took time, but by the following summer (1961) all seemed in readiness, as Cotter and Lynes headed for Zanesville on one of the hottest days of the year for a board of directors meeting. In the meantime, however, the lawyer and the accountant in Zanesville had realized they were about to lose a client, and the general manager of WHS, Bob King, also got to worrying about his future. Cotter offered King a two year contract, which he accepted; but the lawyer and accountant had planted doubts in the directors' minds. Finally, Cotter got in touch with Farley and said, "Gee, I thought we had a deal. But from what I hear down here it doesn't sound like it." Farley stared back at him and said, "We got a deal." That's all he said, but he was good as his word. The next day at the directors' meeting the merger was approved. Ratification by the stockholders followed later and Cotter & Company took over in Zanesville officially on October 11, 1961.

Zanesville, a railroad town about 40 miles east of Columbus, was not well located, so Cotter moved the distribution center to Cleveland in 1962. Yet, WHS had served its purpose. Cotter wanted and needed a nucleus of dealers in place before assuming the expense of opening a branch distribution center.

The Ohio move brought Cotter & Company directly into American Hardware's territory. In the meantime, American had fallen into difficulties of its own. Le Herron, Jr., who had apprenticed with his father at Franklin Hardware, succeeded Zeb Hastings as general manager of American in 1957. Herron faced two intractable problems in Pittsburgh, which made his eight years at the helm stormy and turbulent. The company had a long-term lease at an exorbitant rent in their old, multi-story, public warehouse. To make matters worse, their Teamster local was one of the most militant in the country, and the Teamster shop steward virtually dictated the operational rules in the warehouse. When the union refused to make any cost-saving concessions to management, the company took a long, six-to-eight month strike in 1960-61. Herron determined to move away from these problems and start fresh in a new warehouse with a nonunion staff. American broke ground in suburban Butler, Pa. in March of 1961 and moved in later that year; but, unexpectedly, their landlord at the terminal building in Pittsburgh refused to cancel their existing lease, which ran until 1968. Herron's firm, therefore, paid double rent for a considerable period of time until a sub-lessee could be found.

The union did not give up easily. Though Herron worked out a generous severance pay agreement with Jimmy Hoffa, national president of the Teamsters Union, the militant Pittsburgh local repudiated it and demanded arbitration of the jurisdictional question. They posted an "informational picket line" at the Butler warehouse, and Teamster truck drivers refused to cross it. The company eventually won the right to operate without a union, but the arbitration proceedings and the semi-strike situation dragged on throughout 1962. The net result was, in Herron's words, "five or six lost years at a critical time in American's history." While American was preoccupied with its internal troubles, its nearby rivals, HWI and Cotter & Company, were growing rapidly and picking up some of its dealers.

In the midst of the turmoil, Herron and Cotter were actively planning a merger. American's directors had taken one look at the informational pickets and, remembering the bitterness of the recent strike, had temporarily lost their nerve. They came to Chicago in October of 1961 to hammer out the details of a merger; and on November 10, 1961 a Letter of Understanding was drafted. Under its terms, Cotter & Company would acquire all the assets of American Hardware, would place four American members on its board of directors, and would operate the new Butler warehouse as a distribution center. Thirteen years after Bill Stout had coaxed Cotter into business, Cotter was on the verge of taking over the company that Stout had shaped. Shortly after the first of the year, however, Cotter decided to back off. Both the labor relations problems and the heavy financial obligations of American gave him pause; and in the end, he decided the acquisition might induce corporate indigestion. American's directors, who had recovered their composure in the meantime, were relieved that the deal fell through.

Cotter and Herron became somewhat uneasy rivals. Cotter wrote the younger man, "Free advice is usually not worth much more than it costs, but any time you want to discuss any problems please do not hesitate to give me a call." Herron, however, felt uncomfortable exchanging information as if nothing had happened since the days of

Bill Stout. He wrote Cotter in March, 1962: "No one ever likes to be in a position where they feel they are getting more than they are giving . . . Accordingly, I feel that it is not only proper but my obligation to suggest that we discontinue the regular exchange of financial statements until such time as it might be on a more equal basis." This snapped the last slender thread holding together members of the dealer-owned managers' caucus.

Some had hoped it might work out otherwise. Le Herron, Sr., long urged the managers' caucus to develop more formal ties and forge a nationwide federation of dealer-owned wholesalers. This plan for a "cooperative of cooperatives" had worked well in the grocery trade, and Herron believed it offered the best hope for hardwaremen to compete with discounters. "I said it in 1942 —repeated it in 1951 — I am saying it again! — No one of us is as smart as All of Us! and I might add — No one of us is as *strong* as all of us." Arnold Poole, still trying to breathe some life into the managers' caucus, expressed his willingness "to see all our companies unite as a powerful national group;" but John Cotter disagreed. His experiences with Tru-Test, where the petty jealousies of wholesalers often wrecked Red Oakes' cooperative arrangements, had affected him more negatively than he usually admitted and permanently soured him on plans of federation. So he answered Herron in 1963, "This subject can be discussed at great length either way . . . (but) we set out to go it alone, so to speak."

Canadian Prime Minister Pierre Elliot Trudeau once described Canada's coexistence with the United States as "a mouse sleeping next to an elephant." The managers of other dealer-owned hardware companies must have felt much the same way about Cotter & Company by the 1960s. Cotter, in fact, had no master plan for national dominance of the industry; he remained ever the opportunist, picking up a dealer here, an unemployed sales manager there. Yet he realized that acquiring dealers one by one was a laborious and time-consuming way to expand, so whenever he could land a group of dealers all at once by taking over another firm, he was eager to do so. In the late 1960s, Cotter & Company would swallow several former-members of the dealer-owned caucus, but before then, the whole industry underwent several crises. In the midst of this upheaval in wholesaling, Cotter zeroed in not on the dealer-owned firms but rather on the old-line wholesalers.

CHAPTER SEVEN

THE END
OF AN
ERA

"Eventually — Why Not Now? With the continuing demise of old-line wholesalers all thinking retail hardware dealers must realize that it is only a matter of time before they must become co-owners in a low-cost, dealer-owned organization if they are to survive... There is no substitute for dealer-ownership."
—John Cotter

World War II had brought the old-line wholesalers an unexpected, but welcome, reprieve from economic reality. Despite an extremely tight supply situation, hardware sales increased moderately during the war, then exploded to three times their pre-war level in 1947 and 1948. Profits rode this sales curve to record levels, averaging nearly 5% of sales after taxes in the immediate postwar years. Economic dislocations had pumped up this bubble of prosperity. Due to booming war industries, Americans had money to spend for the first time since the stock market crash of 1929; government rationing restricted supply and inflated prices and profits; and pent-up demand proved so great that no sales effort and very little overhead expense was required to move goods. Saunders Norvell, the dean of the hardware industry, sagely underlined the unreality of the situation at the beginning of 1948:

"During the last four or five years a large number of hardware salesmen have lost the art of selling mainly because they distributed merchandise by allocation at home and spent little or no time on the road. . . Many hardware dealers, particularly in far away territories, report they have not seen a wholesaler's salesman since 1942."

In addition to these favorable circumstances, wholesalers emerged from the war with an exaggerated sense of their own importance; for the government had tried to bypass them in the war mobilization and had failed. Wartime planners thought the wholesale level of industry was inefficient and superfluous, but soon found out otherwise. On the West Coast, for example, the Navy tried to supply Kaiser's massive shipyard on the Columbia River direct from the factories; but as Kaiser geared up to produce an entire Liberty Ship every day, they found they needed a reserve stock of steel and hardware fittings to ensure uninterrupted production. So the government contracted with Marshall-Wells' Portland branch to build up this reserve inventory. After the war, the president of the National Wholesale Hardware Association boasted: "We were the unwanted, the unnecessary, and there were many in Washington who took delight in trying to eliminate us. . . But as the war continued our value as service institutions became apparent."

The old-line wholesalers, however, were headed for a fall. When the last of the wartime emergencies passed, they confronted a more formidable foe than the U.S. government — economic reality. They sent their salesmen back on the road and found that both competition and expenses had increased.

THE WHOLESALERS' AGONY

Hardware wholesalers entered a sort of "Twilight Zone" in the phenomenal fifties and the soaring sixties. They did more business than ever before, as the return of prosperity and the baby boom swelled demand; yet they continually lost market share to new kinds of merchandisers. John Cotter told his dealers, in the early 60s, that "only 20% of the hardware being sold in America passes through hardware stores" (and their wholesale suppliers). This is undoubtedly a low estimate, for Cotter had every reason to exaggerate the erosion of traditional channels; but more impartial surveys, by *Hardware Age* magazine and by the U.S. Census of Business, showed only about half of all hardware passing through the time-worn grooves from manufacturer to wholesaler to retailer. In a 1953 speech, the president of the Southern Wholesale Hardware Association, after listing thirteen new varieties of competition, concluded glumly: "I do not believe that there has ever been an industry which has been invaded as steadily, and to such a great extent, as has the hardware field."

The most important result of this crowded field was the steady erosion of profits. In order to meet competition, wholesalers had to offer lower prices and costly services (such as prepaid freight) to their customers, thus squeezing their profit margins. Wages, salaries, shipping costs, and the expense of keeping salesmen on the road all increased sharply, as inflation settled in as a permanent fixture of the economy. Wholesale profit averages nosedived to 1.85% of sales in 1953, the first year of full decontrol; and they dropped even lower in the next decade. (See Figure 3) Profits in 1963 stood at the same dollar level as 1946, even though sales volume had increased fourfold. Industry spokesmen frequently summed up the situation with an apt phrase — "profitless prosperity."

Responses to these changing conditions ranged from panic to scapegoating, with some creative new approaches as well. Panic and rumors rose to semi-annual crescendoes at the conventions of the National Wholesale Hardware Association in October at Atlantic City and the Southern Wholesale Hardware Association in Florida in the

Figure 3

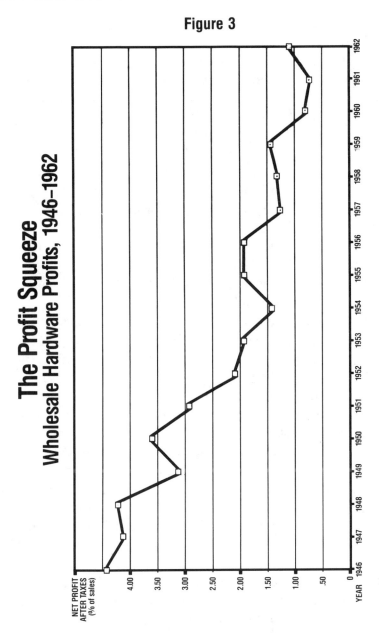

The Profit Squeeze
Wholesale Hardware Profits, 1946–1962

spring. Bill Phair, editor of *Hardware Age,* wrote these reflections on the 1957 Atlantic City meeting:

"What's happening in wholesaling? This is a question that was asked many, many times over the past two weeks. . . . There are a number of distributors who cannot stand too many more profit-less years and still stay in business. . . . If every wholesaler suddenly went out of business, a great many retailers would also be forced to close their doors, particularly the smaller dealers."

Officials of the wholesale associations tended to single out cooperatives as the most blameworthy villains in the competitive picture. Making little distinction between farm coops and dealer-owned wholesalers, they denounced all cooperatives as the first step on the road to socialism. Seth Marshall, president of Marshall-Wells in Duluth, claimed that "in Great Britain coops do 25 per cent of the national volume and they are the strongest political factor in England today. We still have a chance here — but we won't have for long."

Old-line wholesalers particularly resented the tax advantages enjoyed by cooperatives. Coops are not tax-exempt, as is commonly believed, but they are able to avoid the double taxation of dividends which afflicts most corporations. When a regular corporation earns a profit and declares a dividend for its stockholders, the company pays corporate income tax on its earnings and the individual stockholders also pay income tax on their dividends. Thus, corporate profits are taxed twice, once at the corporate rate and once at the individual rate. A cooperative, however, is considered a non-profit institution if it distributes all its earnings to its members in year-end patronage rebates. The coop does not pay any corporate tax on those earnings, but the members do pay income tax on the rebates at their own individual rates. Coop profits, then, are not totally tax-exempt, but they do escape double taxation.

The hardware wholesalers constantly attacked this feature of the tax laws as an unfair business advantage. Coops could pay profits in notes or scrip rather than cash and thus retain their earnings for reinvestment tax-free. In 1943 the NWHA organized a committee on cooperatives under the chairmanship of Seth Marshall and began bankrolling a lobbying effort by the National Tax Equality Association. Marshall sounded the alarm at the hardware conventions and in the trade press:

"Two roads lie before us. One leads to cooperative monopoly and eventually to the Cooperative Commonwealth. The other leads to tax equality.''(Ironically, Marshall's firm, Marshall—Wells of Duluth, did a sizable business supplying hardware to farm coops.)

The anti-coop lobbies petitioned the political parties' national conventions every four years and pressured individual congressmen to introduce tax-law changes imposing full corporate taxation on coops. They obtained a few clarifications in the laws which ensured that individual recipients of patronage dividends paid taxes on them, but farmers' lobbies and the Department of Agriculture prevented any major changes. Finally, in 1962 a compromise tax reform act imposed new regulations on coops but did not substantially change the tax treatment of their profits. The 1962 statute (still in effect today) requires a coop to pay at least 20% of its profits in cash rebates to its members each year; the rest may be paid in notes or stock. The entire rebate, cash plus notes, is considered taxable income for the indvidual recipient, but no corporate tax is paid by the coop. The only major effect of this law, then, was that coops could only retain 80% of their earnings each year rather than 100%.

The wholesalers' tax equality committee, under Marshall's successor, H.L. "Larry" Thompson from Bostwick-Braun of Toledo, considered the 1962 law a step in the right direction; but Congress refused to go any further. Thompson called the coops "legal leeches" and the president of the NWHA dubbed them "pseudo-wholesalers." The association refused to admit Cotter & Company or any of the other dealer-owned companies as members. John Cotter continued to attend the conventions unofficially, working the halls and corridors and social gatherings to maintain his contacts in the industry. Some say he took a perverse pleasure in stationing himself prominently among the potted palms in hotel lobbies, thus forcing convention delegates to make a decision. Manufacturers' executives either had to detour around him or else risk the wholesalers' wrath by shaking his hand in public.

The old line wholesalers didn't spend all their time looking for scapegoats; indeed, many of them tried out new experimental approaches to regain market share and cut costs. The most common innovation by wholesalers in the 1950s was a stores program, an attempt to compete with chain stores by organizing a voluntary chain of independent hardware dealers. The wholesaler offered dealers a common store identification, such as Hibbard's True Value, Janney, Semple, Hill's Service & Quality (S & Q), or Shapleigh's Keen Kutter, plus an advertising program and merchandising aids. In return, the retailer was expected to concentrate his purchases with the sponsoring wholesaler. Stores programs aimed at a closer integration of the wholesaling and retailing functions; and when they were carried to their logical outcome, dealers wrote their own orders and the wholesaler terminated his salesmen.

Few voluntary chains developed that far, however. Janney, Semple, Hill's S & Q program, initiated by Paul Cosgrave in 1952, was fairly typical. Janney offered dealers a Merchandising Kit with standard store modernization plans, advertising suggestions, the S & Q logo, and preprinted order forms for the most commonly ordered hardware items. Beginning in 1954, the Minneapolis wholesaler conducted an annual Retailers' Conference and Market, in imitation of the dealer-owned wholesalers' merchandise shows. Janney hoped to garner nearly all the business from its over 400 S & Q dealers, but the retailers signed no binding contract with the house and many continued to scatter their purchases among competing wholesalers. In the long run, a stores program like S & Q probably increased the wholesaler's costs, since Janney did not eliminate salesmen and retailers did not pay for the increased services. Though the program gave Janney a higher visibility in its market area, it did not improve its competitive position.

Despite their drawbacks, stores programs proliferated in the late 50s and early 60s, riding the crest of the franchising wave in the U.S. Some wholesalers staked their entire future on their stores program and stopped selling hardware to anyone except their programmed, or franchised, dealers. Janney, Semple, Hill, for instance, took this step at the end of 1958. Other wholesalers federated together and organized "super" stores programs along the lines of Red Oakes' old Tru-Test organization. Paul Cosgrave encouraged this trend, leaving Janney in 1954 and establishing PRO Hardware advertising and merchandising group in 1958. By the early 60s, five major wholesalers' federations had emerged — Liberty Distributors, PRO, Sentry, Val-Test, and Allied Hardware Services. These federated, program wholesalers (merchandising groups) were destined to share the future with the dealer-owned companies; for independent, old line wholesalers could no longer compete. The shakeout began in the late 1950s, and is still continuing.

THE SHAKEOUT

Hardware wholesalers muddled through the profitless prosperity of the 1950s as long as sales kept increasing, but when a major recession struck the nation in 1958, the shakeout began. (See Table 6) Two of the Midwestern wholesalers that folded in 1958 were over 100 years old, John Pritzlaff Hardware Co. of Milwaukee and Richards & Conover of Kansas City. The demise of Marshall-Wells, sold off in slices during 1958 (as we shall see in more detail later) rocked the industry, since it was the largest wholesale hardware house in the U.S. Industry spokesmen tried to sound upbeat and optimistic. Bill Phair remarked in a *Hardware Age* editorial: "I think the question we should ask is not 'How many more will disappear?' but rather 'How come only so few have gone out of business?' " Thomas A. Fernley, Jr., who had recently succeeded his uncle George Fernley as managing director of NWHA, issued a reassuring press release: "Only 20 wholesalers who have been members of the NWHA have gone out of business in the past 10 years... In the same period of time, 10 years, 20 new members have been enrolled in the association." But they were whistling in the dark. The wholesalers who folded their tents were long-established, general-line wholesalers; the new ones taking their places were smaller, short-line, specialty jobbers. Even if the industry were just holding its own, as Fernley suggested, that would be nothing to boast about in a period of unprecedented national population and sales expansion.

The end of the '58 recession slowed the shakeout and brought back hopes that the "soaring sixties" would erase all problems. During the first few years of the new decade, however, the economy moved generally sideways, neither lapsing into recession nor taking off quite so rapidly as expected. Not until the Kennedy tax cuts of 1963 did the sixties really soar. In the meantime, the hemorrhaging of old-line wholesalers continued.

Shapleigh Hardware of St. Louis, Saunders Norvell's old firm, had changed ownership several times; most recently, Canadian interests

TABLE 6

THE END OF AN ERA

A Partial List of Midwestern, Old-Line Hardware Wholesalers Who
Went Out of Business,
1953-1963

NAME	LOCATION	Date Business Terminated	Reason for Termination
Rehm Hardware	Chicago, Ill.	1953	Bankruptcy
Sher & Peachin	Chicago, Ill.	1954	Liquidated
Brown Camp Hdwe.	Des Moines, Ia.	1954	Sold to Hibbard, Spencer, Bartlett
Kelley-How-Thomson	Duluth, Minn.	1955	Sold to Marshall Wells
Luethe Hdwe.	Des Moines, Ia.	1956	Liquidated
Tracy Wells	Columbus, Ohio	1957	Liquidated
Michigan Hdwe.	Grand Rapids, Mi.	1957	Bankruptcy
Richards-Conover	Kansas City, Mo.	1958	Liquidated
John Pritzlaff	Milwaukee, Wis.	1958	Liquidated
Peaslee Gaulbert	Louisville, Ky.	1958	Liquidated
Marshall Wells	Duluth, Minn.	1958	Liquidated
Schaberg-Dietrich	Lansing, Mich.	1960	Sold to George Worthington
Shapleigh Hdwe.	St. Louis, Mo.	1960	Liquidated
Buhl Sons	Detroit, Mich.	1960	Sold to Hibbard, Spencer, Bartlett
Paxton & Gallagher	Omaha, Neb.	1960	Liquidated
Janney, Semple, Hill	Minneapolis, Minn.	1960	Liquidated
W. Bingham Co.	Cleveland, Ohio	1961	Liquidated
Hibbard, Spencer, Bartlett Co.	Evanston, Ill.	1962	Sold to Cotter & Company

from Vancouver had bought control in 1956. New management and the Keen Kutter stores program failed to revive the firm's low profits, so the company was liquidated on January 4, 1960, after 117 years in business.

The day after Christmas in 1960, Janney, Semple, Hill of Minneapolis announced that it was selling its general hardware business to the Coast-to-Coast Central Organization. Janney had been the subject of industry rumors for several years. In 1957, Benton J. Case, Janney's president, had made public a notarized statement listing the major stockholders of the firm to quiet speculation of a buyout by corporate raiders. Janney successfully prevented a takeover, but it couldn't stop the flow of red ink, so it closed shop after 91 years in business. In a tragic footnote to Janney's demise, Mr. and Mrs. Ben Case were hit by a car and seriously injured while crossing a Minneapolis street two days after the liquidation announcement.

Another major wholesaler, the 120 year old W. Bingham Co. of Cleveland, closed its doors on May 25, 1961. Bingham's president, Spencer Cram, succinctly summed up the dilemma of the whole industry: "Unsatisfactory net profit after taxes and investment. . . is responsible for this decision." Industry insiders had known that Shapleigh and Janney were in trouble for some time, but the Bingham liquidation came as a surprise. Bill Phair wrote, in a very despondent editorial: "The Bingham case is rather unique. The company was not liquidated to cover heavy financial losses; it was not bankrupt; it had no creditors pressing for past due accounts. Bingham closed its doors due to the cold, inexorable pressure of competition for investors' dollars." In plain English, Bingham's owners realized that there were better ways to invest their stockholders' capital than in a low-profit, old-line hardware wholesale house.

John Cotter, for one, was not surprised by the bloodbath in hardware wholesaling. He had been preaching continually, "Old-line jobbers offer too many costly services that hardware dealers don't need and can't afford." Indeed, he had been keeping a deathwatch on the industry for two decades. From time to time, either Cotter or his sales manager, Herb Haller, issued a mimeographed sheet entitled "End of an Era," which listed all the wholesalers who had liquidated, gone broke, or been taken over in recent years. He sent these bulletins to his members and to prospective dealers, emphasizing the inevitability of dealer-ownership with his slogan — "Eventually — Why Not Now?" Cotter predicted the Shapleigh failure six months in advance, at both his June Toy Show and the November dealer market in 1959. When the news became official, he added, "The end is not yet in sight — there will be still more."

The wholesalers' agony presented a splendid opportunity to Cotter & Company. In 1957 Cotter tried to buy the assets of the bankrupt Michigan Hardware in Grand Rapids, but he was outbid by other interests. When Janney, Semple, Hill closed its doors, he held two recruiting meetings for S & Q dealers just four days later. Besides signing up dealers from the failed stores programs, he also hired the vice presidents, sales managers, and some of the best salesmen from the old line houses. Herb Lendved, v-p from Pritzlaff, Red Lynes, v-p from Marshall-Wells, Rae Murray, executive v-p from Bingham, and George Mclntyre, v-p from Hibbard's, brought several lifetimes of hardware experience to the growing field staff. This gave Cotter a decided advantage in the field, for he had seasoned sales managers competing against green salesmen from other wholesalers. Dave Rolston, himself a former vice president and sales manager of the Edward K. Tryon Co., once counted 23 former vice presidents working for Cotter & Company.

Rae Murray provides a good example of a key personnel acquisition. Murray, like the sales managers of most old-line houses, had long opposed the dealer-owned companies vehemently. After Bingham went out of business, he was in no hurry to join an old rival, such as Cotter & Company; but Bob Morse from True Temper, one of Cotter's major suppliers, constantly urged Murray to talk to John Cotter. After about a year, he finally did so; and when Cotter moved the Ohio distribution center from Zanesville to Cleveland in 1962, Murray signed on. Ironically, Cotter rented space for his Cleveland branch in the former warehouse of Murray's old employer, W. Bingham Co. To compound the irony, the warehouse was owned by Bostwick-Braun, headed by Cotter's arch-opponent, Larry Thompson. It took a while for Murray to get the knack of selling a program, rather than taking orders for merchandise; but once he got the hang of it, he threw himself into the acquisition of dealers like a whirlwind. Cotter named him branch manager of the Cleveland distribution center, and he was largely responsible for the company's rapid growth east of Cleveland. Bob Rose, from Rose, Kimball & Baxter of Elmira, New York, once remarked, "There must be two Rae Murrays, he covers so much territory."

Like an alert linebacker in football, Cotter pounced on the industry's fumbles. He must have found the fumbles of one old-line wholesaler particularly poignant. The last days of Marshall-Wells shocked everyone in the industry and were painful indeed to a Minnesota native.

MARSHALL-WELLS

Minnesota had long been a major center of hardware wholesaling. Though the Upper Midwest, the great plains, and the Rocky Mountain states were sparsely populated, their farms, logging camps, mines and mills all needed tools and implements. The cities of Duluth and Minneapolis, the only population centers of any size in the upper tier of states, both developed a wholesale trade that supplied a quarter of the continent. The U.S. Census of Business in 1948 revealed that Minnesota ranked third behind New York and California in wholesale hardware sales.

Albert M. Marshall came to Duluth from Saginaw, Michigan in 1893, as the Mesabi Iron Range was opening up. He purchased the Chapin & Wells wholesale firm and concentrated on supplying heavy hardware for the logging camps and iron mines of northern Minnesota and the upper peninsula of Michigan. By the turn of the century, he had changed the name to Marshall-Wells, had expanded into general hardware for retail stores, and had become the dominant wholesaler in Duluth. Marshall's son, Seth, succeeded him as president in 1918; and under his leadership, the company's reach stretched across the northern tier of states and into Canada. Eventually, Marshall-Wells opened branch distribution centers in Billings, Montana; Portland, Oregon; Spokane, Washington; and Winnipeg, Manitoba.

To compete with Sears and Ward's, who were opening retail outlets in the 1920s, Seth Marshall instituted the Marshall-Wells franchise dealer plan in 1928. Modeled loosely on the Winchester Stores plan initiated by the arms manufacturer a decade earlier, this was the first stores program sponsored by an old-line hardware wholesaler. Marshall lured 0. E. Stevens away from Sears to help him develop the program, and Stevens brought other Sears people with him, including Red Lynes.

Herbert A. ''Red'' Lynes was born and raised in Fulton, Missouri and went to work for Sears first retail store in the state of Oklahoma, becoming one of Sears' youngest managers in 1933. He served two five-year hitches with Marshall-Wells, the first one during the war and the second in the mid-50s. He also worked at the NRHA in Indianapolis for a time and put in a stint with Red Oakes, John Cotter, and Tru-Test in Chicago. Lynes had a complete background in hardware, with hands-on experience in retail sales, buying, and operations; but his greatest skill was in field management. He could size up the strengths and weaknesses of a retail store or a wholesale warehouse instantly and then outline a systematic, practical plan of operation and management. John Cotter sums him up succinctly as ''a doer,'' and Lynes himself admits that he was often impulsive because he liked to do a job neatly and quickly. Lynes returned to Marshall-Wells in 1952 as sales manager of the Duluth branch, but soon worked his way up to branch manager and then vice president.

When the Marshall-Wells stores program was fully developed, Lynes recalls, dealers could get rebates of 2% on their purchases as a bonus for advertising, 2% more if they used unit controls on stock, and another 2% for large volume purchases. Aggressive dealers who took advantage of the full 6% discounts competed closely with Our Own Hardware, whose costs were relatively high for a dealer-owned firm. By the mid-1950s, Marshall-Wells had nearly 600 stores identified with bold red letters on a white background, half in Canada and half in the U.S., doing an annual volume of over $80 million. They had become the largest wholesale hardware house in the nation, and were as efficient and cost-conscious as an old-line distributor could be. Many years after he retired, Seth Marshall remarked to Red Lynes, ''What John Cotter did is what we tried to do.''

What happened next to Marshall-Wells shouldn't have happened to a dog; a corporate raider took over the firm and sold it off in slices. In May, 1955, Hyman J. Sobiloff acquired majority control of Marshall-Wells' stock from the Marshall family in a complicated stock manipulation. He and his brother, Myer, had made a fortune in the textile business in New York, then in 1952 had sold off their plant and equipment and transformed their family firm into a holding company, called Ambrook Industries. Hardware wholesalers, in the midst of their profitless prosperity, made inviting takeover targets. Due to low profit levels, their stock was undervalued, but their assets — real estate and hardware inventory — were highly valuable and relatively liquid. Hardware doesn't spoil and it rarely depreciates much, so a raider could always cash in on a takeover by selling off the inventory.

At first, however, Sobiloff had no thought of liquidation. In December, 1955, he bought Kelley-How-Thomson, John Cotter's former employer, and ran it as a Marshall-Wells subsidiary. Then he hired Gordon Mead from Firestone Tire and installed him as president, with a five-year contract and a mandate to expand the stores program rapidly. In February, 1956, Sobiloff confidently predicted 1000 dealers and annual sales of $200 million by 1960. He planned to expand far beyond Marshall-Wells' traditional territory. As chancellor of Lakeland College in Florida, Sobiloff had encountered George Jenkins, who owned the Publix Markets grocery chain in that state, and he had decided to install hardware stores in Jenkins' shopping centers. He sent Red Lynes down to Florida to open two test stores, supplying them for a while out of Duluth (!). Lynes worked out careful cost estimates for the opening of a branch distribution center in Florida, predicting substantial losses for the first several years. Sobiloff took one look at the figures and said, "Hell, No." As Lynes recalls, "Sobiloff wanted to make a buck all of a sudden. The hardware business was too slow for him."

In February, 1957, Ambrook Industries struck a deal with Bert Gamble, president of the Gamble-Skogmo hard lines chain, selling Gamble the Canadian operations of Marshall-Wells in return for a controlling interest in Barker Bros., a California furniture company. Through Barker Bros., Ambrook bought W & J Sloane, a 114 year old furniture and floor covering firm in New York. Just 27 months previously, the Sobiloffs had backed another raider in his acquisition of Sloane, but now they turned on him and took over control themselves. By the summer of 1957, Hy Sobiloff was chairman of furniture chains on both coasts and a giant hardware wholesaler in the heartland; but his interest in hardware was waning rapidly. Red Lynes attended a Marshall-Wells board meeting in New York that summer, then went fishing at Sobiloff's home on Long Island. It became evident in the course of conversation that Sobiloff intended to liquidate Marshall-Wells. On his way back through Chicago, Lynes called up John Cotter, met him for lunch, and told him what was up. Cotter hired him on the spot.

Throughout the recession year of 1958, Sobiloff sold off Marshall-Wells piece by piece. The Jensen-Byrd Co., an old-line wholesaler, bought the Spokane branch in April, and Coast-to-Coast acquired the Portland operation in August. After each of these sales, Marshall-Wells management solemnly assured the press that their main operations in Duluth would remain in business, but no one was fooled. The Duluth warehouse closed its doors for the last time in January, 1959. Coast-to-Coast bought the inventory and signed up many of the dealers. Sobiloff retained the Marshall-Wells corporate name, moved its offices to New York, and installed a Boston banker as president. He settled Gordon Mead's unexpired five-year contract by giving him the two Florida hardware stores. Sobiloff had merged his original corporation, Ambrook Industries, with Barker Bros., which controlled Marshall-Wells, which in turn controlled W & J Sloane and the Peaslee-Gaulbert hardware wholesale house in Louisville. Marshall-Wells ended up as merely one level in a paper pyramid of holding companies.

In summing up the melancholy fate of old-line wholesalers, it is important to understand what happened to Marshall-Wells. The firm didn't go broke. It had been a leader of the industry, was well-managed, and took every reasonable measure to keep up with the times. Had its original ownership retained control, it could have stayed in business indefinitely. Instead, a corporate raider took over and terminated Marshall-Wells. Despite the rudeness of his methods, however, Sobiloff had a point. There were easier ways to make money than selling hardware at wholesale. Beginning in 1957 the NWHA started calculating industry profits as a percentage of corporate net worth, a straightforward way of showing the return on investment. In the six years following the Marshall-Wells liquidation, industry profits averaged only 3.89% of net worth. Stockholders could earn a larger return by leaving their money in the bank.

Many of the takeovers and liquidations of hardware wholesalers in the 1950s and 60s represented sensible consolidations of smaller firms into larger ones and could be interpreted as signs of normal growth. But when leading firms, such as Marshall-Wells or Bingham, went out of business, shock waves shook the industry, signalling a deeper, more fundamental weakness. When the next big shock knocked out a major wholesaler, John Cotter was poised and ready to act, and he saw to it that the company had the capital to back him up.

CHAPTER EIGHT
THE
HIBBARD
TAKEOVER

"The decision by Hibbard to go out of the hardware business will undoubtedly be a disappointment to many loyal True Value Members. But this move must be understood as the inevitable result of the many changes which have taken place in the wholesale hardware industry in recent years."
—Edmund S. Kantowicz, George F. McIntyre
   November 21, 1962

John Cotter's older daughter, Mary, ran into Anne Kantowicz one day during her freshman year at St. Mary's College of Notre Dame. In a school filled with the daughters of bankers and lawyers, each was surprised to find that the other had a father in the hardware business. Anne wrote home to ask her father, Edmund S. Kantowicz, v-p and merchandise manager for Hibbard's, whether he knew John Cotter. Kantowicz couldn't wait to write back. He picked up the phone and shouted into the receiver, "Do I know John Cotter? He's the one putting us out of business. Every Monday I go into work and find he's stolen another couple dealers from us during the past week."

The Cotter and Kantowicz families got to know each other at college social affairs. Alice Cotter sensibly decided, "Our husbands can be competitors from nine to five but there's no reason we can't be friendly after that." At Christmastime in 1959, Mary Cotter and Anne Kantowicz were helping to run the Christmas Cordial, a St. Mary's fundraiser at the Ambassador East Hotel. As the two families were waiting around for their daughters at the end of the party, John Cotter suggested they all go down to dinner together in the Buttery. No sooner were they seated than the maitre d' uncorked a bottle of champagne, courtesy of a gentleman at another table. They looked up and saw Jerry Lipson from the Horsman Doll Co., who sold to both Cotter and Hibbard's, smiling and waving at them. After the meal, Lipson walked over to their table and asked, "Who's Taking Over Who?"

No takeover, in fact, was yet in the offing; but John Cotter had been tracking Hibbard's from the first moment he went into business. Hibbard, Spencer, Bartlett, founded in 1855, was one of the leading hardware wholesalers in the nation, and clearly dominated the Chicago market area. Hibbard's recorded over $28 million in sales in 1948, the year Cotter started his company; Ace Hardware, their nearest competitor that year, reached about $10 million. If Cotter wished to make his mark as a Chicago wholesaler, he had to measure himself against the midwestern leader.

THE ORIGINS OF TRUE VALUE

The same month John Cotter moved into North Pier Terminal, June, 1948, Hibbard, Spencer, Bartlett was leaving its fourteen story warehouse just up the street. When the U.S. army air force had commandeered Hibbard's headquarters during the war, the company's president, C. J. Whipple, an engineer by training, studied the government's operations closely and concluded that efficient handling of goods demanded a one-story warehouse. So after the war, he purchased a 35 acre tract of land at the southwestern corner of suburban Evanston and constructed the most modern, one-story warehouse in the country. The new plant contained 19 acres of warehouse and office space under one roof — 840,000 sq.ft. in all — with electrical drag lines, fork lift trucks, and a maze of conveyors to fill orders. Two railroad tracks ran right into the warehouse and a loading dock accommodated fifteen tractor-trailers at a time. An elegant lobby, trimmed with Italian marble, led into the office section of the building, inspiring Hibbard's competitors to dub the whole complex the "Marble Palace."

Hibbard's business methods were as up-to-date as its physical facilities. The company had initiated a stores program about the same time Marshall-Wells did, in the late 20s and 30s. In 1928, the first Toy Parade consumer catalogue appeared, and Hibbard's management invited dealers in for their first Toy Show. Then in 1932, Jack Lacy, v-p and general manager of Peck, Stow & Wilcox in Southington, Conn., agreed to produce a popularly-priced private brand line of hand tools for Hibbard's under the True Value brand name. Though the exact origins of the True Value label are unknown, this is its first definite appearance on Hibbard's merchandise.

Hibbard's expanded its stores program throughout the 1930s, setting up a model store at its headquarters where dealers could pick up merchandising tips, opening a Dealers' Service Department, and producing a complete kit of marketing aids, called Eight Point Service. In 1940, HSB started opening test stores, company-owned "sales and operating laboratories" with the True Value name emblazoned over the door. The first test store, in Chicago Heights, burned to the ground a few hours after the grand opening, but the company opened eight more during the war years. Each store was equipped with up-to-date fixtures, followed an extensive advertising program, and ordered all its merchandise by mail from the parent company. The wholesaler's regular customers resented the competition from these company-owned stores, so Hibbard's closed them down after the war; but Whipple, and his successor, Frank Kaufman, urged dealers to follow the model of the test stores. As Kaufman put it, "We now have the proof that concentration of purchases with one house having a complete merchandising and operating plan is the answer to the problem."

In 1952, Orville W. Ahl, formerly an accountant at Wieboldt's, a Chicago department store, then controller of Hibbard's, ascended to the presidency. With his merchandising manager, Ed Kantowicz, and sales manager, George McIntyre, he systematized the True Value stores program and brought it to a high state of efficiency. Ahl announced the Associate Store Program in December, 1953, a voluntary chain of franchised dealers who would concentrate their purchases with Hibbard's, write their own orders, and utilize the full battery of True Value ads and promotions. Nearly 800 associate store dealers gathered in Evanston for their first merchandise show, March 1 - 3, 1954. The True Value program closely imitated the dealer-owned system. Ahl even rebated a portion of the company's profits to dealers at the end of the year.

Hibbard's sales volume hit an all-time high of $33 million in 1956, but the following year the company voluntarily cut back, reducing its sales volume to $19 million by 1959. Servicing thousands of small accounts in addition to the franchised stores proved too costly, for they were essentially "shipping retail quantities at wholesale prices" to these marginal accounts. So, beginning in 1957, Hibbard's phased out its corps of salesmen, closed out its small accounts, and staked its future in the hardware business squarely on the True Value program. The only essential difference between True Value and a dealer-owned program was the need to earn wholesale profits for stockholders.

CLANDESTINE PLANS

On the surface, Hibbard's condition still appeared very healthy, despite the cutback in sales. The company paid regular quarterly dividends, totalling 3 or 4 dollars per share annually, and accumulated a substantial capital surplus. They also bought up several smaller wholesalers situated strategically around the midwest — Auburn Hardware of Auburn, Indiana, in 1952; Brown-Camp Hardware of Des Moines, Iowa, in 1954; Associated Hardware of St. Louis in 1956; and Buhl Sons of Detroit in 1960. Hibbard's entered the decade of the 1960s with a chain of nearly a thousand dealers, stretching from Denver on the west to the Appalachians on the east, supplied from four distribution centers, in Evanston, St. Louis, Auburn and Detroit.

Yet all was not well behind the scenes at the Marble Palace. Hibbard's hardware sales produced very slender profit margins; and O. W. Ahl, with his accountant's eye, realized he could earn a better return for his stockholders by investing in real estate. From 1956 on, he waged a campaign at every board of directors meeting to liquidate Hibbard's hardware business and transform the company into a real estate investment firm. When the company cut back its extraneous accounts and reduced its volume in 1957 and '58, Ahl moved the executive offices to a corner of the warehouse and rented out the prime office space, with its marble lobby, to an agency of the U.S. government. He acquired other wholesalers for their prime real estate and accumulated tax losses rather than their hardware trade. Such acquisitions provided a perfect cover for Ahl's real intentions. Outsiders looking in saw a leading hardware firm buying out weaker rivals and consolidating its regional dominance; in reality, Ahl was diversifying the business and planning to get out of hardware altogether.

John Cotter was one of the few outsiders who figured out what was going on. Somehow he obtained copies of Hibbard's annual reports about as soon as the stockholders did and he shrewdly read between the lines. He deduced that HSB's net income all derived from real estate and other investments and that in some years the hardware business actually operated at a loss. (See Figure 4).

In 1961, Ahl stepped up his behind-the-scenes campaign. He appointed Howard L. Storch, president of Brown & Storch realtors, to the board of directors so he could extol the profitability of real estate. Kantowicz, McIntyre, and Frank Rodgers, the lone retailer on the board, opposed Ahl vehemently and tried to save the hardware business. They sounded out some True Value store owners about buying the firm and operating it as a dealer-owned, but the dealers' interest cooled considerably when they realized it would require at least $10,000 each. Finally, in 1962, Ahl convinced a majority of the directors to liquidate the hardware business.

In the meantime, John Cotter had been following Hibbard's every move closely. He gathered and saved every scrap of information he could find on his rival's business or financial condition. He ferreted

Figure 4

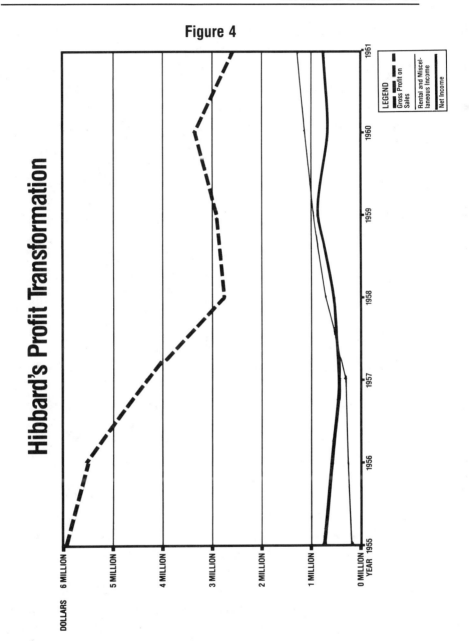

Hibbard's Profit Transformation

out True Value brand merchandise at Walgreen's and Sears, then triumphantly blew the whistle on Hibbard's for selling to the independent dealer's worst enemies. He continually criticized Hibbard's many changes and modifications in their stores program. "Hibbard, Spencer, Bartlett has had about as many plans as the number of years your own wholesaler has been in business," he told his dealers in 1955. HSB, for its part, treated the dealer-owned firm as a deadly enemy. Hibbard's buyers pressured the suppliers not to sell Cotter and led the slander campaigns against the new company. O. W. Ahl highlighted the rivalry in his annual stockholders' reports: "Dealer-owned cooperative wholesalers are each year taking a larger share of the total wholesale hardware market. Under our present tax laws, this type of organization is able to avoid taxation on substantially all of its profits."

After Hibbard's retrenched in the late 1950s, Cotter & Company passed them in sales volume. (See Figure 5) From then on, John Cotter looked for an opportunity to take over his archrival.

He made his first move during the winter of 1960-61, when Hibbard's president, O. W. Ahl, fell seriously ill and was hospitalized for an extended period. Cotter heard of Ahl's condition and asked Ed Kantowicz to meet him in strict secrecy at an Orrington Hotel room in Evanston on a Saturday morning. They talked most of the day, ordering lunch from room service, to avoid any more Jerry Lipson incidents. Cotter told Kantowicz he would like first crack at buying the inventory and acquiring the dealers if Ahl should die and the business were liquidated.

Cotter also talked with the lone retail dealer on Hibbard's board of directors, Frank Rodgers, owner of Carr Hardware in Ames, Iowa. Cotter believed he was partly responsible for Rodger's appointment to the Hibbard board. Back in the fifties, when he was on the road canvassing dealers, Cotter had talked at great length with Rodgers at a convention of the Iowa Retail Hardware Association. George McIntyre, Hibbard's sales manager, had seen them talking, and not long thereafter Rodgers was invited to serve on Hibbard's board. Now in 1961, with rumors flying about Ahl's and Hibbard's condition, Cotter paid Rodgers a visit at his store in Ames. Rodgers told him, "You know I'm a director of Hibbard, Spencer, Bartlett. What are you talking to me for?" Cotter replied politely, "I've heard all sorts of rumors that Hibbard's cannot make up its mind whether to stay in the hardware

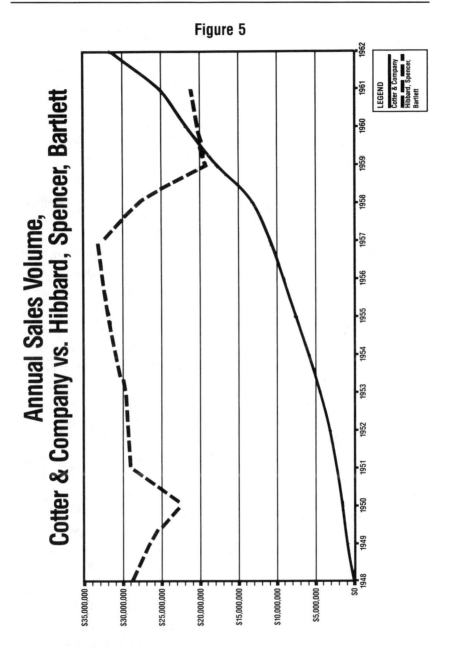

Figure 5

Annual Sales Volume,
Cotter & Company vs. Hibbard, Spencer, Bartlett

business. If anything happens, I'd like you to be fully informed about the Cotter organization.''

Ahl recovered in 1961, so nothing came of this first approach; but when the Hibbard board voted to liquidate the next year, Cotter was their first choice to buy the company's assets. Kantowicz and Rodgers, of course, knew Cotter well by then; and Frank Kaufman, the retired president, lived just down the street from him in Evanston. The other logical candidate, Dick Hesse of Ace, was taboo to the Hibbard people. Hesse often ridiculed Ahl as a "pea-counter," not a real hardware man, and he also branded Hibbard's decision to operate branch distribution centers utter foolishness. So the Hibbard's people wanted to keep Ace out of the picture. In the summer of 1962, Hibbard's board authorized Frank Kaufman to approach John Cotter directly; by August they had reached a verbal agreement. Cotter was so eager to seal the pact and get access to the True Value dealers he agreed to buy Hibbard's inventory at 100% of book value, rather than at a discount.

The Hibbard takeover was one of the best-kept secrets in business history. Only the Hibbard and Cotter directors and about a half-dozen other top-level employees knew of it in advance. All the principals took code names. Cotter used his mother's maiden name, Garrigan; Kantowicz became Cannon. Wives were kept in the dark, so secret meetings had to be held at times and places that would not arouse spousal suspicions. Typically, the two sides met for lunch at the Sheraton on Michigan Avenue or the Howard Johnson's motel at Touhy and Caldwell in Skokie, ordering in from room service to avoid observation. The main purpose of all the secrecy was to prevent any other wholesaler from approaching True Value dealers before Cotter did. John Cotter had initially jotted down on the back of a business card the name of every individual privy to the secret; by the time the deal was announced, he had still not filled up the card.

By mutual agreement, all Hibbard and Cotter personnel who normally attended the hardware show in New York and the wholesale hardware convention in Atlantic City in October showed up as usual, but they tried to avoid being seen together. Yet even the best laid plans can go astray. Max Baer, owner of the Ferum Co., a builders' hardware importer, took Ed Kantowicz to dinner at his favorite New York restaurant, the Brussels. Two minutes after they sat down, Max's brother, Rudy, who ran his own housewares importing firm, walked in with John Cotter and Ed Lanctot. They all greeted one another heartily and tried to act natural, but the Cotter party took seats at the other end of the restaurant.

Original plans called for Cotter to announce the takeover at his fall market, opening on October 29; but additional time proved necessary, so the final decision stipulated a November 23 announcement, the day after Thanksgiving. Cotter's board of directors authorized him in October to pay $250,000 in earnest money and seal the agreement. The final contract provided for a payment of $1,000,000 on the takeover date of January 2, 1963, with the balance payable in two installments, later in January and on June 30. Cotter agreed to buy Hibbard's inventory and accounts receivable at book value and to pay $2500 for the True Value trademark. Acquisition of the True Value label for a nominal sum must surely rank with the purchase of Manhattan Island from the Indians as one of the great bargains in history. The final sum paid for all of Hibbard's assets exceeded $2½ million.

In the weeks leading up to Thanksgiving, George McIntyre, Herb Haller, and Red Lynes conferred frequently, poring over lists of True Value and V & S dealers. They finally targeted about 600 True Value stores as additions to the Cotter membership, eliminating marginal dealers and those whose trading area conflicted with established V & S stores. Kantowicz and Lanctot spent days comparing the two companies' inventories, discovering how many duplicate lines of goods they had, and deciding which lines to drop and which to keep. Kantowicz then faced the delicate task of cancelling orders on discontinued lines without revealing the reason. Both Cotter and Hibbard's carried the True Temper line of garden tools, but Hibbard's had purchased their shovels from the Ames Shovel Co. of West Virginia, not from True Temper. Kantowicz called in Bob Morse, the sales manager of True Temper, and told him that his sales efforts had finally paid off; they were going to drop Ames shovels and buy exclusively from True Temper. Morse was elated and helped Kantowicz close out the Ames stock, selling it off to other wholesalers. When news of the takeover finally broke, Morse called Kantowicz: "You SOB. I thought I was a super salesman. Now I see that I've been had." Enough incidents like this took place in the final weeks that manufacturers grew suspicious and began making some inquiries, but the secret never leaked.

THE THANKSGIVING SURPRISE

As Thanksgving approached, John Cotter wrote three letters of announcement — one to his members, another to the targeted True Value dealers, and a third to manufacturers and other interested parties; O. W. Ahl wrote a letter to True Value dealers. Cotter's communiques were understated and factual — "Hibbard has for years been one of the most respected companies in the wholesale hardware business," (but) "this move is confirmation of an industry trend about which we have told our stockholder-dealers many times." Ahl wrote the simple truth: "It is no longer possible for us to earn a satisfactory profit on the investment." Ed Kantowicz and George McIntyre, who had agreed to join Cotter & Company immediately after the takeover announcement, added a personal note of their own.

All of the letters were dated November 21, prepared secretly by an outside printer, then mailed after the close of business on the day before Thanksgiving. One hitch developed, for the Post Office, amazingly, delivered some letters too quickly. Many manufacturers received their mail at numbered P.O. boxes, where it was posted on Thanksgiving Day itself, rather than the day after. Eager-beavers who picked up their mail on the holiday began spreading the word, so some dealers heard the news in left-handed fashion. Art Quandt, a former Hibbard salesman who owned a True Value store in Riverdale, Illinois, was one of those informed indirectly. He called up Ed Kantowicz, a long-time personal friend, at 10:00 PM on Thanksgiving night and vented his hurt feelings. Quandt felt betrayed, since no one had informed him in advance, and he would not be placated; he eventually signed on with Ace rather than Cotter. (Though Quandt never reconciled with True Value, one of his sons, Thomas, later bought a True Value store in Glenwood, Illinois.)

The day after Thanksgiving, as most of the True Value and V & S dealers were reading their announcements in the morning mail, the Hibbard and Cotter field men reported to the O'Hare Inn for what they thought were routine sales meetings. Adjoining rooms had been booked, and when the salesmen read the bulletin boards in the hotel lobby they began to put two and two together. After separate announcements to the two forces, the meetings were combined and Cotter hired the Hibbard's field men on the spot. Speed was essential, for Cotter wanted the Hibbard men to help him recruit True Value dealers before other competitors found out what was afoot. A series of dealer information meetings began on Monday, November 26 and continued for two weeks in cities across the midwest. The first week, Ed Kantowicz teamed with Herb Haller for four meetings, while George McIntyre worked with Red Lynes at four others, plus an extra Sunday meeting in Denver. The second week they switched partners — Kantowicz working with Lynes and McIntyre with Haller. Most of the True Value dealers turned out for these meetings and some of them grumbled and complained. A November 28 letter from John Cotter, assuring the former-Hibbard dealers they could retain their True Value store identification, helped immensely in damping down opposition. Cotter could not sign these dealers immediately, since he needed SEC approval for such a large influx of new stockholders, but he got verbal commitments from the majority. Most True Value dealers had made up their minds before Ace's field men ever contacted them.

Shock waves from Cotter's coup rippled through the industry, and letters of congratulations and amazement rolled in. Cotter's friends savored the irony — upstart newcomer takes over entrenched archrival.

—"I can't help but smile when I recall that about twelve or so years ago the top management of a certain company threatened to throw my Vise Grip Wrenches out completely if I continued to sell Cotter & Company."

—"John, I know besides the prestige and so forth this must give you a great deal of personal satisfaction, for in your early years Hibbard tried their best to bring pressure to bear."

—"I can still recall the day just a few short years ago being herded into the head man's office by the buyer and the merchandise manager of OVB and told to either stop selling John or out you go."

Le Herron, Jr. sent a two line letter: "You never cease to amaze me. Congratulations on what is most obviously another big step forward for you and Cotter & Company." Bill Phair penned a curiously muted editorial in *Hardware Age* which mentioned neither Hibbard's nor Cotter & Company by name. But he did pay Cotter an indirect tribute:

"Recently a long-established wholesale firm was sold. In two weeks following the sale, our office-and other offices- received more news releases and other information about the company than we had received in five years from the old company. The new firm understands the value of creating a good image.''

Characteristically, John Cotter celebrated quietly at home, but his family remembers the Hibbard takeover as a peak moment, one of the proudest days of his life.

COTTER – TV HARDWARE

During the transition period, before he was authorized to formally sign True Value dealers, Cotter organized a wholly-owned subsidiary to supply them out of the former-Hibbard warehouse which he leased for the token sum of one dollar. Frank Greenberg, his attorney, suggested several names for the subsidiary, such as Rettoc Hardware (Cotter spelled backwards) or Cotter NSD (for non-stockholder dealer), but he added sensibly, ''the name we pick doesn't have to have any cosmic significance.'' In the end, John Cotter simply combined his own name with True Value's initials to form Cotter—TV Hardware.

The new subsidiary began its brief life on the takeover date, January 2, 1963, with Ed Kantowicz as operations manager and George McIntyre as sales manager. Kantowicz had worked for Hibbard's all his life, starting as a stock boy in 1925, selling cutlery during the depths of the Depression, then working his way up through the buying ranks. In 1952 he became vice-president and merchandise manager. Though he had no operations experience, as head buyer he knew the inventory and the people in the warehouse. The pressure of his new and uncertain role, managing a branch whose main task was to go out of business, caused him to break out in a rash which didn't go away completely until Cotter—TV Hardware faded out. Kantowicz remembers the electricity in the air when he, a former archrival, walked into his first department managers' meeting at Cotter & Company. The managers were presenting final reports on the October Market, and one stared directly at Kantowicz while announcing he had shipped 19 carloads of lawn furniture. Without flinching, Kantowicz shot back the news that Hibbard's recently delivered 24 carloads. A bit later, Frank Morman stopped speaking to him for several days. Kantowicz confided to Harold Ost, ''I'm worried. Frank Morman won't talk to me.'' Ost reassured him, "Why should you be any different from the rest of us?"

George McIntyre had started with Hibbard's as a mail clerk in the early 30s, then went on the road as a salesman in 1939. He jumped to general sales manager in 1951 and vice-president the following year. An Irishman born with the gift of gab, an orphan at an early age who had to make his own way in the world, McIntyre knew all there was to know about sales technique. Yet, as sales manager at Hibbard's, he had abandoned the psychology of the quick sale and pursued a longer-range program of aiding and assisting the True Value dealers. McIntyre deemphasized the word "selling," preferring to say that he and his field staff were "servicing" the independent dealers. With such a background, "Mac" smoothly integrated the True Value stores into Cotter's program.

Cotter—TV Hardware conducted the last Hibbard show in Evanston, from January 20 to the 22nd. John Cotter held a get-acquainted dinner for the dealers at the Orrington Hotel, Sunday night before the show, and announced that he had just received authorization from the SEC to sell new memberships. Monday morning at the opening of the show, True Value dealers formed six lines, many with $1000 cash in hand, to pay their stock subscriptions and formally join Cotter & Company. The temperature outside plunged to minus 20 the first day of the show and Cotter—TV people spent much of their time working the parking lot with jumper cables and frozen fingers. When the arctic temperatures eased, a blizzard struck; but with much pushing, towing, and shovelling all the True Value members finally got started and made it home.

So many store owners signed on and began taking shipments direct from Cotter & Company that there weren't enough price books to go around. Frank Morman and his staff worked many hours of overtime seven days a week to supply the demand. The sales volume of the subsidiary dropped off steadily, so Kantowicz and McIntyre began closing it down. Moving and integrating the inventory proved complex, but the subsidiary finally passed out of existence on March 29, three months ahead of schedule.

John Cotter hired about 50 former-Hibbard employees and worked them into his organization as smoothly as possible. The warehouse men from Hibbard's ultramodern plant found the Clybourn Avenue operations primitive; in return, the long-time Cotter employees baited the newcomers mercilessly as beaten men from a failed operation. Bob Klein, who had started at Hibbard's in 1924, took over as buyer of electrical supplies but other Hibbard's buyers became assistant buyers at Cotter & Company. Ed Kantowicz was named Manager of the Buying Department, effectively the *merchandise* manager, while Ed Lanctot remained merchan*dising* or advertising manager. Cotter divided the enlarged field staff into eastern and western divisions, with Red Lynes as eastern field manager, working out of Cleveland, George McIntyre western field manager, stationed in Chicago, and Herb Haller as national sales manager. A few years later, when Lynes moved on to special assignments, Herb Haller and George McIntyre divided up the membership and field men as co-equal sales managers. This division of responsibility, though rife with potential conflicts, worked smoothly most of the time.

Usually when an old line wholesale house liquidated, no one knew where its business went, as the former-customers scattered their purchases among many competing wholesalers. But Cotter secured the lion's share of Hibbard's trade. Out of 900 True Value stores, Cotter went after 600 and signed about 400. *Hardware Merchandiser* published a follow-up survey six months later, revealing that only 69 True Value stores affiliated with Ace. A few dealers expressed regret at Hibbard's passing. An Evanston dealer said, ''I never looked into joining Cotter before because I was happy with Hibbard. They had an excellent stock of merchandise and their orders were shipped 95% complete. Also, they were very nice people to deal with.'' But most were delighted at the lower prices and ''the contagious enthusiasm that runs through the whole Cotter organization.'' A Wilmette dealer reported, ''My father was one of the first store owners approached by John Cotter when he started out in '47. My father said it sounded like a good idea— but prove it. He has.''

The Hibbard takeover put Cotter & Company on the map. The acquisition of 400 ''housebroken'' True Value dealers, who were accustomed to writing their own orders and didn't need extensive orientation, along with Hibbard's experienced hardware personnel marked the most important milestone in the history of Cotter & Company. Sales volume, which had been increasing steadily at an average rate of 23%

a year, leaped 56% between 1962 and 1963. The True Value label gave Cotter stores greater name recognition, for the brand had been heavily advertised in the midwest for 30 years. V & S and True Value coexisted for a few years after the takeover, but Cotter gradually phased out the V & S name and retained True Value as his trademark. (Years later, V & S was revived for the Cotter variety stores division.)

Bitter irony marked the passing of Hibbard, Spencer, Bartlett after 107 years in the hardware trade. O. W. Ahl died on August 2, 1964, less than two years after the takeover. Had Hibbard's board held out against him a little longer, Kantowicz and McIntyre might have been able to gain control after Ahl's death and convert Hibbard's into a dealer-owned firm. Had that taken place, the three-way Chicago hardware war between True Value, V & S, and Ace would have continued, with results no one could predict. As it actually turned out, however, HSB became a real estate investment trust, administered by a part-time president and one secretary in a law office. The trust finally sold all its real estate in 1985 and the Hibbard corporate name ceased to exist. John Cotter, in the meantime, took Hibbard's best known trademark, True Value, and transformed it into a national brand.

CHAPTER NINE
GROWTH
THROUGH
CONSOLIDATION

"Everything is to your advantage with growth. First of all, you increase your buying power. Secondly, you must have national distribution in order to have national advertising. Finally, everything you do, with rare exceptions, improves because of volume.

We called them consolidations; I didn't want to flaunt a takeover in the face of anybody."
—John Cotter

"Grow or Die" is a law of life. When a tree stops adding growth rings, it starts to rot. When a human body reaches full size, it begins to disintegrate, as any middle-aged person can attest. If a company attempts to stand still, it falls backward. Pop star Bob Dylan said it best: "He who is not busy being born is busy dying."

Cotter & Company took about two years to digest the True Value acquisition, but John Cotter was still looking to extend the company's geographic reach. He followed no master plan, adhered to no timetable; instead, he carefully studied changing conditions, played his hunches, and capitalized on circumstances. "Timing," he says, "is the key. You got to make the decision and you got to move. You got to be used to change 'cause change is gonna keep coming."

Money proved as important as timing. Most of the early dealer-owned firms (with the exception of Our Own Hardware) had been undercapitalized; and at the time Cotter began looking for takeover candidates, they still were. Cotter, on the other hand, had always been careful to build a sound capital structure as a foundation.

Every dealer-member put up $1000 in initial capital for 10 voting shares of Class A stock. The rest of the capital was accumulated through retention of patronage dividends. At the end of the year, each member received 20% (later raised to 30%) of his accrued dividends in cash. Another approximate 10% was converted to non-voting, no-dividend Class B stock until a certain limit was reached. This Class B stock functioned as a deposit to ensure payment for each member's purchases. Finally, the remainder of the dividends were paid in five-year subordinated notes which earned a market rate of interest. Thus a member received most of his shared profits in cash or interest-bearing notes, and Cotter & Company got the use of substantial working capital. This capital accumulation not only ensured the stability of the company but permitted growth through acquisitions.

DALLAS AND PHILADELPHIA

Cotter had long looked southwest as a direction to expand. When the Walter H. Allen Co. of Dallas abandoned its small branch warehouse in St. Louis in 1953, he signed a few of the dealers Allen had formerly supplied. Since Cotter marketed a much more complete line of toys than Allen did, some Allen dealers came all the way from Texas to attend Cotter's June Toy Shows. Cotter kept his eye on General Mercantile, a partially dealer-owned wholesaler of St. Louis, throughout the 1960s as a logical takeover candidate. He even advanced to the "letter of understanding" level with that firm at one point, but the deal fell through. St. Louis posed some thorny labor difficulties; and a Teamster leader in Chicago warned Cotter against entering the area. So as it turned out, Cotter's first move to the southwest went further afield than St. Louis.

Red Lynes, Cotter's special assignments man and troubleshooter throughout the expansion drive, explains how the leap to Texas began:

"We heard that Coast-to-Coast had made overtures to take over Walter Allen, but John didn't want to go straight down there and tell Walter we'd heard about it. Well, Sears had just put in a new conveyor system down in their mail order plant in Dallas, so l asked my nephew, Ron King (who worked for Sears) to get Cotter an invite to see the operation. That's the way he got into Dallas and just 'happened' to call Walter Allen and ask him to have lunch. John started to talk about Coast-to-Coast and Walter admitted they had made overtures."

This roundabout entry into Dallas took place at the end of August, 1964.

It's not clear whether Allen seriously considered Coast-to-Coast's offers. As a pioneer of the dealer-owned movement, he would have found it painful to sell out to a conglomerate (Household Finance had recently purchased Coast). Yet he was 77 years old and his brother, George, had just reached 65; their business was standing still and just about breaking even. So when Cotter told them he would be interested in consolidating with them, they jumped at the opportunity. After consulting with Carl Monk, the key dealer on the board of directors, the Allens made a deal and presented it to their full board of directors for approval on November 5. No cash would change hands in the transaction. Dealer-members would simply exchange their stock in the Walter H. Allen Co. for stock in Cotter & Company, and Cotter would assume all the assets and the liabilities of Allen.

This was as friendly a takeover as could be imagined. Walter Allen had known Cotter since his days at Tru-Test, for the Allen Co. had been one of Red Oakes' member wholesalers. Then for nearly 15 years they had sat down together and freely exchanged information at the dealer-owned managers' caucus meetings. Now Cotter made the takeover as painless as possible. He agreed to call his Dallas operation the "Walter H. Allen Division" of Cotter & Company, left the Walter Allen sign on the building, and appointed Walter Allen and Carl Monk to his board of directors. He granted both Walter and George Allen lifetime pensions. Cotter, McIntyre, and Lynes conducted a dealer-meeting on November 16 to explain the advantages of the takeover to the members. They pointed out that Cotter's operating expense averaged about 7% lower than Allen's and this cost difference would be passed on to them in lower merchandise prices once they were integrated into the True Value program.

Yet nothing ever goes exactly according to plan. W. E. "Gene" Smith, president of Oklahoma Hardware and a long-time foe of the dealer-owned movement, got word of the proposed transaction and set out to prevent it. The very day Cotter was in Dallas talking to the Allen dealers, November 16, Smith sent a telegram to Allen's directors: "Oklahoma Hardware Company is interested in submitting to your stockholders an offer for the acquisition of your business. Are you accepting offers other than Cotter's?" Allen turned him down flat, so Smith tried to stir up opposition to Cotter's deal. He inspired an anonymous letter, dated November 27 and purportedly written by disgruntled Allen dealers, which raised some questions — "Why, all of a sudden, has the Management decided Walter H. Allen Company should be sold?" — "Who assumes the expense and liability for providing a 'Lifetime Contract' to Mr. Walter H. Allen and Mr. George R. Allen?" — "What kind of company is Cotter & Company of Chicago?" The letter closed with this hint, "Bear in mind that if members choose not to sell to Cotter and still want to liquidate . . . there are other wholesalers interested." A second letter, dated December 1 and signed by seven Allen members, invited their fellow members to an informal breakfast, at their own expense, the morning of the scheduled stockholders' meeting on December 8.

Gene Smith had arranged to make his pitch to the Allen members at this breakfast meeting in the Marriott motel. John Cotter, Walter Allen and Carl Monk attended the meeting; but they needn't have bothered, for few dealers showed up. The price of the meal was about $4.50, and John knew that very few hardware dealers would spend that much for a breakfast. The room was lined with row after row of empty tables, neatly set for breakfast with a glass of orange juice at each place. As Smith's hopes fizzled out, John Cotter dubbed the Oklahoma interloper "Orange Juice" Smith. Later in the day at the Allen stockholders' meeting, Orange Juice's forces could muster only 3.8% of the votes. Cotter's merger plan was approved by a vote of 89.7% for, 3.8% against, with the remainder spoiled proxies or abstentions.

Gene Smith was not finished yet. He complained to the U.S. Justice Department that Cotter's acquisition in Dallas violated the anti-trust laws and constituted a conspiracy to restrain trade. American anti-trust policy, based on the Sherman Act of 1890 and the Clayton Act of 1914, is enormously complex and confusing. The most commonly used provision of anti-trust law is Section 7 of the Clayton Act which forbids "any corporation engaged in interstate commerce to acquire any part of the capital stock of another corporation likewise engaged, where the effect may be to substantially lessen competition or to restrain such commerce in any section or community or tend to create a monopoly of any line of commerce." Interpretations of Section 7 are many and varied; and the government rarely inquires or prosecutes unless someone complains, as Smith did in this case. The assistant attorney general of the anti-trust division, William H. Orrick, Jr., sent Cotter a letter on February 9, 1965 asking for enormous amounts of information on Cotter's and Allen's business. Cotter's lawyers forwarded the material a month later, and the case dragged through the bureaucracy all summer. Then in August, President Johnson appointed Donald F. Turner, a former Harvard Law School professor, as his new chief of the anti-trust division. Turner held more tolerant views of corporate mergers than his predecessor did. In Turner's opinion, if two companies had not previously competed in the same market area, their merger constituted a "market extension," not a monopoly, and was thus legal. The inquiry into Cotter & Company was terminated with no charges resulting.

"Market extension" aptly described Cotter's move into Dallas. Walter H. Allen Co. had 370 members in the states of Texas, Oklahoma, New Mexico, Arkansas and Louisiana, and one each in Missouri and Arizona. Cotter signed about 320 of them, decisively projecting himself into a new area of the country.

The acquisition, however, posed some formidable operations problems. Cotter left Red Lynes in charge in Dallas for over a year after the formal takeover on January 2, 1965, and Lynes found the 190,000 sq.ft. Allen facility "the dirtiest warehouse I've ever seen." Lynes recalls:

"When we started turning that thing around it was one hell of a mess. They had twice as many employees as they needed, hardly any equipment, and a towveyor that didn't work. We had to keep holding dealer meetings to assure the dealers that this wasn't going to last forever. But for a year or so, we had a chaotic situation because we had to do that warehouse over completely. We figured we'd lose money the first year, and we did."

Only about 60% of Walter Allen's inventory matched the Cotter stock, so the other 40% had to be weeded out and sold off at reduced prices. Lynes then increased and expanded the inventory by ordering almost a million dollars worth of popular, fast-selling goods. He dismissed 23 employees at the Allen division, offering them a week's pay for each year of service up to a maximum of 12. Despite the severance pay, Lynes earned a reputation as Cotter's hatchet man, a reputation which grew with later takeovers. Finally, in the second year, the Allen division reached the million dollars a month in shipments it needed to break even, and Lynes gradually eased out of Dallas, leaving Winston MacNutt, the former Allen warehouse superintendent, in charge as distribution center manager.

Besides the additional dealers and increased business, Cotter received one other permanent benefit from Walter Allen. In contemplating expansion, Cotter had been troubled by the problem of differential freight rates and the seeming need for separate price books in different parts of the country, as Western dealers traditionally paid a premium on shipments from the East. Separate price books would greatly complicate dealer-owned accounting and would also compromise Cotter's low-cost image. Walter Allen suggested a solution, as Cotter explains:

"He said, 'Well, there's only about a 2% actual difference in freight. Sell them at your price and deduct the difference out of their patronage dividends at the end of the year.' Well, I looked in the mirror at that dummy Cotter and said, 'Why the hell didn't you think of that?' The policy worked fine. So now we had a pattern to do the West Coast. And that is how we unified the Cotter price book all across the U.S.''

Instead of moving on to the West Coast immediately, however, Cotter next turned East. Ever since he had moved into Ohio in 1961 and challenged American Hardware on their own territory, Cotter had wanted to push on and acquire dealers on the East Coast. He would have liked to buy Franklin Hardware in Philadelphia when they liquidated in 1962, but Le Herron, Jr., then president of American Hardware, had the inside track to his father's firm and American picked up most of Franklin's dealers. In 1964 Cotter established a field staff in Philadelphia and set them a target of 180 dealers before he would open a regional distribution center there. As a matter of policy, he always wanted a dealer base organized first before incurring the expense of a new warehouse.

Then on March 8, 1965, Tryon-Supplee-Biddle, a combination of two century-old wholesalers in Philadelphia, filed for bankruptcy under Chapter 11 of the Bankruptcy Act. Cotter still had only 147 dealers in the area, but he decided to go ahead anyway and open a regional distribution center. Bill Stout wrote him confidentially from his retirement, "E. Penna., Delaware, Maryland, D.C., New Jersey, *wide open* for dealer-owned. Now served only by small specialty jobbers." Everyone else advised against it — Philadelphia was a different world, Cotter's name was unknown there, American Hardware had recovered from its problems and was entrenched in Pennsylvania. But Cotter played a hunch that hardware retailers in Philly were looking for low cost distribution in the wake of Supplee-Biddle's failure, and if he didn't provide it someone else would. "When the time is right, you got to do it." So Cotter took Marty Seplak, his warehouse superintendent from Clybourn Ave., with him to Philadelphia in March of 1965 to look for a warehouse. They settled on the former Frankford Grocery building in the northeastern part of the city, and Cotter left Seplak behind to set it up. (Coincidentally, Frankford Grocery is reputed to be the earliest dealer-owned grocery wholesaler, founded in 1888.) The Philadelphia branch opened on July 1, 1965; but it needed about 200 dealers to make it a viable operation. By the end of the year, it had 198; the gamble paid off.

Opening a regional distribution center from scratch posed greater risks and larger initial overhead costs. Cotter much preferred to take over an existing firm and acquire its ready-made base of dealers, as he did in the case of WHS, Hibbard's, and Walter H. Allen. Yet opening a new warehouse, even in an old building, did prove easier, from an operational standpoint, than cleaning up someone else's mess. In less than a year, Marty Seplak had Philadelphia running efficiently. By the end of 1965, Cotter & Company was serving over 1700 members in 36 states, from four distribution centers; and they were arguing with Belknap of Louisville over who deserved the title of "largest hardware wholesaler in the U.S." Cotter's next move, to the West Coast, settled that issue.

LOS ANGELES AND PORTLAND

Arnie Poole, general manager of Great Western Hardware, John Cotter's admiring acolyte on the West Coast, guessed early in the game that Cotter was headed his way. He alternated between offers to cooperate and good-natured vows to fight him hand to hand. After Cotter's takeover of Hibbard's, Poole wrote him: "Maybe you are now ready to consider a West Coast operation, and I am just the guy to put you in touch with the proper people . . . Just think Cotter & Company — V & S Division, T. V. Division, G.W.H. Division." When he heard of the Walter H. Allen merger in Dallas, Poole commented, "I am no longer surprised when I get news of new growth and expansion of Cotter & Company . . . This brings about a strange turn of events with a Cotter & Company store less than twenty miles from our Phoenix warehouse. You may be up against the toughest competition you ever faced because, don't forget, I was trained by the master himself." After this show of bravado, Poole lapsed back into a cooperative mood, "Seriously, if I can ever do anything to help, you may be sure that you can count on me. Through my propaganda most dealers in this area know more about you than they do about me so together we should be able to get all of them."

Cotter didn't rush to acquire a foothold on the West Coast. Cautious as always, waiting for the right opportunity, he told those who inquired about his intentions, "I have repeatedly told myself we better stay east of the Rocky Mountains." Yet circumstances in the mid-1960s slowly changed his mind. Poole, perhaps trying too hard to impress his mentor, over-extended Great Western Hardware. He sold merchandise to members below his own cost, he spent money he didn't have on a costly computer system, and he diversified into variety merchandise, everything from collapsible umbrellas to plastic flowers. As the company's finances deteriorated in 1967, Poole fired his merchandise manager, who wrote to Cotter, "A little over a year ago . . . Arnold started doing right things, but at the wrong time. In other words, we did things that we couldn't afford to do, and it has caught up with us and I don't believe the company can survive." Ed Rea, a Great Western member, confirmed the seriousness of the situation when he met Cotter at the NRHA Convention that year. Then William Claypool, III, a Great Western member in Needles, California and chairman of GWH's board of directors, called Cotter the day after Christmas, 1967, with a similar message, and asked him to save them.

In the meantime, other developments on the Coast aroused Cotter's interest and concern. Ace Hardware, his archrival now that Hibbard's was gone, had preceded him to California. Ace signed two disgruntled Great Western dealers at the beginning of 1964, then in the summer of that year made a concerted push to acquire more. Dick Hesse and his heir-apparent, Arthur Krausman, held a series of meetings in L.A. in August, and Krausman remained on the Coast to buttonhole dealers. By the end of that year, Ace had signed 33 dealers, whom Arnie Poole described sourly as "discounters, troublemakers, Hebes, and in one case, the leader of the Get Poole movement." Ace experienced difficulties supplying California stores from its single warehouse in Chicago, so Hesse finally withdrew his long-standing opposition to branch distribution centers. Finding the right facility and acquiring enough dealers to support it took Ace longer than anticipated and they did not open their branch at Benecia, California, outside San Francisco, until late in 1968.

With Ace actively working the West Coast and Great Western in danger of going under, Cotter felt he had to make his move. Just as in the Philadelphia case, if he didn't fill the vacuum someone else would. So Bill Claypool, Arnie Poole, Ed Rea, and John Cotter arranged a consolidation of Great Western with Cotter & Company. Cotter presented a merger proposal to a secret meeting of Great Western directors at Saddleback Inn on January 23, 1968, bringing Walter

Allen with him to confirm the success of his last merger. He then made a public pitch to the dealer-members at a meeting on February 12. One dealer opposed the merger vociferously, but Great Western's banker quieted him by stating that the only alternative to merger was bankruptcy. If the members turned down Cotter's offer, the banker would call a $700,000 loan which was past due. The February meeting resulted in an agreement in principle, the directors then hammered out a contract on March 12, and 96.4% of the members approved on April 8. The final contract provided an exchange of Great Western stock for Cotter & Company stock, as in the Walter Allen merger; but due to the perilous financial state of GWH, the members' stock had to be discounted and they did not receive a 100% share-for-share investment in Cotter & Company.

Cotter took over Great Western on May 1, 1968, leaving Red Lynes in California to work with Poole. Lynes found the Great Western warehouse in Santa Fe Springs even more disorderly than the Allen facility had been. "Operations were terrible. They didn't have a watchman at night. All the truck drivers had keys to the warehouse." Cotter remembers that, "Red called me up from time to time and said he wanted to jump in the Pacific Ocean after working with Poole." About 90 days after the takeover, Lynes and Cotter realized that Poole had burned himself out and couldn't run the operation, so they had to let him go. Marty Seplak came out from Philadelphia to assist Lynes as operations manager.

Shaping up the California operation required a lot of time and money. As John Cotter puts it: "That was big money for us in those days. We paid off the bank $700,000. We paid off the past due bills to manufacturers, and that was another $700,000. And then we had to take another million and a half and put it into inventory so we'd have something to sell besides imported umbrellas."

The Santa Fe Springs warehouse had only 105,000 sq.ft., and land for an addition proved very costly. Cotter paid $53,500 an acre for 13 acres, and then built a 100,000 sq.ft. addition for about $500,000. The title company had overlooked the fact that the City of Santa Fe Springs held mineral rights on the property; so when the city engineer discovered a functioning artesian well on the site, he demanded a large fee to settle the mineral rights. Lynes remembers, "The city attorney wanted to be reasonable but the city engineer was holier-than-thou and wanted 'to protect the people.' He wanted 35 to 40 thousand for that well. We finally got him down to $16,000.'' There was also a large water storage tank on the site, formerly used to supply sprinklers in the area; Cotter & Company had to buy that twice, once from the propertyholders, then from the city, and pay to have it dismantled and carted away. Somebody once asked John Cotter why he put up with all this just to build a small warehouse addition. Why didn't he move to another site in the L.A. area? Cotter replied, ''That horse was so sick that if you did anything but spoonfeed it, it would have died on you.''

Despite all the hassle, Cotter believes the Great Western takeover was well worthwhile; for it provided him a substantial beachhead of 257 dealers on the West Coast.

In order to consolidate this beachhead, Cotter now looked to the Pacific Northwest. Red Lynes knew the area well from his wartime days with Marshall-Wells in Portland and still retained many friends and contacts. Lynes learned that Seattle Hardware was folding its unsuccessful stores program and some of the dealers were looking for a better deal. More importantly, Northern Hardware, the dealer-owned wholesaler in Portland, seemed ripe for a merger. The company was not in financial trouble, as Great Western had been. Northern recorded its first million dollar sales month in March, 1966; then in 1968 it enjoyed its best year ever, with sales over $8 million and patronage rebates exceeding 4%. A Dun & Bradstreet report in 1969 summed up Northern's condition: ''Record, Clean; Condition, Strong; Trend, Up.'' But Don Foss, general manager since 1953, wanted to retire and there was no obvious successor in the organization. Furthermore, Northern's warehouse was inadequate, a multi-story building in downtown Portland. (John Cotter characterized it as ''doing business out of a chimney.'') Northern lacked the financial resources to build a more modern facility.

With all this in mind, Lynes headed north from L.A. in the summer of 1969 to look over the situation. He compiled a list of the leading dealers in the Northwest; and he and Jim Craig, a Northern dealer from Vancouver, Washington, whom Lynes knew well, each called up 25 of them. They invited these fifty dealers to a dinner meeting and a slide presentation on Cotter's True Value program. Twenty-seven dealers showed up for the dinner, and though Lynes didn't know it at the time, Harley Bailey and Gerry Ronald from Northern sat in the hotel lobby and recorded all the Northern dealers as they walked in. The dinner meeting in Portland was intended as a fishing expedition, but Lynes soon found himself with two very big fish on his line. Len Farr, a Northern dealer and board member from Coos Bay, Oregon, talked to Lynes after the meeting and encouraged him to see Northern's president, T. Hedley Dingle, in Coeur d'Alene, Idaho. At Farr's urging, Lynes flew to Spokane, rented a car, and drove to Idaho. Dingle, who had known John Cotter for years, was enthusiastic about joining True Value and wanted to move immediately on a merger. Lynes knew he was in over his head, so he called John Cotter back in Chicago. Cotter authorized him to proceed.

Phone calls and correspondence between Farr, Dingle, and Foss on the one side and Cotter and Lynes on the other continued through the fall of 1969 until a tentative agreement was reached at the end of the year. Cotter assured the Northern dealers that he would continue their annual show in February, stock various lines of merchandise locally popular in the Northwest, and move as rapidly as possible to build or acquire a new warehouse. He struck a personal agreement with Foss to retain him as a consultant at $1000 per month through 1977.

Everything proceeded smoothly towards a friendly takeover, until the stockholders' meeting on February 24, 1970. At the last minute, Northern's attorney requested Cotter to put his promise of a new warehouse into binding contract language. Cotter had already paid $50,000 into escrow to bind the purchase of the Oliver White parts depot in Portland and was buying up adjacent Union Pacific land so he could expand to 400,000 sq.ft. But he got mad and refused the lawyer's request for a signed promise. He said, "Look, we got a deal here and got it all worked out and we're gonna build you a building. But you're gonna have to trust me to run this, and you're gonna start trusting me today." Taken aback, the lawyer caucused with the Northern board members, who then approved the agreement in principle. Some opposition continued, particularly from small dealers who feared they might be lost in Cotter's large organization. But the final vote at another stockholder meeting on April 20 approved the consolidation with 86.5%

in favor. Cotter & Company took over on June 1, 1970. Gerry Ronald, who had worked with Red Lynes at Marshall-Wells, became branch manager; but Ronald died just a year later and was succeeded by Harley Bailey.

IS BIGGER BETTER?

The acquisition of dealer-owned companies in Zanesville, Dallas, Los Angeles, and Portland, along with the opening of branch distribution centers in Cleveland and Philadelphia, transformed Cotter & Company into a national firm. By the end of 1970, Cotter had 3687 True Value members, in all fifty states, including Alaska and Hawaii. The company recorded $225 million in sales in 1970. The Hibbard takeover put Cotter on the map; the other takeovers spread the map across the continent.

No two takeovers were exactly alike, but a common pattern emerged in the acquisition of the smaller dealer-owned firms. Either the inadequacy of the general manager or his impending retirement caused a crisis in the company, and one or two strong directors, who dominated the board of directors, then pushed for a merger. In Zanesville, David Farley took the lead; in Dallas, Carl Monk was the catalyst; in L.A., Bill Claypool and Ed Rea; and in Portland, Len Farr and Hedley Dingle. These dominant dealers facilitated a friendly takeover by Cotter & Company, but at the same time they posed a problem to John Cotter as general manager and to the new branch manager he installed. Cotter, and his troubleshooter Red Lynes, had to convince these dealers to step farther into the background and let management manage.

Not every attempted takeover proved successful. We have already seen that Cotter failed to consummate the purchase of American Hardware in Pittsburgh and General Mercantile in St. Louis. Also, throughout the 1960s, he had been keeping an eye on the Whitlock Corporation of Yonkers, N.Y., a well-run regional wholesaler, closely held by Henry R. Stein and his family. Cotter talked informally with Stein as early as 1964, but nothing developed until Whitlock's new warehouse in Carlstadt, New Jersey, was hit by a strike late in 1968. Whitlock's former sales manager, Bill Earnest, had signed on with Cotter as a field man, and one day he visited Henry Stein in his struck plant. Stein told him to inform John Cotter he had had enough; he sold his inventory to Cotter and went out of business. Whitlock belonged to the PRO merchandising group and had a voluntary chain of about 50 dealers under the PRO banner. Cotter held a meeting for these dealers at the Hilton Inn in Tarrytown, New York, but did not succeed in signing very many. The New York dealers didn't know or trust Cotter and his people; they shared the usual New Yorker's condescension to the "second city" and considered the Chicagoans little better than Capone gangsters. Herb Haller recalls that this was the only time he ever saw John Cotter lose control of a meeting; Bill Earnest says he had never seen Cotter so mad. As a result, Rose, Kimball & Baxter of Elmira, New York, another wholesaler affiliated with PRO, signed 43 of 52 Whitlock members. Still, the effort was not in vain. Both Bill Earnest and Pat Casey, Cotter & Company's current eastern and western sales managers, came from Whitlock.

After 1970, Cotter executed only one more takeover. He bought the Van Camp Hardware Co. of Indianapolis in 1976 in order to obtain a new regional distribution center and relieve the very severe overcrowding at Chicago. This proved to be his least successful acquisition, as he signed up only one of the Van Camp salesmen, Gary Hoover, and very few dealers. Bostwick-Braun of Toledo moved in swiftly and hired 18 Van Camp salesmen. Even the warehouse, which was the primary reason for Cotter's purchase, has proven less than ideal. (As Herb Haller put it, "We wanted the mine but we got the shaft.")

Since 1970, Cotter has gradually filled in his national distribution network by building new regional warehouses from the ground up, as the number of dealers and volume of sales has continued to grow steadily. Warehouses opened in Atlanta and Kansas City in 1971, Manchester, New Hampshire in 1973, Mankato, Minnesota in 1977, and Denver, Colorado in 1984. The two newest centers, in Woodland, California and Henderson, North Carolina, have recently come on line. In addition, some of the older distribution centers have moved to new facilities in suburban areas, including the parent warehouse which relocated from Clybourn Avenue in Chicago to Harvard, Illinois in 1982. (See Table 7) Ben Maze, who began working for Cotter as a warehouse employee in 1954, rose through the ranks to become Tool Department Manager. He later moved the Zanesville operation to

TABLE 7
COTTER & COMPANY REGIONAL DISTRIBUTION CENTERS

LOCATION	DATE OPENED	SQUARE FOOTAGE	MANAGER	COMMENTS
Harvard, Ill.	1982	440,000	Jim Eller	Moved from Clybourn Avenue
Cleveland, Ohio	1962	405,000	Ed Meyer	Moved from Zanesville, Ohio
Allentown, Pa.	1976	420,000	Bob Halsey	Moved from Philadelphia
Corsicana, Texas	1983	450,000	Dave Van Buskirk	Moved from Dallas
Pomona, Calif.	1979	320,000	Vince Haan	Moved from Santa Fe Springs
Portland, Ore.	1971	405,000	Tom Statham	Built after acquisition of Northern Hardware
Atlanta, Ga.	1971	360,000	Charlie Foell	
Kansas City, Mo.	1971	415,000	Andy Leonard	
Manchester, N.H.	1973	415,000	Dick Rae	
Indianapolis, Ind.	1976	420,000	John Semkus	Acquired from Van Camp Hardware
Mankato, Minn.	1977	320,000	Bill Livingston	
Denver, Col.	1984	310,000	Ken Sturgill	
Woodland, Calif.	1985	320,000	Homer Clark	
Henderson, N.C.	1986	300,000	Roger Hansen	

Figure 6

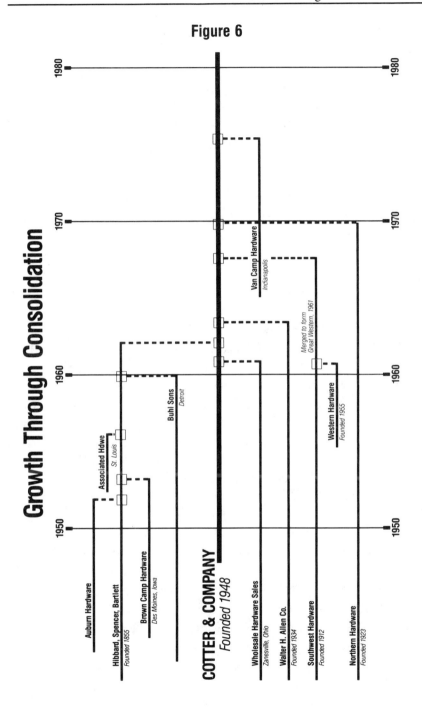

Growth Through Consolidation

Cleveland and became operations manager. Using the experience he gained there, he has planned and built all new regional distribution centers.

Is bigger always better? Until recently, few Americans would have hesitated before answering, ''Yes;'' but in the last fifteen years, there has been widespread discussion of ''limits to growth'' and a belief in some quarters that ''small is beautiful.'' In the process of interviewing John Cotter and his associates, I probed frequently for limits to growth or disadvantages of bigness; but no one at Cotter & Company admitted to any. Indeed, Cotter answered me vehemently with the statement quoted at the head of this chapter: ''Everything is to your advantage with growth . . . Buying power . . . National distribution . . . National advertising . . . Everything you do, with rare exceptions, improves because of volume.''

Cotter worked and planned to avoid those rare exceptions. The operation of branch distribution centers is a tricky and costly business, which the wholesale hardware industry had avoided for most of its history. During the heyday of the old-line wholesalers, only Simmons of St. Louis and Marshall-Wells of Duluth attempted a multi-warehouse operation. When Hibbard's surrounded the Midwest with branch warehouses in the 1950s, Dick Hesse of Ace ridiculed the decision mercilessly; but he was only echoing the conventional wisdom. John Cotter broke out of the regional wholesaling mentality with his usual mixture of caution and daring. Though no corporate raider in the mold of Hyman Sobiloff, he clearly enjoyed the hunt and the chase of takeovers and the prestige which successful acquisitions brought him. Yet he had a more practical reason for buying out other companies. A distribution center needs at least 200 or 300 dealers to support itself. Taking over a dealer-owned firm or a program wholesaler and signing its dealers en masse is the most efficient way of providing this dealer base. Cotter believes that Ace, once it abandoned Hesse's prejudice against branch warehouses, went to the opposite extreme, using a warehouse to open up and create a new territory, not to serve an already established group of dealers. Cotter's policy of growth through consolidation was, at one and the same time, more cautious and more spectacular.

Regional distribution centers can lead to costly duplication of services; but Cotter has tried to avoid this by centralizing all the buying and financial decisions in Chicago. The distribution center manager is responsible for the operation of his warehouse, keeping it clean and orderly and shipping merchandise to members in his area on time. Everything else is handled at headquarters. If the branch manager starts acting like a sales manager, he gets himself and his operation in trouble. Low cost distribution cannot afford decentralization of decision-making or duplication of functions.

Dealer-members have often expressed regret at the loss of intimacy and familiarity as Cotter & Company grew. At the time of the Hibbard takeover, one dealer, who asked to remain anonymous, told *Hardware Merchandiser:* "Cotter & Company . . . are a small business that grew up fast. I wonder how big they can get before forgetting the small retailer." Similar fears that "there is a penalty to be small in the Cotter organization" arose among some Northern Hardware dealers prior to Cotter's Portland acquisition. Herb Haller encountered these sentiments out in the field all the time. "Now that you're so big are you going to forget all about us?" This danger is real in any large organization, and it's impossible to avoid some negative consequences of bigness. John Cotter himself feels frustrated occasionally since he can't personally oversee every decision and know every member by name.

Herb Haller has, perhaps, furnished the best answer to these negative assessments of growth. Whenever a dealer-member started complaining about how big and impersonal Cotter & Company had become, Haller would ask him to look around his own store. "Do you remember when you had a 25' storefront, and you and your wife were the only staff? You could stand in the center of the store waiting on customers and practically touch the shelves on all four walls. Now you have 15,000 or 20,000 square feet and a staff of 50 or more. You spend most of your time in an office at the back of the store, doing paperwork. You've lost some of the old coziness, but do you really want to go back?" Few are nostalgic enough to trade the lower merchandise costs, national recognition and advertising, plus countless other benefits of present size for the supposed intimacy of past smallness.

Without question, however, there is one downside to rapid growth and large size; it makes you a target. The general manager of Our Own Hardware told a trade magazine in 1978, "Perhaps not being as big as the national hardware coops has been an advantage to us. Some deal-ers who have switched to us say one of the reasons was our personal approach; they didn't feel like they were just numbers here." United Hardware published a full page ad in a recent issue of *Hardware Age,* blaring out in huge headlines: "Most Americans No Longer Assume Bigger is Better. But Our Competition Still Does." Most everyone takes potshots at No. 1.

The most spectacular potshot came back in 1966, when the presi-dent of the National Wholesale Hardware Association delivered a sen-sational speech, denouncing John Cotter by name. Cotter & Company's flurry of takeovers and its drive toward nationwide distribution stirred the NWHA to dig in for a last stand against dealer-owned wholesalers.

CHAPTER TEN
MR. SHEFFIELD
GIVES A
SPEECH

"It's a fact that John Cotter has actually referred to himself as the P. T. Barnum of the Hardware Industry, and frankly, that's a very accurate and apt description. I'm not implying that he exemplifies Barnum's statement that 'a sucker is born every minute,' but I am implying that he is a great showman . . . On the other hand, I am saying he has no secret formula for reducing expenses. I am knocking and criticizing the ethics being used by Cotter in his effort to sell his service package to hardware retailers. I see no reason for making half true statements."
—John W. Sheffield, Annual Address of the President
  of the National Wholesale Hardware Association,
  October 17, 1966

John Sheffield's personal attack on John Cotter at the 1966 NWHA convention in Atlantic City did not come out of nowhere, like a bolt from the blue. It was the culmination of a long guerrilla war between John Cotter and the old-line hardware wholesalers represented by the trade association. Article 3 of the NWHA constitution limited membership to "full-line, full-function" wholesalers. This clause barred both small, short-line, specialty jobbers, who generally didn't desire membership, and the dealer-owned wholesalers, such as Cotter, American, and Our Own, who sought it eagerly.

In October, 1957, the newly-elected NWHA president, John Stiles from Morley-Murphey in Green Bay, Wisconsin, had defended these exclusions, proclaiming that any jobber "who does not have an active sales force . . . who does not carry adequate warehouse stock" is a "pseudo-wholesaler." Stiles spoke rather cautiously in generalities and he named no names, but John Cotter took it personally. The following August, while on vacation in Wisconsin, Cotter decided to pay a call on Mr. Stiles. As he tells the story:

"I happened to be in Green Bay so I prepared myself a little speech and went down to his office. If the devil himself had appeared at his front door he couldn't have been more surprised. I had with me our financial statement. He looked at it, apologized and said he hadn't realized we had such an extensive inventory."

Stiles may have apologized when Cotter caught him off guard, but he didn't change his tune. In his 1959 swan-song as president, he again contrasted the "full-function wholesalers" with these "parasites who come closer to being brokers than wholesalers." There the matter rested for a number of years, with John Cotter regularly appearing uninvited in Atlantic City, and the association just as regularly pretending he didn't exist.

After Cotter's takeover of Hibbard's in 1962 caught the full attention of the industry, the battle moved out into the field where it mattered most. In 1964 and '65, a number of anonymous pamphlets began showing up in the hands of wholesale salesmen when they talked to dealers. One of them, prepared by Dick Snow, sales manager of Van Camp Hardware in Indianapolis, compared the "Full Function Wholesaler vs. Dealer-Owned Wholesaler." Three others, eventually traced back to Gene "Orange Juice" Smith of Oklahoma Hardware, carried such titles as: "It's a Good Deal for John, Is It Good for the Retailer?"; "You Can Believe It! There Really is a Difference;" and "Speak for Yourself, John. Low Cost? Prove It!" All of Smith's pamphlets, which were nearly identical, purported to separate "Fact from Fantasy" in Cotter's claims of low-cost wholesaling. They listed 15 or 16 "hidden charges" which supposedly inflated the costs of Cotter's members and they included a personal attack on John Cotter's earnings of about $200,000 in 1965. Salesmen didn't generally hand out these propaganda leaflets but read selected passages to dealers in order to plant doubts in their minds. Nevertheless, a few Cotter members secured copies and forwarded them to John Cotter or Herb Haller.

Cotter, for his part, carried on his own propaganda barrage against the old-line wholesalers. His field men circulated the list of wholesalers who had gone out of business and Cotter continually predicted that others would follow. He also distributed a striking graph comparing the high overhead costs of traditional wholesalers with his own company's rock-bottom operating costs. (See Figure 7) John Cotter, then, had been embroiled in a long-running controversy with competing wholesalers; the question of operating costs formed the focus of debate.

EARL LIFSHEY LIGHTS THE FUSE

On June 13, 1966 Earl Lifshey, a highly respected columnist for *Home Furnishings Daily,* brought the controversy over wholesaling costs out into the open. In his daily column, "If You Ask Me," Lifshey wrote:

"The so-called retailing revolution . . . is against waste in distribution . . . When the talk gets around to cutting costs — and waste — at the wholesale level . . . the evidence there is so impressive as to almost border on the sensational in one particular case . . . Cotter & Company . . . In 1950, Cotter reports, its operating cost was 10.52 per cent. Last year that dropped down to 6.97 per cent and, on the basis of current calculation, it will go down as far as 5.97 per cent by next year.

In comparison — or contrast! — the operating expenses of the so-called old-line wholesalers functioning in the usual manner, have continued to increase in recent years from 15 to 18.74 per cent . . ."

To make the point more graphically, Lifshey printed a copy of Cot-

Figure 7

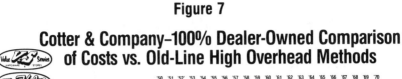

Cotter & Company–100% Dealer-Owned Comparison of Costs vs. Old-Line High Overhead Methods

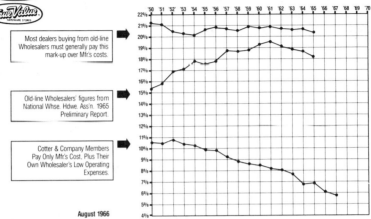

Most dealers buying from old-line Wholesalers must generally pay this mark-up over Mfr.'s costs.

Old-line Wholesalers' figures from National Whse. Hdwe. Ass'n. 1965 Preliminary Report.

Cotter & Company Members Pay Only Mfr.'s Cost, Plus Their Own Wholesaler's Low Operating Expenses.

August 1966

ter's own chart showing "Operating Cost Comparisons."

Lifshey received a deluge of mail about this column. Gene Smith wrote him on June 16 with his usual point-by-point litany of "hidden charges," lifted directly from his pamphlets. John W. Sheffield, Sr., president of Sheffield Hardware in Americus, Georgia, and the current president of NWHA, wrote him, as did Thomas A. Fernley, Jr., managing director of NWHA. Fernley complained about Cotter and Lifshey's unauthorized use of association cost statistics.

On July 5 and 6, Lifshey published two follow-up columns on the cost controversy. He began the first with a tongue-in-cheek statement: "All that noise you heard yesterday wasn't Fourth-of-July fireworks. It was the bombardment the National Wholesale Hardware Association and its members have been directing at me ever since my column of June 13 about Cotter & Company." He then went on to disclaim any collusion with John Cotter: "Let me say for the record as emphatically as I can that John Cotter didn't 'snow' me or solicit any mention here whatever." This may have been true, but Lifshey did share his correspondence concerning the June 13th column with Cotter, and

Cotter did freely circulate reprints of the column to his friends.

In his final column, Lifshey wouldn't let the old-line wholesalers off the hook:

"As I read and re-read the numerous lengthy letters they continue to send me dissecting and denouncing the Cotter methods, I can't escape the feeling that they're looking down their noses at Cotter — with the greatest envy. I can't help recalling too that according to Dun & Bradstreet, over 270 (many long-established) wholesalers have gone out of business in the last 10 years *despite* all their tradition. Or could it perhaps be *because* of it?

I think Tom Fernley, managing director of the National Wholesale Hardware Association, expressed — perhaps inadvertently — one of the basics of the whole matter in his letter to me in which he says, 'There are a number of items in our Overhead Expense Report which could indeed be reduced appreciably if our members could operate under the quite strict rules which prevail under the Cotter & Company arrangement.' (Note that If!)"

Lifshey closed his column sadly, "I have many good friends among the wholesalers and it disturbs me to see them squirm and run scared in this fashion."

This very public airing of dirty linen proved too much for the officers of NWHA. John Sheffield and Gene Smith got together and decided to answer Lifshey and Cotter openly. Perhaps they were envious or running scared, as Lifshey suggested; more likely they were just angry. John Cotter was an abrasive, outspoken competitor who freely predicted that "eventually most merchandise sold by independent hardware dealers will be distributed through dealer-owned organizations or there will be few, if any, independent dealers." This was more than competition, it was a battle for the hearts and minds of retailers, with survival at stake. So when a high-profile trade columnist, such as Lifshey, took Cotter's side so strongly, the other side felt it had to reply.

JOHN SHEFFIELD THROWS THE BOMB

Sheffield's response to Lifshey came in two stages. On July 12 he delivered a hard-hitting, but still diplomatically-worded, address to the National Retail Hardware Association at the Fontainebleu Hotel in Miami. Then in Atlantic City in October, at his own convention of the

NWHA, he let loose a full-scale personal blast at John Cotter, calling him by name and displaying and dissecting Cotter & Company cost figures.

In his Miami speech, Sheffield emphasized one main point, that wholesale salesmen were not an expensive luxury which could be dispensed with but an important service to retailers. "Who explains to you and your clerks the product knowledge and sales features of new products?" he asked. "Who suggests better ways to display new merchandise? Who helps out in your store . . . in an emergency? . . . Obviously, the answer to all these questions is the wholesale salesman."

Sheffield didn't mention either Lifshey or Cotter by name in his NRHA speech, but towards the end of it he showed his irritation and edged close to a personal attack:

"Frankly, I like competition . . . I think it is all part of the game to do everything you can to get a retailer's business . . . but not by trying to make the retailer think your competitor is a skunk . . . In a talk made some months ago by the president of one of the short-service distribution houses, the speaker made the statement that, 'The old, full-line, full-service, salesman travelling wholesale hardware business is dead. The only trouble is they just don't know it and won't roll over.'

I don't think it's Retailer-Oriented to resort to this type of competition."

Sheffield's presidential address in Atlantic City was far longer, more detailed, and more pointed than the Miami curtainraiser. And this time he named names. He introduced his talk as a response to Earl Lifshey's June 13th column, which he called "an insult to the intelligence of all of Mr. Lifshey's readers." His references to John Cotter throughout the speech were sarcastic and cutting. He termed Cotter "a self admitted big shot" and "the P.T. Barnum of the Hardware Industry" and charged him with "half true statements" and "the big lie of the hardware industry today."

Rhetoric aside, Sheffield devoted the heart of his speech to a detailed cost comparison between Cotter & Company and the NWHA's average wholesaler member, presented in nine graphic charts. The main chart displayed Cotter's sales, cost of goods, gross margin, and cost of operation side by side with the NWHA average for all large wholesalers. Column A showed Cotter's gross margin at 10.53% of sales and cost of operation at 6.97%; Column B revealed corresponding NWHA figures of 19.69% and 16.34%, respectively. Sheffield spent the rest of his speech trying to explain away the 9% difference in costs and he ascribed most of it to "tricky bookkeeping."

Sheffield argued that all comparisons between Cotter & Company cost figures and those for NWHA members were invalid since they operated their businesses in a totally different manner. Cotter & Company travelled no salesmen, paid no income tax, and provided fewer free services (such as prepaid freight) so of course his costs were lower. Sheffield quoted a hometown CPA back in Americus, Georgia, who had looked over his figures, and said it was like trying to compare apples and oranges. Furthermore, Sheffield alleged, most of the costs Cotter dispensed with were not truly eliminated, but simply shifted to someone else, usually the retailer. The retail-member of a dealer-owned wholesaler had to spend his own valuable time writing up orders rather than letting a salesman do it, he had to pay his own freight, and, of course, he and every other taxpayer had to make up the taxes which the coop wholesaler didn't pay. In addition, Sheffield detailed Gene Smith's long list of "hidden charges" which a retailer in a dealer-owned company had to absorb. Among these charges were a $7.50 per month catalogue fee, a 2% per month penalty for unpaid bills, a $22.50 per month penalty for not buying enough merchandise, a 4% broken carton charge for small purchases, and a stiff penalty for returning merchandise or cancelling a pool order.

Sheffield ascribed the different manners of doing business and handling operating costs primarily to the difference in tax status. A traditional, profit-making wholesaler would absorb freight charges, catalogue costs, and many other costs because they used them as business deductions on their corporate income tax returns. A non-profit corporation received no tax benefit from these costs so it shifted them to the retailer. Sheffield summarized his argument this way:

"In columns A and B you are really looking at the end product of two schools of thought in bookkeeping. Column A showing Cotter's figures represents the desire to impress their Members with the fact that they operate on a small margin, and at a low cost of doing business.

While Column B being the taxpaying Members of our Association are doing everything they can in their bookkeeping to lower the cost of merchandise and to be certain that every penny is added to the proper expense account . . . I don't think there is anything dishonest in either method — it's just a case of Cotter trying to impress his Members and our people trying to impress the Internal Revenue Department . . .''

Sheffield closed with some ''tricky bookkeeping'' of his own. With the help of his anonymous CPA from Americus, he estimated what Cotter's true costs of operations would be if he did business the same way an NWHA member did. He ended up with a cost figure 1% higher than the NWHA's. He concluded:

''Gentlemen, I have tried to show you how, by using an arbitrary method of applying funds, Cotter brings his cost of operations down to a ridiculous figure . . . I want it clearly understood I'm not making this talk in an effort to knock or criticize Cotter's operation . . . On the other hand . . . I am knocking and criticizing the ethics being used by Cotter in his effort to sell his service package to hardware retailers. I see no reason for making half true statements.''

A COST ANALYSIS

John Sheffield's controversial speech was long, tangled, and not always completely clear; but it does present an opportunity to look over Cotter & Company's mature system of operation and attempt an independent cost analysis.

Sheffield's two main points, 1) that a profit-making business has every reason, for tax purposes, to exaggerate its expenses whereas a cooperative business tries to minimize its expenses; and 2) that wholesale costs and functions can never be truly eliminated, only shifted, both have some validity, as far as they go.

Of course, a traditional corporation will pad its expense account as much as legally possible, and of course, Cotter will use every possible device to impress his members with his low costs. In fact, Cotter did exclude two small expenses from his cost of operation figure, interest paid, .57% of sales, and bad debts, .07%, reporting them separately as adjustments to his profit. (The NWHA included bad debts in its operating cost figure, but it too handled interest cost separately as an adjustment.) Leaving these two charges aside allowed Cotter to quote an operating cost figure below 7%, which no doubt sounded better to his members than 7.61% would. Yet the difference is small and not of major significance.

John Cotter, too, would agree that some wholesaling functions were shifted in his system; he often quoted the phrase, "you can eliminate the jobber but you can't eliminate the job." For instance, some one has to write the retailers' orders; if a wholesale salesman doesn't do it, the dealers themselves must. This function is shifted to their shoulders, and some of them can't handle it. Not every storeowner is organized and disciplined enough to write his own orders without a major waste of time and money.

So, Sheffield's two main points are basically true; in fact, they are so obvious they approach the status of truisms. The dealer-owned system *is* different from old-line wholesaling; comparison between them *is* like comparing apples and oranges. But Sheffield completely ignored the crucial question: "Which system provides a better deal for the retailer?" A close comparison indicates that dealer-ownership does produce definite cost savings. (See Table 8) Cotter's warehouse and office overhead fell substantially below the NWHA average, but an excellent manager of a traditional wholesaler could produce comparable results if he made operating efficiency a top priority. Dealer-ownership provides no automatic advantage in that matter, John Cotter just happened to be a good manager. Three items in Table 8, however, do represent cost savings inherent in the dealer-owned system — selling expense, income tax, and net profit.

Travelling a sales force is expensive. As long as a wholesaler sends out salesmen, he will always have expenses about 4 or 5 per cent higher than a dealer-owned firm. Of course, it is comfortable and convenient for the retailer to let the salesman do some of his work for him; but if he is disciplined enough to write his own orders, that 4 or 5 per cent can come right off the cost of his goods. In a highly competitive situation, he cannot forego that 4%, he cannot afford the luxury of dealing with, and paying for, travelling salesmen. As John Cotter preaches continually, "Old-line wholesalers were providing services the dealers didn't really need and could no longer afford."

TABLE 8

1965 COST COMPARISON
COTTER & COMPANY vs. NWHA AVERAGE

	COTTER	NWHA (members with over $12 million in sales)
Sales	100%	100%
Cost of Goods	89.47%	79.99%
Gross Margin	10.53%	20.01%
Operating Expenses		
Warehouse	3.72%	4.53%
Administrative	2.53%	5.32%
Selling	.72%	4.88%
Other	0	2.56%
TOTAL	**6.97%**	**17.29%**
Net Margin	3.56%	2.72%
Adjustments		
Subtract		
Interest Paid	.57%	.28%
Subtract bad debts	.07%	0
Subtract income tax	0	1.22%
And others	0	.20%
TOTAL	**.64%**	**1.30%**
Net Profit	**2.92%**	**1.42%**

Income tax, too, is a burden that a traditional wholesaler bears and a dealer-owned firm doesn't, and the traditional wholesalers never let anyone forget it. Just for the record, it's worth noting that the tax advantage is not all that large. Corporations use every legal deduction to reduce their taxable profit, so in 1965 the average large NWHA member paid taxes equivalent to only 1.22% of sales. Still, there is no reason to deny this is a disadvantage for traditional firms. Tax equality is a legitimate issue, as all businesses in the same industry should compete on a "level playing field." Yet, as Earl Lifshey pointed out in one of his columns, "If the law is bad the place to complain is Congress — not Cotter." Furthermore, as tax reformers have been arguing for decades, the better way to equalize tax treatment would be to eliminate double taxation of dividends from all corporations rather than reimpose it on cooperatives. In any case, as the tax laws are currently written, a dealer-owned firm does enjoy a tax advantage which can be applied to lower the cost of goods.

The final cost advantage for a retail member of a dealer-owned wholesaler lies in year-end patronage rebates. All of Cotter & Company's net profit of 2.92% of sales in 1965 was paid out to its members, whereas traditional wholesalers paid out profits to their stockholders. True, only 20% of the patronage rebates were paid in cash, the rest in notes and stock, but the money ultimately belonged to the members. If they were willing to look at their dividends as long-term investments, they had no trouble recognizing them as a bottom-line advantage.

In sum, then, a dealer-owned company develops a 7% inherent cost advantage over an old-line wholesaler — 4% from elimination of salesmen, 1½% from tax advantages, and 1½% from rebate of profits. An excellent manager, such as John Cotter, can increase the advantage by lowering costs elsewhere, and a poor manager could squander the advantage by operating inefficiently. But the bottom-line is a basic 7% advantage in the system of dealer-ownership.

What of the "hidden charges" to the retailer alleged by Gene Smith, John Sheffield, and others? There are a lot of extra fees in the dealer-owned system — a broken carton charge, a penalty charge for failing to meet the minimum monthly purchase level, and a stiff service charge for late payment, to name a few. Yet these fees are *deterrent charges,* intended to discourage behavior which is detrimental to the retailer and to his dealer-owned wholesaler. An efficient member who follows the system, concentrates his purchases, and pays his bills on time *will never pay any of these* deterrent charges.

Some costs are, indeed, shifted to the retailer. A Cotter member pays his own freight costs and pays a monthly fee for the use of his catalogue and price book. These do represent out-of-pocket costs to the member, but they form part of Cotter's policy of each member paying his own way. Does anyone believe that freight pre-paid by the wholesaler is truly free? The wholesaler builds the freight cost — and any other ''free'' services — into the cost of goods. The old-line wholesaler who advertises such ''free'' services is the one with ''hidden charges.'' In the Cotter & Company dealer-owned system, any necessary fees are straightforward and charged directly to the dealer incurring them, not spread among all the dealers or hidden in the merchandise prices.

In sum, the Gene Smith litany of hidden charges and the John Sheffield allegations of tricky bookkeeping were both ''red herrings.'' Dealer-ownership did produce cost advantages for the hardware retailer and did reduce the cost of his goods.

JOHN COTTER'S RESPONSE TO SHEFFIELD

Though this dispassionate cost analysis would seem to indicate that Cotter had nothing to fear from Sheffield's address, John Cotter did not act so calmly at the time. In fact, he got furious; and he threatened to sue Sheffield if he did not immediately retract his libelous statements. On November 17, a month after the presidential address, Sheffield circulated an apology of sorts and his statement was published in the trade press. Sheffield avowed:

''I did not mean to charge Cotter & Company or Mr. Cotter personally with unlawful accounting practices or otherwise to impugn the personal integrity of Mr. Cotter. I had no intention of using strong and intemperate language . . .''

Cotter did not consider Sheffield's statement a ''wholehearted forthright retraction'' so he instructed his lawyers to pursue the matter further. He wanted a detailed retraction of ''false financial statements'' made by Mr. Sheffield and he also wanted the NWHA to stop all fur-

further circulation of anti-Cotter pamphlets or statements. This second point is particularly important, for it probably explains why Cotter proved so uncharacteristically litigation-minded in this case. Cotter did not view Sheffield's address as an isolated incident, but rather as the culmination of a propaganda and disinformation campaign against him. He decided to use Sheffield's indiscretion as a weapon to end the whole campaign.

Ron Aronberg, Cotter's legal counsel, and Jack Lahr, from the NWHA's law firm, wrote back and forth for nearly a year, trying to discover a mutually agreeable form of words. Cotter intended that John Sheffield should sign any retraction both as an individual and in his capacity as president of NWHA. When he heard through the grapevine that Tom Fernley had ghostwritten all or part of the speech, he insisted that Fernley sign any agreement as well. (John Sheffield denies that Fernley wrote any part of the speech; the folksy and pungent style of the writing would seem to support him in this.) Cotter believed the disavowals of the American Hardware Manufacturers' Association, co-sponsors of the October convention with the NWHA, that they had no foreknowledge of the contents of Sheffield's speech. Cotter, therefore, did not include AHMA in any of the threatened legal action.

The legal dickering became so tangled, Cotter had to hire a Philadelphia lawyer to unravel it. In April, 1967, he engaged the Philadelphia law firm of Ballard, Spahr, Andrews & Ingersoll, specialists in libel litigation, to file and prosecute a lawsuit against the NWHA and each of its officers. Apparently one of the Ballard partners lived near Tom Fernley on the Main Line, so he applied some informal pressure to induce a settlement. After further negotiations over the summer, NWHA finally produced a settlement statement which satisfied Cotter.

On October 6, 1967, nearly a year after the offending speech, John Sheffield, Tom Fernley, and John Cotter signed a four-paragraph statement which brought the controversy to a close. Sheffield affirmed:

"I apologize for the strong, and perhaps intemperate, language in my October 17, 1966 speech . . . Moreover, in order to provide you with the assurances you feel to be necessary to effect the settlement, neither I nor NWHA will distribute directly nor encourage the NWHA membership to distribute, untrue and defamatory statements, oral or written, about your Company, its

financial statements, business operations and practices, promotional materials, or its conduct otherwise being illegal.''
Cotter accepted this letter rather than the more lengthy and formal agreement, filled with "whereases" and legal jargon, that he had insisted on earlier. He also dropped his demand that the settlement letter be sent to every NWHA member. Charles Thompson, Cotter's Philadelphia lawyer from the Ballard firm, finally convinced him "that the NWHA letter in its present form has the flavor of 'eating crow' and should be accepted as written."

AFTERMATH OF THE CONTROVERSY

In retrospect, the Sheffield controversy appears to be a case of overkill on one side and overreaction on the other. It is difficult to understand why the president of a trade association would depart so markedly from the usual banal generalities of convention rhetoric and leave himself wide open for a libel suit. The publishers of the trade press couldn't understand it either. They treated the whole incident with kid gloves, not even publishing the customary transcript of the speech lest they be drawn into the legal action. It's also difficult to understand why John Cotter pursued litigation so long and vigorously. Perhaps the long guerrilla war within the hardware industry had simply taken its toll. Both sides, however, got what they wanted. Cotter put a stop to the pamphlets attacking him and Sheffield claims that Cotter muffled his rhetoric against the traditional wholesalers.

The controversy did have one unforeseen, happy result. Like the lancing of a boil, the Sheffield affair seemed to provide a catharsis, a sense of release to the industry. From that time on, John Cotter was no longer a "non-person." His name began to appear more frequently and more favorably in *Hardware Age* and *Hardware Retailing.* As a result of this publicity in the trade press, many of the most prestigious members of the American Hardware Manufacturers Association, who were enjoying an ever-increasing business from Cotter and other dealer-owned wholesalers, began to seriously question the logic of their largest customers not being permitted to join the National Wholesale Hardware Association.

The movement to cease treating Cotter like a pariah gathered momentum after John J. Sullivan was named editor of *Hardware Age* in June

of 1968. During his first week on the job, Sullivan made an appointment to see Cotter. As he was ushered into the office, Cotter said:
"Your magazine hasn't paid a damn bit of attention to us for five years.
What the hell are you doing here now?" Sullivan answered, "I can't
be responsible for what happened more than five days ago. But I don't
think that any publication that purports to represent our industry can
do it without being deeply involved with you and your people."

Sullivan proved as good as his word. The following year, in an
October 1, 1969 *Hardware Age* editorial, he publicly called for the
admission of Cotter & Company, and other dealer-owned wholesalers,
to the NWHA. Sullivan wrote:

"Two years ago one young Southern wholesaler stood up at an
industry seminar and exclaimed: 'We've wasted too much time
and energy hating the John Cotters in this business when we should
have been learning from them.!'"

Sullivan closed the editorial with one of John Cotter's favorite phrases:
"So I ask: If eventually, why not now?"

Sullivan's plea wasn't answered immediately, but small symbolic
steps were taken. In the spring of 1970, the Southern Wholesale Hardware Association invited Don Wolf, the president of HWI in Fort
Wayne, to address their convention. This was the first time a dealer-
owned manager had ever participated formally in an official hardware
industry program. (The question of membership had never come up
in the Southern association since no dealer-owned firms were head-
quartered in the South.) Then in August of the same year, John Cotter
himself addressed the NRHA convention in Toronto. (NRHA, under
the leadership first of Russ Mueller then of Bill Mashaw, was more
favorably disposed to dealer-ownership; but they had never before invited a dealer-owned manager to speak.) Cotter's Toronto speech put a
few noses out of joint. Rather than talk in pious generalities or fawn
over his hosts for the privilege of addressing them, Cotter delivered
a hard-hitting speech asking the retail dealers to "re-think their source
of supply." He delivered an undisguised sales pitch for dealer-
ownership and for his own company. John Sullivan called him later
and suggested the speech wasn't very "statesmanlike." Cotter replied
in his best "aw-shucks" manner: "Well, you know me. I just got carried away. Besides, most of what I said was true."

Finally, at the October, 1973 convention, the NWHA membership voted to amend its constitution and admit all wholesalers of hardware and related lines to membership, regardless of their corporate structure. Dan Cotter sent a check for $4,110 to cover the initiation fee and annual dues on January 4, 1974. At long last, after so many years of ostracism, the largest hardware wholesaler in the country, a part of the most rapidly growing segment of the industry, could take its place as a member of the National Wholesale Hardware Association.

CHAPTER ELEVEN
LOCALIZING
NATIONAL
ADVERTISING

"Every day of the year, advertising for True Value Hardware Stores and Home Centers appears in newspapers and magazines and on radio and television. But, direct mail is the foundation of True Value advertising. Its strength is seen in the over 200 million copies of True Value tabloids and catalogues distributed annually."

—Pat Summerall, at True Value's 76th Semi-Annual Red Carpet Market, October, 1985

The low cost of goods and vigorous, incessant advertising — these have been the twin pillars of success for True Value Hardware Stores. The cost of goods issue drew most attention throughout the industry in the 1950s and 60s, culminating in the Sheffield controversy; but in recent years, advertising has pushed to the fore. Cotter & Company's expansion into a national distributor by 1970 made possible a national advertising campaign unprecedented in hardware. Pat Summerall, True Value's electronic spokesman, has given the hardware store a consistent, credible voice on radio and TV. Throughout the 1970s and 80s he engaged in a highly visible media war against a series of blonde bombshells and assorted pitchmen from the competition. As a result, True Value became a household name.

Manufacturers of brand name goods have always faced a major problem when they advertised their wares nationwide. They could attract the consumer's attention, arouse his interest, and imprint a brand name in his memory, but they couldn't tell him where, in his own home town or local neighborhood, he could find the goods. Local, independent retailers, for their part, had few effective ways of "tying in" with national ads. Cotter & Company has brought the two together — national advertising and local retailers. True Value provides a recognizable name of a local outlet where the consumer can find the manufacturer's goods.

The oldest adage in advertising holds that, "Half of the money I spend on advertising is wasted, and the trouble is I don't know which half." True Value eliminates this uncertainty by helping the hardware manufacturer "localize" his national ads. With almost 7000 True Value hardware stores located in all fifty states, a manufacturer of tools or housewares can be certain the customer will easily find the merchandise he advertises in partnership with Cotter & Company. By a creative use of cooperative advertising agreements, John Cotter has transformed hardware advertising as he has so many other features of the trade.

Cotter did not wait until True Value had spread nationwide to begin advertising; he emphasized it right from the beginning. And in Ed Lanctot, he found the perfect impresario to orchestrate the earliest effective advertising in the hardware industry. It all began with direct mail catalogues, which still form the backbone of True Value advertising.

DIRECT MAIL

Like so much else in the dealer-owned system of management, Hall Hardware of Minnesota pioneered direct mail advertising, in order to counteract the Sears catalogue in the rural trade. The 32-page Our Own catalogues, begun in 1933, were colorful and effective. They did not furnish a mail order coupon, as Sears did; but at least they alerted the farm family to the wide range of merchandise available from their hardware store on their next trip to town. Our Own's mailers did a particularly good job of selling paint, establishing the private brand Supermix Paint as a dominant seller in the Upper Midwest before World War II. Other dealer-owned wholesalers, such as American in Pittsburgh, imitated the Our Own catalogues, as did Marshall-Wells and Hibbard's, traditional wholesalers with stores programs.

John Cotter promised the hardware retailers gathered at Sycamore and at his other organizational meetings in 1947 that he would establish a direct mail program as soon as possible. He fulfilled his promise with a 32-page rotogravure catalogue in fall, 1948. The cover displayed a brown and orange autumn scene, flanked by a listing of 31 major manufacturers; and it was personalized with the individual hardware dealer's store name. Succeeding editions retained the seasonal motif on the cover, but merchandise was superimposed over it.

John Cotter gives Ed Lanctot 100% of the credit for getting the first direct mail out the door, though he adds, with a twinkle in his eye, "It was late as always." The general public identifies True Value Hardware with Pat Summerall, but industry insiders know that next to John Cotter, no one is more responsible for True Value's success than Ed Lanctot. Lanctot and Cotter did much of the layout and preparation of the first catalogue themselves and then used their contacts from Oakes & Co. to get the final artwork done economically. A committee of dealer-members spent an entire day with Lanctot selecting merchandise for the catalogue. Preparing direct mail was, and is, tedious, time-consuming labor, but Lanctot has shown the stamina to stick with it over the years. He recalls that he missed the birth of his first son since he had to chair a dealers' advertising meeting that day. Though he absorbs the hard work, Lanctot also thrives on the deal-making involved with selecting merchandise bargains. He virtually lives on the telephone. In fact, Pat Summerall has dubbed the invention of the mobile telephone "the best thing that ever happened to Lanctot." Now he can even make phone calls from airplanes.

Cotter members circulated 68,000 copies of the first catalogue, either mailing them to local lists of customers or else hiring neighborhood children to take them door to door. The delivered cost of each catalogue worked out to about 6¢ a copy for the dealer. Cotter & Company followed up this first advertising endeavor with regular spring and fall catalogues every year thereafter, gradually adding others throughout the year as well. In order to make a maximum impression on both dealers and consumers, Cotter promoted the second catalogue, in April, 1949, with a full-page ad in the *Chicago Tribune*. The newspaper ad pictured the spring catalogue and listed names and addresses of all participating dealers. This unprecedented ad was only a one-shot deal, for Cotter did not move consistently into newspaper advertising for another ten years; but it did help to establish the direct mail program on a firm footing. Circulation of the mailers increased rapidly; by 1954, a Mid-Summer circular appeared in 700,000 copies.

Cotter and Lanctot's success with direct mail caught the attention of other dealer-owned managers. Bill Stout, in particular, raised the roof at American Hardware when he discovered that Cotter was producing catalogues at nearly half the cost of his own. Cotter proposed to Stout, and his treasurer Zeb Hastings, that they pool their efforts and attain even greater economies by putting out a joint catalogue. For a number of years in the mid-50s, the two companies did circulate a common advertising catalogue, but the complicated logistics of producing it eventually outweighed the cost saving. The joint venture was terminated by mutual agreement in 1957.

In the early years, Cotter and Lanctot devised many other inexpensive forms of advertising and promotion to raise the visibility of hardware stores and increase sales. Cotter constantly harped on the need for members to identify their stores with V & S (Value & Service) signs (he did not acquire the True Value name until 1963), and Lanctot provided a flood of V & S decals, in-store banners, even V & S wrapping paper. Around 1958, they adopted another Our Own Hardware innovation, the "Bargain of the Month" promotion. Lanctot would secure some hardware or housewares item at nearly manufacturer's cost, then pass it on to the dealer with no wholesale markup in order to provide a low cost traffic builder. Local dealers were urged to order large quantities of the bargain item and promote it heavily with window banners, local newspaper ads, and later, of course, with radio and TV. These promotions have been expanded in recent years with the addition of the Hardware Value of the Month and the True Value of the Month.

Yet, direct mail has always been the workhorse of the Cotter advertising program. Ed Lanctot believes that a newspaper-style circular, or a bargain of the month promotion, may have more "pulling power" in the short run, but a consumer catalogue has more "staying power." A catalogue proves particularly useful in widening the range of merchandise which a regular customer purchases. The average customer, a do-it-yourself homeowner, goes to a hardware store for a specific tool or accessory he needs and gives no thought to the wide variety of other goods available there. But if a direct mail catalogue has been sitting in his living room, his wife may notice the housewares and his children the toys and they may all accompany him on his next visit to the hardware store. Pyrex, Sunbeam, Rubbermaid and many other brands are well known from national ads and customer satisfaction. A Cotter & Company direct mailer reminds the customer that he or she can find them at the hardware store. It localizes and focuses the brand name advertising.

A trade publication on direct mail methods, published about the time John Cotter started his company, pointed out succinctly the unique value of direct mail: "The difference between direct mail advertising and other forms of advertising is the difference between the telephone and the radio. The telephone is selective — the radio broadcasts." Another advertising authority notes that well-targeted direct mail turns up "prospects not suspects."

Today, True Value distributes a different consumer catalogue each month of the year, beginning with True Value Days in January, continuing with the largest promotions — Hardware Week in March, Spring and Summer Values in April, and the Fall Shopper in September — then ending with Christmas gift ideas in November and December. All told, 200 million copies reach an estimated 592 million readers in a year. Cotter, Lanctot, and the member advertising councils have fine-tuned the catalogues and circulars so that each appears in several editions, one with only basic hardware in it, another for stores that emphasize housewares, and so on. Some editions are tailored to a specific region; for example, the Southern edition of True Value Days in January includes a lawn and garden insert which is obviously unnecessary up North at that time of year.

Other forms of advertising, particularly radio and TV, may be more glamorous, but direct mail remains the foundation for True Value's entire ad program. All other media support and promote the goods listed in the direct mail.

COOP ADVERTISING IN NEWSPAPERS AND MAGAZINES

Cotter & Company did not invent direct mail advertising, they simply refined and expanded upon ideas developed by others. In newspaper and magazine advertising, however, they were truly innovative, tapping a pool of manufacturers' coop advertising funds for an unprecedented array of print ads. The idea of ''coop advertising'' is central to this development, and so merits some explanation before continuing the narrative.

Cooperative advertising is widespread and commonplace in the marketplace; current estimates of its magnitude range from 4 to 10 billion dollars annually. Basically, coop advertising entails an agreement between manufacturer and retailer to share the cost of advertising on some fixed percentage basis, often 50/50, up to a specified maximum, usually 3 or 4 per cent of purchases. Examples of coop arrangements abound: a product display card in a store window — the manufacturer supplies the card, the retailer the space; product listings in the Yellow Pages — the manufacturer pays the phone company to list his trademark, each retailer pays for his own store listing under the trademark. Yet the most common form of coop advertising has always been the local newspaper ad. When a manufacturer wishes to promote a specific group of products, he prepares a sample ad and supplies it to the retailer who adds his store name and buys space in the local paper. The storeowner sends a receipt and a sample tearsheet of the ad to the manufacturer who then reimburses him for half the cost. Coop advertising was an early attempt to localize national ads. It spread the manufacturer's money farther and, presumably, put it to work where it could do the most good.

Coop advertising, however, has always been subject to abuse. Large retailers, particularly department stores, rely heavily on it and have frequently tried to use their large volume to monopolize the lion's share of it. Some dealers, too, consider the ad allowances as disguised discounts and simply pocket the money without buying any advertising. If the dealer represents a large account, manufacturers may tolerate this. The Robinson-Patman Act of 1936, which attempted to ban all discriminatory pricing practices, devised elaborate rules to regulate coop advertising. Specifically, the law required that advertising allowances be made available to all competing retailers on proportionately equal terms. That is, if a housewares manufacturer gives a department store a 4% ad allowance, he must offer the same terms to hardware stores, discounters, and any other competing merchants who carry his line. Despite the Robinson-Patman Act, however, abuses continued and large retailers often retained an advantage. As a result, many smaller retailers rarely bothered with coop ads; and as much as ⅓ of the manufacturers' funds available in any one year went unused.

John Cotter and Ed Lanctot tapped into these coop ad funds in new and creative ways, allowing smaller retailers to compete with department stores and mass merchandisers. A group of member-retailers together under the V & S or True Value umbrella could qualify for a much larger ad allowance than any one storeowner, and an ad listing scores of participating dealers maximized the manufacturer's investment. Cotter's first *Chicago Tribune* ad, in April 1949, was financed in this way, perhaps the first time a voluntary hardware chain had used coop money for this purpose. Then, in April, 1958, Cotter initiated a continuing newspaper ad campaign in Chicago and other midwestern city dailies. Beginning with a monthly quarter-page in the *Chicago Daily News* and *Chicago Tribune,* the ads expanded to full-page by the end of 1958, and spread to Appleton, Green Bay, and Milwaukee, Wisconsin, and Grand Rapids, Michigan in 1959. Such regional newspaper ads, with costs shared by manufacturers and retailers, have become regular features of the hardware industry. Cotter & Company currently sponsors such advertisements, often featuring Bargain of the Month or other promotional goods, in newspapers nationwide.

Coop ads in newspapers, at least on a piecemeal basis, had been common long before Cotter & Company started; but hardware advertising in magazines was largely unknown. The national scope of most consumer magazines made it impossible to arrange coop deals with local retailers or regional wholesalers; and few hardware manufacturers produced any brand name advertising on their own. What little advertising they did was confined to the trade press and aimed at retailers, not ultimate consumers.

The National Retail Hardware Association began the first consumer-oriented hardware ads in 1953. Each year thereafter, NRHA purchased two-page, fold-out, "gatefold" ads in *Life, Look,* and *Saturday Evening Post* as part of their "Hardware Week" in April, and again in October. Manufacturers of the goods featured in these ads paid the full cost; and NRHA urged all independent hardware stores to tie-in with the promotions by posting the ads in their windows. The NRHA ads, however, posed the same problem that all national advertising does; it didn't specify where the consumer could find the goods. The manufacturers found this unsatisfactory and decided in 1963 to drop their support; the NRHA, a trade association which purchased no goods itself, had no influence or clout to change their minds.

John Cotter had criticized some aspects of NRHA's national promotions. In 1954, for instance, he thought it completely inappropriate to begin Hardware Week on Easter Sunday: "It just seems to us when all the 'mamas' and 'gals' are thinking about Easter bonnets and shoes for the kids it would be a good time to 'lay off' promoting hardware." Nonetheless, he loyally backed all the campaigns, requesting his members to tie-in; and his company regularly made the NRHA's list of the top ten cooperating wholesalers. So when he heard that the manufacturers were planning to cancel NRHA's magazine ads, he decided to use his buying power and apply some pressure. He convinced the major hardware manufacturers, who by this time had ceased to boycott him and valued his business highly, to reverse their decision.

This good deed was not totally altruistic. As Cotter himself phrases it, "Everything has its price." He asked Russ Mueller, managing director of NRHA, whether he'd mind if Cotter & Company placed its own ads in the same edition of *Look* to tie-in with Hardware Week. Mueller, of course, could hardly object; so Cotter & Company ran a two-page color ad, featuring 23 products, in the May 5, 1964 issue of *Look*. They had chosen *Look* for this new venture since that magazine offered a regionalized advertising service. Not yet a national distributor in 1964, V & S and True Value (both names were used in the ad) ran its ad in 13 states. The manufacturers paid for both the NRHA and the V & S—True Value ads and found the combination produced more sales than the former Hardware Week promotion had. Cotter continued to run the *Look* ads every spring and fall, and he quickly expanded to other consumer magazines as well. "So in doing something good for the association," he concluded, "we got something started that was very good for True Value hardware stores." (Incidentally, the extremely awkward look of two store logos — V & S and True Value — in national ads hastened the changeover solely to True Value.)

Cotter & Company was the first hardware wholesaler to advertise in national consumer magazines. A Kansas City ad agency, Christenson, Barclay, and Shaw, had contacted Cotter and Lanctot in the fall of 1963, at the very time they were mulling over NRHA's predicament, and proposed that they consider magazine ads. Bob Shaw and Jerry Christenson convinced them that manufacturers' money would be available if they went after it aggressively. Christenson's agency has managed Cotter's magazine advertising program ever since, though most other True Value advertising is produced in-house.

In 1971, NRHA decided to drop out of *Look* and switch their annual ads to *Reader's Digest*. Ironically, True Value planned to take over the gatefold position that year and expand to fully national coverage in the magazine, when *Look* announced it was going out of business. Christenson quickly booked space in other national magazines to replace it. Currently, 70 True Value ads appear in 14 different magazines, ranging from *Better Homes & Gardens* to *Sports Illustrated*. These ads reach an estimated readership of 1,192,000,000.

"HI, THIS IS PAT SUMMERALL"

In the early 1970s, Cotter & Company had become a national distributor, it had phased out its earlier V & S store identification in favor of True Value, and extensive magazine and newspaper advertising had spread this name across the country. Yet something was still missing. John Cotter recalls, "I got talking to Lanctot. We need something more. We need a voice." They had already experimented a bit with the electronic media. Herb Lendved, the Wisconsin field representative, had arranged the first local TV spots in November, 1969 in Green Bay, and True Value spots had run periodically on local radio, particularly on WGN in Chicago. But Lanctot had his hands full with direct mail and print ads and was reluctant to expand farther into a new area.

Then, sometime in 1972, CBS' Chicago sales representative, Dick Game, walked into Lanctot's office with an attractive offer on network radio spots. Cotter and Lanctot decided to grab the offer, but they were still groping for a suitable format and spokesman. While in New York for the hardware show, in the fall of '72, they scheduled a meeting with CBS executives to work out details. George Arkedis, the general manager of CBS, stopped in briefly to get acquainted and fell to reminiscing with Lanctot. Arkedis had formerly worked in Chicago and, he discovered, had lived near Lanctot in Park Ridge and had attended the same church. Arkedis stayed longer than he planned and eventually suggested to Lanctot and Cotter that they might want to use Pat Summerall, a sports reporter on New York radio and TV.

Lanctot had heard Summerall's voice on radio during previous trips to New York, and he had been especially impressed by his eulogy of Paul Christman, a Chicago Cardinal quarterback, also a Park Ridge neighbor. Cotter and Lanctot sealed the deal with CBS, and Pat Summerall delivered his first True Value commercial on CBS network radio October 2, 1972. Cotter & Company booked an initial series of 20 commercials per week, airing on 240 CBS stations. These early spots, concentrated in morning and evening "drive time" for maximum exposure, presented mainly "institutional advertising" to familiarize listeners with the True Value name; but before Christmas, the schedule was stepped up to 42 spots per week and featured promotional merchandise. CBS produced this first series of radio ads in New York; and Cotter and Lanctot did not even meet Pat Summerall until several months later, when he stopped by in Chicago to say hello.

Summerall first appeared on TV for True Value in October, 1974, on a regional spot in Milwaukee. Lanctot never lets Pat forget that he cut his finger on a carpenter's plane during the filming. As Summerall's TV commercials grew more numerous, CBS Sports executives began to object to his appearances on stations outside the CBS network; but after a change in management at the sports department, CBS permitted Summerall to work directly for True Value and appear on other networks. Ed Lanctot and Summerall sealed the new agreement with a handshake.

True Value Hardware expanded its media exposure rapidly in the 1970s and 80s and hired other spokesmen — Frank Blair on the NBC Today show, and Paul Harvey, the conservative commentator, on ABC Mutual Radio. Currently, True Value runs 614 network television commercials annually as well as 1110 syndicated participations on daytime talk and game shows. In addition, an estimated 8 billion adults 18 years and over are reached by True Value radio spots each year. Pat Summerall couldn't possibly handle all this electronic coverage, but he remains the preeminent, and most readily identifiable, spokesman, appearing on all the major networks, both radio and TV.

Pat Summerall was born in Lake City, Florida, and worked in his uncle's hardware store as a boy. He attended the University of Arkansas, earning letters in three sports, and was drafted by the baseball Cardinals to play first base. After one year in the minor leagues, however, Summerall and his manager both discovered that he could hit the fast ball, but he couldn't hit the curve. Football, where he could kick field goals and play in the line, seemed more promising. He played five years, 1952 to 1957, with the football Cardinals, who were then in Chicago. One year the Cardinals endured a miserable 1-11 season, but their only victory came against their crosstown rivals, the hated Chicago Bears. In 1958, the Cardinals traded Summerall to the New York Giants, where he finished his sports career, retiring in 1962. Two years before he hung up his cleats, in 1960, he and three Giant teammates auditioned for a five minute CBS radio sports show. Summerall won the job, and has been with CBS ever since, currently broadcasting football, golf, and tennis for the TV network.

Summerall's association with True Value Hardware has been sometimes gruelling, but mutually rewarding for him and for True Value. He generally comes to Chicago at least two days a month to tape commercials. All the True Value ads are prepared by Lanctot's staff in-house and recorded at various studios around Chicago. Summerall averages about 155 or 160 ads in two days, but he has recorded as many as 180 in this short time period. Network spots require exact timing, so he holds a stopwatch in one hand and reads several lines ahead to get the emphasis and timing just right. Usually he can do the commercials in a "blind read," the first time through, but it is intensive, fatiguing work. Summerall is paid on a piecework basis, but he tapes so many pieces that he earns a handsome income. Summerall also serves as True Value spokesman in many other capacities. He nearly always addresses one of the member meetings at semi-annual dealer markets; and in his words, he appears around the country "as often as Lanctot can get me trapped into something."

The life of a television spokesman has its amusing, and embarrassing, moments. Many True Value hardware stores display a life-size cardboard cutout of Summerall in their window or among the merchandise. Pat reports that his friends often violate these mannequins in unspeakable ways. One New Year's Eve, Tom Brookshier, then Summerall's partner on CBS Football, found a Summerall cutout in his garage at 3:00 AM. Brookshier didn't hesitate, he gunned the motor and ran Pat down. Occasionally, too, local police making their nightly rounds have shot at the cardboard Summerall thinking it an intruder in the store.

On at least one occasion, however, the cardboard mannequin rescued Summerall when he needed help. Pat narrates:

"Back when I first started doing Cotter TV ads . . . I was rushing to the Jacksonville airport to catch a plane to Dallas for a playoff game. I was late and I was going too fast, so the police stopped me. I still had a New Jersey driver's license, with my real name on it, George A. Summerall, Jr. The officer looked at it and said, 'Summerall, that's an unusual name. Are you related to Pat?'
I said, 'I am Pat.'
The officer wouldn't believe me. He said, 'I know Pat Summerall. He has black hair.'
So I said, 'Well, things change.'
But he wasn't buying any of it. He thought I was some sort of impostor and that maybe I was up to something serious. So he called another officer to drive my car, put me in the back seat of his police car, and was taking me to the courthouse. We happened to pass a True Value hardware store, so I got his attention and asked him to stop to look at my picture in the window. He stopped, looked, and agreed to let me go."

John Cotter believes that Pat Summerall "has a good, pleasant, listenable voice, and he has credibility." Summerall returns the compliment. He says he has made lifelong friends in the hardware business, "the kind of people you want to spend time with and hold up to your kids as models." When he first began in broadcasting, someone warned him, "Look out for the mice, because the mice become rats eventually." But he has encountered no rats at Cotter & Company, and he ascribes that to the example of the man at the top.

Assessing the usefulness of a celebrity spokesman for a commercial product can be a tricky business. Pat Summerall's advantages appear to be his low-key, friendly manner, his calm, reassuring voice, and his consistent identification with True Value products. Some celebrity pitchmen will sell anything, and therefore become overexposed and lose credibility. One ad executive has remarked, "Seeing a commercial by Ed McMahon is almost like looking at a TV test pattern." Pat Summerall has avoided this problem by working exclusively for True Value.

A recent article in the advertising trade press suggests:
"Creating a good campaign that features a celebrity is an inexact science, to say the least. The main guidelines, say the experts, are to use a fresh face, have a logical connection between the person and the product, and a good creative spot."
One could object that there is no obvious connection between Pat Summerall, an ex-football player, and hardware; but the connection is more subliminal than logical — he projects an image of reliability and credibility. AT&T spokesmen explain a similar bond between Cliff Robertson and the phone company: "Robertson has the same kind of image we have as a company — comfortable, warm, honest, someone you would invite into your living room." Ditto for Pat Summerall and True Value Hardware Stores. True Value localizes hardware advertising, and Pat Summerall personalizes it with "Say Pat Summerall sent you."

HARDWARE WARS

Summerall's comfortable, reliable image contrasts strongly with some of the electronic advertising aired by True Value's archrival, Ace Hardware. In 1974, Ace, which Cotter employees characterized as twice as old but half as large, began a concerted campaign to catch up. Dick Hesse, the last surviving founder, consummated a plan he had first announced in 1957 to sell all his company stock to individual Ace dealers and convert to dealer-ownership. Hesse died about a year after this disinvestment, on October 12, 1975.

Once free of Hesse's conservative, authoritarian hand, Ace president Arthur Krausman and his new officers and directors embarked on an ambitious expansion program. They began opening numerous branch distribution centers across the country, they announced a move of the corporate executive offices to posh suburban Oak Brook, Illinois in order to "help attract talented young executives by offering a (better) business environment," and they hired Chicago ad agency D'Arcy-McManus-Masius to launch a media campaign. A year and half after Pat Summerall started True Value radio ads, Ace countered by hiring former baseball catcher Joe Garagiola as their spokesman on NBC network radio. Ace also ran its first national magazine ads in 1974 and mounted its first multi-market newspaper advertising in 1976.

Television, however, witnessed the biggest splash of the new Ace ad campaign — the blonde bombshell and the "helpful hardware man." The D'Arcy agency hired actress Connie Stevens in 1974 to sing and dance and catch the viewer's attention on Ace commercials. While actor Lou Fant stood stolidly, attired in his red Ace uniform, a provocatively-clad Connie bounced around him singing, "Ace is the place with the helpful hardware man." These Ace TV spots represented "institutional advertising" with a vengeance, designed to catch maximum attention and broadcast the Ace name with a catchy slogan and a pretty face. Connie Stevens, who reportedly started with a one year contract in the range of 50 to 75 thousand dollars, was pulling in about $150,000 annually when she was released by Ace in 1978. The ad agency, however, continued the same campaign with a fresh face, Suzanne Somers, star of TV sitcom "Three's Company." Somers' manager negotiated a million dollar contract for Ace's newest blonde bombshell.

Celebrity advertising can sometimes prove risky. As the advertising trade paper, *Marketing & Media Decisions,* points out: "While a well-known personality may help create an immediate identity or persona for a product, the benefits may turn into a minus if the spokesperson suddenly plummets in popularity, gets into an embarrassing scrape, or loses credibility . . ." Suzanne Somers got into an embarrassing scrape immediately after Ace hired her in 1979. The February, 1980 issue of *Playboy* ran a ten page feature on Somers, using, without her permission, nude photos taken years previously when she was an unknown. Ace immediately dropped all of Somers' commercials, while stating they would honor the financial obligations of her two-year contract; but they later reinstated her and renewed her contract through 1982. At the end of 1982, Ace finally ended their relationship with Somers, dismissed the D'Arcy—McManus ad agency, and retrenched to more sober, traditional advertising featuring product and price.

In romancing the consumer Ace did the cancan, while True Value danced the waltz. John Cotter preferred the slower, steadier tempo and took undisguised pleasure in the "perils of Pauline" which eight years of blondes caused Ace. Still, the Ace ads did capture attention, which was their primary purpose. Ace spokesmen claimed, in the advertising trade press, that they had raised their company's name recognition to a level comparable with True Value. Name recognition, however, doesn't automatically translate into sales. As one ad executive has pungently phrased it, "You can get high recall by passing wind noisily at an elegant dinner party. But you may not improve your social standing." Ace remains almost literally half as large as True Value in annual sales.

One feature of the Ace ads often overlooked was the phrase "helpful hardware man." First used by the National Retail Hardware Association in 1954, the phrase does emphasize the right image for an independent hardware dealer; and Connie Stevens always underlined it by crooning, "I don't know anything about hardware, but I know someone who does." Ace could also capitalize on the rhyme-ability of their three letter name. Dick Hesse had often used the slogan, "Ace Sets the Pace;" the new jingle, "Ace is the Place," proved equally memorable.

Be that as it may, someone once said that imitation is the sincerest form of flattery; and in national advertising True Value "sets the pace" and Ace scrambles to catch up. Like Hertz and Avis, McDonald's and Burger King, True Value and Ace compete head to head in the marketplace and in the media; but True Value definitely remains the McDonald's or the Hertz of the industry. The listing of the "Top 200 Brands" for 1984, in *Marketing & Media Decisions,* ranked True Value 85th among national advertisers, just ahead of Winston cigarettes and the U.S. Army. On network radio, where Pat Summerall seems to be everywhere, True Value ranks consistently in the top five. Ace did not make the list at all; in fact, the only other hardware firm listed was Black & Decker, ranked 174th. The magazine sets True Value's media billings for 1984 at $41 million, but this figure does not include expenditures for newspapers or direct mail. The true total may be 2 or 3 times the $41 million figure. Even that sum, of course, remains far below the $633 million expended by Sears, the nation's No. 1 advertiser; and Sears sells a lot of hardware, along with its other merchandise. Yet, among groups of independent hardware stores, True Value has been the advertising pioneer.

In looking back at nearly forty years of Cotter & Company advertising, the outstanding characteristic is consistency. Direct mail has always been the foundation for True Value hardware stores; the other media built upon it. Once Cotter & Company began using other media — newspapers, magazines, radio, and TV — they have stayed with them and continually expanded their coverage. Pat Summerall has anchored a steady, dependable presence on the TV screen for almost fifteen years. By contrast, Sears launched a ''blockbuster'' magazine campaign in 1977, only to scale it back to half the size two years later. Ace has moved in and out of radio from time to time, and has changed TV spokespersons frequently.

The main effect of True Value's consistent advertising, and its competition's attempts to imitate it, has been to raise the image and the visibility of all hardware stores. Forty years ago, hardware stores did little advertising, except for a few direct mail broadsides and some local coop newspaper ads; and hardware manufacturers only placed their ads in the trade press. Today, True Value, Ace, and many of the merchandising groups, such as Sentry, Trustworthy, etc., trumpet their own names and many hardware brand names nationwide. This has produced an unintended side effect. With more and more hardware advertising aimed at the consumer, less money is available for ads in the trade press, and both *Hardware Age* and *DIY Retailing* have felt the pinch of reduced ad volume. Yet as Rick Lambert, *DIY Retailing's* publisher, has admitted, the trend toward consumer advertising has been a mixed blessing for his magazine, but it has been very good for the industry as a whole.

The independent hardware store owner — whom Ace calls the

"helpful hardware man" and John Cotter terms a "P.H.D.," professional hardware dealer — enjoys a new status and a more secure future. Thanks to national advertising, the general public now views the hardware store as a dependable, affordable, convenient source of a vast selection of goods. True Value's pathbreaking advertising has not only benefitted their own stores, but hardware stores generally. The consumer often fails to distinguish among competing stores; a customer will walk into an Ace store, on occasion, and ask for the "Pat Summerall paint" he saw on TV. By "localizing national advertising" John Cotter, Ed Lanctot, and Pat Summerall have built a more secure niche for all independent hardware stores. The editors of *Hardware Retailing* (called *DIY Retailing* today) summed it up a few years ago: "National advertising promotes the entire hardware/home center form of retailing. It gives the industry a stature in the marketplace on a par with national retail chains."

CHAPTER TWELVE
COMPETITIVE
EDGES FOR
HARDWARE RETAILERS

"Our principal finding is clear and simple. Organizations that do branch out (whether by acquisition or internal diversification) but stick very close to their knitting outperform the others . . . Thus it would appear that some diversification is a basis for stability through adaptation, but that willy-nilly diversification doesn't pay — by any measure."
—Thomas J. Peters, Robert H. Waterman, Jr.,
  In Search of Excellence

"Stick to the Knitting" is one of the basic principles of excellent companies, according to the best-selling management study, *In Search of Excellence,* by Thomas Peters and Robert Waterman. John Cotter has always preached and exemplified this same philosophy; diversification is not one of his favorite words. Yet a company that never diversifies, never changes or adapts, will likely cease to grow and thus will die. There is a fundamental tension between two commonsense business maxims, "grow or die" and "stick to the knitting;" and it requires delicate management to strike a proper balance. Peters and Waterman acknowledge this in the quotation at the head of this chapter; a successful company needs to branch out while still staying in touch with its primary business.

In the late 1960s and early 70s, as Cotter & Company rapidly expanded its geographic reach, it also increased its internal complexity and branched out into new ventures that no one could have foreseen just a few years earlier. Cotter & Company acquired its own fleet of trucks to deliver merchandise, it developed a member insurance program, travel and real estate agencies, and a complete slate of retail-member services, from selling store fixtures to computerized accounting services. Then in an unprecedented series of moves, Cotter established two member-owned manufacturing facilities — a paint factory and a lawn mower factory — and also eased into general merchandising by forming a separate variety stores division.

In thus branching out, John Cotter rejected his own previous advice to the contrary. As late as 1968, he wrote his members with his usual vehemence:

"Apparently because of the enormous enthusiasm of True Value dealers, management receives an endless series of suggestions . . . to make available such services as credit cards, dealer financing, pension plans, fixture manufacturing, fire insurance, liability insurance, etc. . . . Your own wholesaler is exactly what the name implies and must be extremely careful, for the benefit of all dealers, to continue as just that, rather than attempt to become a service bureau or get into fields in which management has no experience."

Yet in less than ten years, Cotter had initiated just about all the services listed above and many more as well. Each of the new services, however, grew out of Cotter's passion for lowering costs and related directly to his company's prime mission, saving money for the hardware retailer. Ever the entrepreneur, he was quite willing, whenever circumstances dictated, to start a new venture and help his retailer-members earn more profit. Rather than apologize for his seeming lack of consistency, Cotter heralded his new departures as "competitive edges" for the hardware retailer.

MEMBER SERVICES

Company trucking is, perhaps, the best place to start, for it shows clearly how circumstances prompted Cotter in a new direction; and it also illustrates his incremental, step-by-step approach to diversification.

Shortly after he had moved the company to its permanent headquarters on Clybourn Avenue, John Cotter began looking for ways to improve efficiency and lower costs. One Monday in August, 1961, his warehouse superintendent reported that over 100 different truck lines had called at the warehouse that day to pick up orders and deliver them to the stores. Phoning and scheduling so many independent truck companies proved costly and complicated, so Cotter ordered his personnel manager, Bob Hansen, to conduct a study and see if the number of truck lines could be consolidated and cut in half. The study dragged on for years, and repeated attempts to reduce the number of common carriers never cut it much below 80. So, in November, 1966, Cotter & Company bought several tractor trailers and began hauling its own goods on a limited, experimental basis from the Chicago warehouse to the Indianapolis area. The trucking program expanded gradually through the Midwest to areas with heavy concentrations of members, then eventually to the Cleveland, Dallas, Philadelphia, and all subsequent distribution centers. By 1970 the newly-established traffic department was running 66 tractors and 114 trailers from coast to coast; currently, the fleet numbers over 300 tractors and 700 trailers.

John Cotter kept a sharp eye on the costs of this truck fleet at all times. Whenever possible, delivery routes were scheduled so that the trucks could backhaul new goods from the manufacturers rather than returning to the distribution centers empty. Retailers were charged a deposit on merchandise tote boxes so that they would return them regularly rather than stack them in a corner or toss them out. As the truck fleet aged, the maintenance force completely dismantled and rebuilt tractors after about 450,000 miles. Rebuilt tractors cost about half the price of new ones.

The truck fleet also did double duty as a medium of institutional advertising. Beginning in 1970, all company trailers displayed $4' x 6'$ advertising panels on front, rear, and sides, showing the True Value logo and selected exclusive brand merchandise, such as Tru-Test Paints and Lawn Chief Mowers. Scale models of the True Value tractor-trailers were purchased from a toy manufacturer and offered as promotional items at Christmastime.

The member insurance program similarly grew in a gradual, step-by-step manner. Most hardware stores had covered their insurance needs through one of the hardware mutual companies founded in the Midwest around the turn of the century. As we have seen previously, the hardware mutuals also furnished a crucial model for the organization of the earliest dealer-owned hardware wholesalers. Over the years, however, the mutual insurance companies had grown enormously and begun writing an extensive amount of general insurance, outside the hardware field. As they wandered farther from their prime mission, their overhead and expenses grew. John Cotter remembers being overwhelmed by the lavish appointments of one hardware mutual firm he visited. So beginning in 1972, he organized a member insurance program to reduce the costs charged to retailers. Bill Voss, the True Value Insurance Center manager, and his staff acted as insurance brokers for the Cotter members, obtaining the best possible rates from the established companies through volume discounts. All underwriting profits they earned were returned to the members at year-end as patronage rebates. In the first year of operation, 1972, the program issued over 2000 policies and took in over $3 million in premiums. By 1976 over half the True Value members participated in the insurance program.

Then on January 1, 1981, Cotter & Company incorporated its own mutual insurance company, Cotter Member Insurance, Ltd., based offshore in Bermuda. By owning their own insurance company, participating True Value members share not only in the underwriting profits but also in the investment profits. Cotter Insurance consultants work exclusively for Cotter members, and they are paid on a salary rather than a commission basis to eliminate any incentives for the selling of unnecessary coverage. Formation of a separate mutual insurance company proved timely for Cotter members in protecting them against the recent escalation in general insurance rates.

Trucking and insurance are run by separate departments of Cotter & Company, indeed Cotter Insurance is a distinct corporation; but the Member Services Department also offers, by my count, 33 services for members. Begun in the late 1960s by Don Glaholt, who came over from Coast-to-Coast, and now under Don Neely, also from Coast, Member Services provides information, counselling, and troubleshooting assistance to keep retailers competitive. This is the same sort of advice and counsel that old-line wholesale salesmen used to take pride in offering, but at a fraction of the cost. Many True Value members check out the new store fixtures or services available at each market, and in between markets they can contact field men for in-store consultation. Member Services charges a $100 per day consultation fee, the same charge as ten years ago; this fee doesn't defray all costs but it serves to capture the retailer's full attention and make the consultation more businesslike and productive. Currently, Member Services is offering a full-scale store modernization program to help the True Value hardware store become, and remain, "The Store of First Choice" in its locality.

Cotter member services are more extensive than most, but not all that different from those traditionally offered by the national or state retail hardware associations or by other progressive wholesalers. Common, too, is Cotter's promotion of private (which he terms "exclusive") brands in members' stores. Exclusive brand goods are produced on contract by a manufacturer especially for a distributor and his group of customers. Though similar in type and quality to national brand goods, exclusive brands are sold only in one group of stores, such as True Value Hardware Stores. By contracting for exclusive brands, True Value, or any other distributor, can help maintain the retail margin and protect against ruthless price-cutting by discounters. Often, exclusive brands offer the best of both worlds, a lower price to the consumer and a profitable margin for the retailer.

Private brands have been used most extensively by grocery chains; in the hardware field, Sears pioneered with its own Craftsman line of tools. Cotter & Company distributed a number of exclusive brand products in the 1960s under the Tru-Test and Servess labels. More recently, as its buying power with manufacturers increased, it has established extensive lines of merchandise under such exclusive names as Master Mechanic, Master Plumber, and Master Electrician.

Cotter has largely followed industry-wide trends in the expansion of member services and the use of exclusive brands. His decision, however, to integrate backward into manufacturing was unprecedented. In establishing a member-owned paint factory and lawn mower factory, John Cotter showed anew his entrepreneurial flair and carried the dealer-owned concept farther than anyone else.

GENERAL PAINT AND CHEMICAL CO.

Paint and painting supplies have always been staples on hardware store shelves, though many old-fashioned hardware stores did not promote their sale as vigorously as they might have. John Cotter recalls that paint sales were very important at Dayton's Bluff Hardware, where he worked as a boy; he personally moved the paint department from the back of the store to the front, so paints would sell better, and he washed the labels to make them look new. Ever since then, Cotter has labored to make paint a front-of-the-store, high volume, high profit seller in hardware stores.

In the early years of his company, Cotter did not insist that members carry an exclusive paint line; but he believed he "had to have a bucket of paint in the direct mail catalogue," so he contracted with a small manufacturer on Chicago's south side to sell him a plain white paint with a V & S label on it. This early private brand paint, however, yielded a slender volume of sales; in 1952, Cotter's best members only purchased a couple thousand dollars worth each. In searching for a better source of supply, Cotter discovered General Paint & Chemical Co. in the early 1950s.

General Paint was founded in 1922 by F. R. Bigelow and two partners, who bought an old paint factory on Mendell St., along the north branch of the Chicago River, near Armitage Ave. In 1931 they acquired the Wheeler Varnish Works and brought Don Allen aboard as sales manager; in the meantime, too, Bigelow's son, Jack, had joined the company. By the time John Cotter discovered General Paint, all the original founders had died, Jack Bigelow was chairman of the board,

Don Allen president, and C. V. "Chris" Christensen sales manager. When Cotter inquired, they expressed a strong interest in private paint business and began producing a line of V & S paint. A high quality outdoor white paint, called LZT (lead, zinc, titanium), proved particularly satisfactory.

The relationship between General Paint and Cotter & Company nearly ended in 1961. Two persuasive vice presidents from Sherwin-Williams offered to sell Cotter their complete line of nationally known paint at an attractive price if he would drop his other lines and promote Sherwin-Williams exclusively. Cotter agreed to the deal, but Sherwin-Williams' president vetoed it, offering only a few secondary lines. In retrospect, Cotter is grateful the Sherwin-Williams contract fell through. Price deals change as executives move in and out; the arrangement he finally made, buying his own paint factory, has provided a more stable solution.

Cotter was pleased with the quality, price, and service General Paint offered him. When he took over Hibbard, Spencer, Bartlett in 1963, he consolidated their True Value paint with his own V & S line under a new label, Tru-Test, which he had recently bought from Red Oakes for a few hundred dollars. Within a few years, Tru-Test Paints accounted for 70% of General Paint's production. This made Cotter nervous. General Paint was closely held by Jack Bigelow and his family and a few other stockholders; and Cotter feared that Bigelow might sell out to a conglomerate. Normally, when a large company bought a paint manufacturer, it paid the depreciated book value of the firm's assets plus a certain amount per retail account. True Value's large number of retail outlets would make General Paint an attractive acquisition, and such a sale would provide quite a financial windfall for Bigelow.

One day in 1967, over lunch at the Ivanhoe Restaurant, Cotter was discussing with Bigelow the advisability of owning his own paint factory. Bigelow offered to sell him General. Cotter hesitated, "No, you'll want too much blue sky in the price, and we probably wouldn't be able to afford your management fees either." But Bigelow offered to sell at depreciated book value and promised that he and his staff would stay on at the same salaries they were then earning. So Cotter & Company purchased General Paint on November 1, 1967 for $1,977,185. The purchase price fell due in four equal annual installments, but the paint factory paid for itself in only 18 months. Jack Bigelow, Don Allen, and the other principals remained with the company until retirement, and all factory employees retained their full seniority.

Cotter's purchase of General Paint surprised the industry nearly as much as his takeover of Hibbard's had. The president of a local paint company ate lunch with Cotter shortly before he sealed the deal and tried to convince him he was making a terrible mistake. He also urged other paint manufacturers to call and dissuade Cotter. "Being stupid enough to ignore all their advice," Cotter says, he went ahead anyway. Shortly thereafter, the paint man called again and offered to buy the factory for twice what Cotter paid for it, in order to save him from his horrible folly of diversification. Cotter just laughed.

General Paint has proven very profitable under Cotter & Company ownership, paying a double-digit patronage dividend to True Value members every year. Paint sales totalled 1½ million gallons in the first year of ownership, 1968, and exceeded 10 million gallons in 1985. Cotter purchased an old brewery building on Blackhawk St. in 1972 to accommodate General Paint's expanded production, then in 1976 he moved the latex production to a new one-story facility in Cary, Illinois. The original Mendell St. factory was recently closed and demolished, so today General Paint produces its latex paints, which provide about 75% of sales, in Cary, and its oil-based paints on Blackhawk St. in Chicago. The Cary facility, which is highly automated, contains virtually four factories under one roof; besides latex paint, it also produces specialty chemicals and caulking compounds, and runs a line to fill aerosol cans. The Cary factory has a capacity of 50,000 gallons per day, but this could be expanded by running double shifts, if demand should make it necessary.

John Cotter is intensely proud of the paint factories. Shortly after the purchase of General Paint, he ran ads in the trade press proclaiming — "They said: 'To get costs any lower, you'll have to own the paint factory.' So the nation's No. 1 group of independent hardware dealers *bought it.*" He instructed his top executives and his ad agency, "Please make certain that reference is made to the paint factories and pictures used in all advertising and promotions." The year he bought General Paint, Cotter surveyed his members and discovered they were selling 175 different lines of paint. He immediately set out to change this, writing to all members, ''Any member-dealer not concentrating on Tru-Test Paint to the exclusion of all other paint brands is simply throwing money away.'' In the years since, he has continued to hammer on this same theme, trying to convince True Value members to carry Tru-Test Paint exclusively and make it a high visibility commodity in the stores. ''If you needed a hammer at home,'' he wrote in 1977, ''you'd surely take one from your store rather than buying one from a competitor. Yet 21% of True Value members still do not feature Tru-Test Paint. Still others do not sell Tru-Test exclusively.''

To put more push in the paint marketing program, Cotter hired Irv Rose in July, 1978. General Paint's management was highly competent technically, but always lagged a bit in promotional energy. Rose had worked with Coast-to-Coast for 18 years before HFC took it over; and while with Coast, he had secured 92% participation of dealers in the direct mail program. Cotter was looking for similar numbers with Tru-Test Paint. Rose came aboard as director of marketing for paint; and when Cliff Hesness, the last of Jack Bigelow's team of executives, retired, Rose succeeded him as general manager at Cary. He has promoted the Tru-Test line vigorously and now reports that ''foreign brands'' comprise only 6% of the paint sold in True Value stores. Echoing John Cotter, Rose says he would like to be remembered as the man who prompted most True Value dealers to move paint to the front of the store. ''First of all, it is a profitable, high volume item. Moreover, people who purchase paints are also more than likely to buy brushes, rollers, sandpaper, putty . . . We've also found that the paint customer is frequently a repeat customer.''

John Cotter's unorthodox decision to diversify into paint manufacturing has proven an unalloyed success. Ace Hardware paid him the usual compliment by imitating him and opening their own paint factory. His other manufacturing venture, however, has had a more rocky career.

GENERAL POWER AND EQUIPMENT CO.

Cotter bought General Paint in order to protect and perpetuate a generally happy relationship with his supplier, but his decision to build lawn mowers grew out of the lack of any suitable supplier for outdoor power equipment. General Paint was a successful, going concern when Cotter bought it, but he had to develop his mower factory from scratch. The production of paint is a relatively simple process, but manufacturing power mowers is a more complicated operation. Paint can be produced and sold year round, but lawn equipment is highly seasonal. For all these reasons, Cotter's leap into the outdoor power equipment business required greater audacity and entailed greater risk than his earlier move into paint manufacturing.

Outdoor power equipment, a relatively new industry developed after World War II, did not have the same traditional connection with the hardware store that paint did. Many hardware dealers did not want to bother with the complicated service and safety requirements of lawn mowers and so left the business to Sears and to specialized lawn and garden stores. But John Cotter never wanted hardware stores to abdicate any line of merchandise voluntarily; so from the earliest days of his company, he offered power mowers under private brand names. He struck his first supply deal with Foley Manufacturing Co. of Minneapolis; but when they went out of the mower business, the Southland Mower Co. of Selma, Alabama became his principal supplier.

Cotter never felt satisfied with the quality of mowers that Southland produced. One day Harry Debo's hardware store in Peru, Illinois received a pre-season shipment in February; when Debo opened the cartons, he found one mower missing three wheels, another without a handle, and so on. Cotter couldn't find any other manufacturer to offer him better quality or service. He came close with Atlas Tool Co. of St. Louis. Atlas sold him a good line of snow throwers and rototillers, as well as some mowers; but the sales manager refused an exclusive deal for mowers. He wanted to sell Ace, HWI, and other wholesalers as well. Cotter told him to forget it.

Encouraged by his successful experience with paint manufacturing, and aware that he could start by simply assembling components made by others, he decided to give lawn mower production a try. First he made certain that Briggs & Stratton, the principal manufacturer of engines, would sell to him. When he inquired, he discovered that Briggs & Stratton's vice president, Bill Sheely, was an Irish Catholic graduate of Cretin High School in St. Paul. Needless to say, they hit it off well and Sheely agreed to sell him as soon as he set up a factory. So

Cotter ran an ad for a manager in the *Wall Street Journal* and hired Sy Taub, who was running a small power mower factory in Indiana. They found a 60,000 sq.ft. factory in Carpentersville, Illinois and equipped it with used equipment. On September 15, 1971, the General Power and Equipment Co., a wholly-owned subsidiary of Cotter & Company, produced its first rotary lawn mowers, under the Tru-Test brand name. Production was concentrated on popularly-priced, promotional models, and roughly 175,000 were manufactured the first year. A Wheeler Manufacturing Division (the name borrowed from Wheeler Varnish, a part of General Paint) was established to sell mowers to outside accounts, a necessary expedient to attain sufficient volume.

All seemed to go fairly well for awhile, though the mower factory did not earn sufficient profit to pay a patronage dividend in the first years. Then, in 1975, Cotter renamed his lawn mower line Lawn Chief, reserving the Tru-Test label primarily for paint, and announced the move to a new 260,000 sq.ft. factory in Cary, Illinois, side by side with General Paint. The move to larger quarters and expansion into a greater variety of models, however, overextended Lawn Chief in a generally bad sales year for the outdoor power industry. Cotter dismissed Sy Taub and began to look for help.

He asked Dave Rolston, the only man in his organization with an engineering degree and manufacturing experience, to take over at Cary. Rolston, a Philadelphia native who had worked for several hardware manufacturers and wholesalers in the East before joining Cotter & Company in 1969, had recently replaced Herb Haller as national sales manager and was reluctant to give up the post. But Cotter asked him to help out in Cary for 90 days, promising to hire another general manager within that time. He was negotiating for the purchase of Atlas Tool of St. Louis and hoped to acquire their expert personnel shortly, but Atlas' owners were not ready to sell. So Dave Rolston's temporary stint as manager of General Power and Wheeler Manufacturing lasted 9½ years.

Rolston faced a difficult situation when he took over in April, 1976. General Power had lost over $3 million the preceding year, the factory was overstocked with inventory, and outside sales through Wheeler Mfg. exceeded sales to True Value stores by more than 5 to 1. They needed better quality and more products, particularly countercyclical products that could take up the seasonal slack when lawn mower assembly lines lay idle. In order to move into year-round production, Rolston knew he had to go beyond a mere assembly operation, buy some heavy equipment, and become a full-fledged manufacturer. But General Power owned no manufacturing equipment whatsoever. Then, in 1979, a former employee called him up and said he was liquidating a factory on Chicago's south side. Rolston looked over the roomful of machines, but he had no idea how much to offer. The liquidator told him, "I'll sell you the lot for $4400." Rolston didn't even check with Cotter. He bought 44 stamping presses for that price, later selling off 24 of them and recouping nearly the whole purchase price.

After 1979 General Power introduced several new product lines — wheelbarrows, snow shovels, electric heaters — which occupied the stamping machines and assembly lines year-round. Rolston kept the inventory in line, sales and profits increased modestly, and the ratio of outside sales to True Value sales came into better balance. Then on August 1, 1983, Cotter finally acquired Atlas Tool Co., and with it their popular lines of tillers and snow throwers, several gigantic stamping presses, and a number of experienced managers. Glenn Alexander, the president of Atlas, became sales manager of General Power, and then succeeded Rolston as general manager when he retired in 1985.

Cotter & Company's experience with General Power illustrates some of the perils of diversification, especially the difficulty of starting a completely new business from scratch. John Cotter always preferred to expand by acquiring the assets and expertise of others. In this case, he didn't succeed in doing this until 12 years after he began lawn mower manufacturing. Outdoor power equipment proved far more complicated and, in the short run, less profitable, than paint. General Power still operates at far less than its capacity in the new 832,000 sq.ft. factory it occupied in Harvard, Illinois in 1981. John Cotter is convinced, however, that the lawn mower factory, in the long run, provides another competitive edge for True Value hardware stores. He believes the exclusiveness of Lawn Chief Mowers is vital, as it is with Tru-Test Paints. "You got to romance this business," he says, "and give the dealer something of his own, or else he won't put his heart in it." And, of course, the True Value members share the profits at all three levels of operation — manufacturing, wholesaling, retailing. Cotter's goal is to make the Lawn Chief factory run 16 hours a day, 11 months a year. "When we get there, we'll make money like a bandit."

V & S VARIETY STORES

In 1972 John Cotter resurrected his original store program name, V & S, to christen a new division of Cotter & Company. This time V & S carried a double meaning, not only Value & Service, but also Variety and Soft Lines. Many hardware stores, particularly in small towns, had traditionally operated combination stores, retailing drugs, liquor, or general merchandise in addition to hardware. After Cotter & Company had demonstrated that dealer-ownership cuts costs and saves money for the retailer, these owners of combination stores frequently asked John Cotter to apply the same system to their other lines of merchandise. Cotter initially turned down all such requests to divert him from hardware, and he still rejects any notion of selling drugs or liquor; but eventually he took a second look at variety and soft lines, the traditional "five and dime" merchandise so important on Main Streets everywhere.

Al Rafuse and Harry Goodbar, retired executives from Ben Franklin stores, a nationwide chain of franchised dime stores, had been doing some consulting work for Cotter; and they convinced him that the details of variety distribution could be handled in similar fashion to hardware. So Cotter conducted a survey and found that over 10% of True Value members, some 500 to 700 storeowners, already operated combination hardware and variety stores. Furthermore, about 40% of the items sold in variety outlets were available from Cotter & Company distribution centers. With both a dealer and a merchandise base in place, Cotter would not need to build a variety division completely from scratch. On July 25, 1972, therefore, Cotter met with a delegation of combination store owners and laid plans for the new division. The board of directors approved in October, and Cotter hired his first four variety employees, field men Clyde Reed and Ken Waity, and buyers Chuck Hedblom and Vern Gerdes.

The growth of V & S Variety recapitulated the early development of Cotter & Company, but in a greatly telescoped time frame. V & S signed 1000 members in just five years, whereas Cotter required 15 years to recruit his first thousand hardware members. Variety sales reached $3 million in less than two years, compared to five years for Cotter's early hardware sales. In greatly accelerated fashion, Cotter introduced all the features of the dealer-owned system to variety distribution. For the first two years, merchandise was available only on a direct-ship and relay basis, but in November, 1974 variety inventory was added to stock in the Chicago and Atlanta distribution centers. As variety membership grew, new inventory was introduced in all the other distribution centers as well. Variety dealers visited their first market in May, 1974, and then twice a year thereafter, and distributed their first direct mail circular in August, 1974. In February, 1979, V & S initiated a Variety Value of the Month promotion, similar to the long-standing hardware Bargain of the Month.

John Cotter even tried to expand V & S the same way he had his hardware business, by taking over other wholesalers. In January, 1976 he bought the assets of the Hildebrand Co. of Louisville, Kentucky, dispatching his trusted field troubleshooter, Red Lynes, to wrap up the details of consolidation. Similarly, in September, 1981 he took over the Kling Co., another Louisville variety wholesaler. Both acquisitions brought experienced variety personnel into the Cotter organization and solidified V & S' already strong dealer base in what Cotter calls the "Highway 41 corridor" between Chicago and Florida. Yet neither proved comparable to the Hibbard takeover in the hardware field. Acquisition of the True Value name and True Value chain of dealers was a unique event, probably never to be repeated.

Cotter's timing for the startup of a variety division proved sharp, as usual. The five and dime store business had been declining for some years as costs increased and regional discounters, such as Arkansas-based Wal-Mart, muscled into their traditional small town bastions. W. T. Grant, one of the original "Big Five" dime store chains, went out of business in 1974, and Ben Franklin found it harder and harder to collect their traditional high markup from franchised dealers. John Cotter preached his usual themes to prospective V & S members: "The variety store today is as necessary as ever. It is an important necessity in every community. The owner of a variety store can make a good living — but *there is only one way. He must own his own low-cost wholesaler.*" The experience of Gagnon's V & S in Rockford, Illinois, illustrates how dealer-ownership ultimately sold itself. Gagnon's initially retained its Ben Franklin affiliation since they offered many convenient services and an easy ordering system which was comfortable and familiar to the store employees. But when the owner introduced a profit-sharing plan in his store, the employees began comparing wholesale prices and urged him to purchase more from V & S. Gagnon's became the earliest leader of the V & S Ten High list.

The V & S Variety division encountered more internal organizational difficulties at Cotter & Company than it did external resistance in the marketplace. The earliest variety employees did not thoroughly understand the Cotter system, and the long-time Cotter people did not understand variety. Indeed, old-time hardware men looked down on "lotions and potions" and "buttons and bows." They had a hard time learning to write "wear" rather than "ware."

Building a separate division which mirrored and duplicated the hardware business in many ways required numerous decisions and constant adjustments. John Cotter insisted on a clear, physical separation between V & S Variety Stores and True Value Hardware Stores at the retail level, so as not to blur the image of the hardware store he had spent so much time and labor building up. A hardware retailer could not simply order a few cartons of dime store items and place them on a rack in his store. Likewise, a variety member could not order True Value, Tru-Test, or other exclusive hardware brands. Cotter hired a separate buying staff to purchase variety lines such as greeting cards and stationery, health and beauty aids, and women's and children's apparel; but the True Value buyers handled small appliances, tools, and toys, which were sold in both hardware and variety outlets. Originally, variety dealers came to headquarters for a separate market before the main True Value markets. The variety staff finally felt they had fully arrived at Cotter & Company when, in the late 1970s, the markets were combined and the V & S logo stayed up permanently in the exhibition area right next to True Value. Cotter initially built a separate field staff to sign up and service variety members, but this proved too costly and unwieldy, so in 1985 he consolidated both field staffs into one. The resultant profit improvement for the variety division was dramatic.

The variety division may have grown too quickly for its own good.

Stocking variety merchandise in all distribution centers and carrying a separate field staff overextended the division and drained profits. Dan Cotter admits: "We did with the variety division something that we generally preach against; we tried to anticipate and create the market rather than follow it conservatively." Nevertheless, both John and Dan Cotter now believe that V & S is on a firm footing and both are bullish about its future growth and profits. Dan Cotter thinks that variety has a potential equal to hardware; he predicts it will eventually be a billion dollar business. Variety is not only a profit center in its own right, but a good complement to hardware. Over 80% of variety store customers are women or children, many of whom might never set foot in a hardware store; a combination hardware and variety store builds more traffic for both ends of the business.

Cotter & Company's diversification into paint and lawn mower manufacturing and variety goods merchandising added a completely new dimension to dealer-owned hardware distribution. General Paint and General Power both rank among the top ten manufacturers in their industries, and V & S Variety ranks number 2 behind Ben Franklin Stores. The paint business proved successful immediately, but the lawn mower factory and variety division needed much nursing. Only a manager with an entrepreneurial streak, someone who is restlessly looking for every competitive edge, would have attempted any of these ventures; and only an entrepreneur as patient and persistent as John Cotter would have persevered until all of them paid off. It's time to take a closer, more personal look at John Cotter — entrepreneur and manager.

CHAPTER THIRTEEN
JOHN COTTER,
MAN AND
MANAGER

"An effective leader must be the master of two ends of the spectrum; ideas at the highest level of abstraction and actions at the most mundane level of detail. The value-shaping leader is concerned, on the one hand, with soaring, lofty visions that will generate excitement and enthusiasm for tens or hundreds of thousands of people . . . That's where the pathfinding role is critically important. On the other hand, it seems the only way to instill enthusiasm is through scores of daily events, with the value-shaping manager becoming an implementer par excellence. In this role, the leader is a bug for detail, and directly instills values through deeds rather than words; no opportunity is too small. So it is at once attention to ideas and attention to detail."
—Thomas Peters, Robert Waterman,
In Search of Excellence

In January, 1978, John Cotter assumed the post of Chairman of the Board and his son, Dan, became President of Cotter & Company. Five years later, in 1983, the company founder stepped further into the background, relinquishing the title of Chief Executive Officer to Dan and creating the post of Executive Vice-President and Chief Operating Officer for his son-in-law, Paul Fee. Since then he has never made a major decision without consulting Dan and, usually, Paul too. Many have remarked that he has mellowed considerably, that he shows his Irish temper less often, that he is more patient and more willing to admit a mistake. He has even slowed his pace a bit, spending two months every winter in Florida. But John Cotter did not retire. When not in Florida, he still works six days a week at Clybourn Avenue; and even in the southland, he remains in constant touch with the office via a WATS line. Dan Cotter admits candidly: "No one will kid you; the ultimate authority still rests with the chairman. He's been very good about working with me in most areas, but if he wants something and I say it's not a good idea and he still wants it, he's gonna go ahead and do it." John Cotter still exhibits the same restless energy and the same compulsive work habits he has developed over a lifetime.

A DAY IN THE LIFE

John Cotter and his wife, Alice, are both early risers, awaking before six every morning. While he showers and shaves, she sets out his breakfast — toast and orange juice, cereal with fruit. He leaves their north Evanston home about seven to drive to the office.

The Cotters have lived in north Evanston, an upper-middle class neighborhood of tree-lined streets, ever since they moved to the Chicago area in 1942. Their present home on Thayer Street, their third in the neighborhood, is a large two-story stone house on a triple-sized city lot. Their younger daughter, Patti, calls the purchase of this house "the most impulsive thing" her father ever did. One Thursday evening in 1960, Cotter was reading the *Evanston Review,* a community newspaper highly prized for its classified ads, when he blurted out: "The Ashton house is for sale. I always liked that place; why don't we buy it?" He made an appointment with the realtor the next day, and the whole family inspected the house on Saturday. Cotter paced back and forth for an hour or two, then wrote out a check. He believed that Alice and the kids deserved something better than the square Colonial house they had lived in for twenty years. Their new house, though clearly the most handsome on the block, is hardly palatial. One could easily drive by it without thinking that a movie star or a tycoon lived there.

Leaving this house each morning, John Cotter drives himself to work, though in bad weather he may hitch a ride with Paul Fee. Cotter has always fancied automobiles. He doesn't tinker with auto innards; but he loves the look, the lines, the feel of autos. And he adores racing cars. As a boy he never missed the races at the Minnesota State Fair. When he bought his first car, he showed such respect for the machine that he put it up on blocks throughout the long Minnesota winter; he and Alice hopped a streetcar on their dates. As a father he took his son Dan to Chicago's Soldier Field for stock car events; and in 1948, he gave Dan a trip to the Indianapolis 500 for his eighth grade graduation present. Dan has been hooked ever since, and now owns a team of Indy cars and race drivers as his principal recreation. Dan's racing team won the Indianapolis 500 in 1983. His father, no doubt, takes vicarious pleasure in Dan's hobby; but he has never indulged himself with his own cars. Only in 1985 did the family finally convince him to buy a Cadillac, and then he bought a downsized model at that.

Cotter arrives at his Clybourn Avenue headquarters about 7:30 or 7:45 each day. The area directly east, towards Lincoln Park, has turned into a fashionable, "gentrified" neighborhood for "yuppies;" but the immediate vicinity, along the north branch of the Chicago River, remains an industrial district. Lathrop Homes, a Chicago Housing Authority project, lies due west. Cotter & Company has long supported the work of the Chicago Boys Club in the project and surrounding area. The Insane Unknowns street gang have emblazoned their insignia on nearly every building in the neighborhood; but Cotter & Company's walls are always clean and freshly painted. Cotter's own "graffiti" — True Value, Tru-Test, and V & S logos — decorate the nearby railroad viaducts and parking lot fences.

Though the Chicago distribution center moved all its activities to Harvard, Illinois in 1982, the Cotter office complex on Clybourn still looks like the warehouse it once was. The interior is spartan, functional, and obsessively clean; painted brick walls, even in the chairman's office, plainly recall the building's origins. An animated seasonal display — Christmas elves, Valentine lovers, St. Patrick's Day leprechauns — greets the visitor as he walks in; and the second floor waiting room is lined with trophies and plaques presented by hardware manufacturers. The trophy cases contain what looks to be the largest collection of Steuben glass figurines in the U.S., mostly presented to Cotter by Corning Glass Works.

Cotter & Company offices are open for business from 8:00 AM to 4:30 PM. The chairman, usually garbed in a cardigan sweater, spends most of those hours in meetings or on the phone. A steady stream of employees will want to talk to him and he will usually see them immediately. He's as likely to wander over to their offices as to summon them to his. He used to go out for lunch with department managers and manufacturers' reps at one of the many German restaurants in the Lincoln Park district, or at the Svithiod club, before it closed. Now, however, he rarely eats out; he says it takes too much time and is bad for his diet. He brings a sandwich and an apple from home, as well as something for his sweet tooth, draws the curtains in his office, reads the *Wall Street Journal,* then stretches out his lanky frame for a nap. The daily nap is not a recent concession to age, but a longtime part of his orderly routine. He must possess an internal clock, for he drops off to sleep immediately, wakes without an alarm about 40 or 45 minutes later, then rises refreshed and clearheaded. He spends the afternoon as he did the morning — talking, listening, keeping in touch with every aspect of the business.

About 5:00 PM or a little later, Cotter eases his red Cadillac out of the lot and heads north to Evanston. He may take another brief nap before dinner, then he'll read the mail, the newspaper, and some trade magazines in the evening. He used to like an occasional drink before or after dinner, but more than thirty years ago his doctor diagnosed a case of gout; so he has avoided alcohol since then. Mrs. Cotter emphasizes, almost apologetically, that napping is her husband's favorite recreation. Any time he is at home, he's likely to say, ''Al, I feel a nap coming on.''

Cotter's four children confirm that his routine has always been similar. He was usually home for dinner, in the years they were growing up, though business might occasionally keep him out. He tried not to talk shop at the dinner table, chatting instead about family matters or telling a funny story about something that happened that day. He rarely watched TV in the evenings; in fact, they were the last family on the block to buy a television set, somewhere around 1952. The Cotters didn't belong to a country club, rarely attended plays or shows, and didn't entertain guests very often. John was handy around the house and liked to tinker with things, but he had no hobbies or avocations. He always worked at least a half day on Saturdays, and he still does, but Sunday is a time for church and family. He resists suggestions to begin the markets or schedule business meetings on Sundays.

At least one week a year, the whole family would pack up and escape to Wisconsin, where they would meet Alice's parents at a lake and then idle away the time fishing, swimming, or just floating on inner tubes. The drives there and back, however, took an eternity; for Cotter stopped off at every hardware store along the way. The children recall spending endless hours waiting in the car on a town square, or playing in the town park; they all express amazement at their mother's infinite patience. In addition to these family excursions, Alice Cotter accompanied her husband to conventions, and, in later years, on cruises or trips to Europe. The Cotters employed live-in help to assist Alice in her daily chores and to care for the children while they were away.

Work, family, and religion define John Cotter's life; but he is not showy or demonstrative about either his family or his faith. The Cotters are not a "touchy-feely" family; John's sons say there was "no hugging him." Family roles were utterly traditional: John worked hard to support them; Alice tended the house and garden and mediated most family crises; Dan, the oldest child, was ever the cut-up, always in some mischief, whereas Mary, the older daughter, resembled her father, the conscientious perfectionist; Patti was the easy-going, happy-go-lucky daughter and Michael, the youngest, the sensitive artist and family rebel. John Cotter never coached a Little League team or led a Boy Scout troop, he rarely helped his kids with their homework or got involved in their activities. Yet none of them considered him an absentee father; he was there if they needed him. One daughter remembers him as "a very strict father with an Irish temper," but the other calls him "basically a soft touch," easy to wheedle favors from.

Family members disagree about whether John Cotter is a "workaholic." It all depends on how you define the word. All concur that

Cotter paces himself well, takes his naps, and guards his health carefully; and no one suggests that his work habits ever harmed his family. Yet they admit, on the other hand, that hardware is John Cotter's life, the company is his pride and joy, almost like another child.

Cotter himself takes pride in being a "full-time manager," and he disparages businessmen who get too diverted into other activities. "People can get intoxicated with the damnedest things besides alcohol," he avows. In 1961, Cotter accepted an appointment to the board of directors of the Lake View Bank, but some years later he found that it took too much of his time. Reading reports, attending the monthly meeting, then socializing at lunch with the other directors occupied a day and a half per month he preferred to devote to his own business. So he resigned from the board and has steadfastly refused all other invitations to sit on corporate or foundation boards. He does, however, practice considerable private philanthropy. He underwrote the entire cost of painting and renovating St. Athanasius church, his home parish in Evanston; he helped build a small country church in Black Duck, Minnesota and another in Tomahawk, Wisconsin as memorials to his parents; and he donates regularly to his alma mater, Cretin High School in St. Paul. When a young priest in Iowa, a distant relative of his, wrote him asking for a donation to his "outdoor ministry," Cotter wrote a check for an acre of "Catholic campground." Since he is always working, he has no time to volunteer for church or charity, but he gives lavishly of the money his hard work earns. He does his good deeds in private, however, wanting only to be remembered for his full-time management of Cotter & Company.

IDEAS, DETAILS, PEOPLE

I have never seen an organizational chart of Cotter & Company; I doubt if one has ever existed. The informal division of labor at the top management level, however, is reasonably clear and straightforward. Dan Cotter, the president, who grew up in the company and has done nearly every job in the place, manages the basics of hardware distribution and acts as external ambassador, Mr. Outside, staying in touch with the dealers, the field men, the manufacturers, and the hardware associations. Paul Fee, executive vice-president, serves more as Mr. Inside, fine tuning such in-house departments as insurance, accounting, data processing, and member services. Ed Lanctot, whose official titles are secretary/treasurer of the corporation and merchandising manager, continues to oversee every detail of advertising and promotion, as he always has. The national sales managers, Bill Earnest and Pat Casey, divide the country in two geographically; while the buying managers, Nick Arena and Jerry Thompson, allocate their work by product categories, with Arena managing basic hardware and Thompson the specialty lines. Within, over, and around this simple management structure, John Cotter does whatever he wants to, inquiring or intervening at will; but in recent years, he has spent more and more of his time nursing the paint and lawn mower factories. Irv Rose and Glenn Alexander deal directly with him more than most other department managers do.

In his management style, John Cotter follows instinctively most of the basic principles of excellent companies prescribed by Thomas Peters and Robert Waterman. He's an action-oriented, hands on manager who likes to wander around the company and see what is going on. He's informal and unpretentious and thinks nothing of going two or three levels down in the hierarchy to talk over a problem with the person responsible. He's always open and accessible. His secretary recalls a small but illuminating incident. Two women in the direct mail department wanted to change an order form, but their supervisor wouldn't let them because he believed that Mr. Cotter had personally designed that form. The women came to see Cotter, explained their proposed improvement, and he approved it without fuss or delay.

Above all, however, three qualities of Cotter's management stand out as preeminent: attention to ideas and values, attention to details, and attention to people.

1. Attention to Ideas and Values. At first glance, it may seem strange to ascribe much interest in ideas to John Cotter. He is intensely practical, usually affects a down-home folksiness, and expresses a healthy distrust for most intellectuals. He reads voraciously, but his reading matter falls within a fairly narrow range, mainly newspapers, trade magazines and business publications, business history, and biographies of corporate leaders. Despite considerable drawing ability, he has no time for art or literature. Dan gave him a set of oil paints for his 70th birthday, but doesn't think he ever took them out of the box. His views

on politics and economics are shaped by standard Republican trickle-down theory. He harbors strong opinions on many subjects, but he devotes most of his time and attention to hardware.

Yet within his own field of business, he manifests a shrewd strategic instinct and a breathtaking sense of vision. Few have understood the plight of the independent hardware dealer better or conceptualized the solution more brilliantly. He always sees the big picture, detecting long-range trends before others do; and he appreciates the value of history as a form of institutional memory. Not every company founder would commission a full and honest history and open to the historian both his private mementoes and company records. Over the years, Cotter has gathered and saved the most extensive archives in the hardware industry. He knows where he and the company fit within the overall scheme of things.

Peters and Waterman emphasize, throughout their book *In Search of Excellence,* the primacy of ideas, values, and vision. "Let us suppose that we were asked for one all-purpose bit of advice for management," they write. "We might be tempted to reply: 'Figure out your value system. Decide what your company *stands for.*'" John Cotter knows what his company stands for and he preaches it on every possible occasion: "We provide the independent hardware dealer with the right goods at the right price at the right time. We treat every retail-member the same, and we keep the overhead costs down." Low-cost distribution is so fundamental it can never be taken for granted. Le Herron believes that Cotter's single-minded dedication to it explains his success: "He understood better than any of the other managers the central point of dealer-ownership, getting the goods in the store at the lowest possible cost. Everything else is secondary."

Cotter's messianic dedication to the gospel of low-cost distribution strikes some observers as close-minded. Actually, he is very inquisitive, curious, and open to new ideas, up to a point. Le Herron says, "He has a mind like a sponge that soaks up ideas;" Bill Phair recalls that Cotter used to inquire, "Bill, what are we doing wrong? You get around in the industry. What mistakes have we made?"; and Paul Fee concludes simply, "He is constantly processing input." Yet once Cotter has gathered all the ideas he can, if one of them fits his organization and promises to provide an edge for his members, he will decide swiftly and stick to his decision tenaciously. Once he makes up his mind, he rarely changes it; and he's not shy about preaching, "Ours is the Only Way."

He finds his primary pulpit for inculcating ideas and shaping values at the semi-annual markets. Twice a year, the dealer-members gather at True Value headquarters for a three-day event that is one part revival meeting, one part business seminar, and four parts of hard, tedious merchandise ordering. Each morning at the market opens with a pep talk from John (or, in recent years, Dan) Cotter; and in the evening, at the end of each session, the chairman delivers an accounting of his stewardship and unveils his plans for the future. Cotter still thinks like the retailer he once was in Eau Claire, Wisconsin, and the members sense his rapport with them. As a result he can urge them to greater discipline and dedication without their taking offense. He makes himself totally available at market time, mingling at lunch and dinner, walking the merchandise aisles, and keeping his office door wide open. He postpones all but the most essential business during each market, so he can devote himself to the retailer. Charisma is an overworked word; let's call John Cotter, in Peters' and Waterman's phrase, a value-shaping leader.

2. Attention to Details. Cotter preaches to his members that "retailing is detailing," and he follows his own philosophy. Again, the semi-annual markets provide a good example. Twice a year, several thousand dealers converge on Chicago; so nothing is left to chance in the planning of their pilgrimage. In 1970, Cotter established a travel agency to serve the members; his son Michael joined the agency as sales manager in 1977 and became general manager in 1986. Though it is legally separate from Cotter & Company and it solicits some outside corporate and personal clients, Galaxy Travel devotes six or seven months each year to the travel arrangements for dealers attending the markets. Galaxy books most of them into the Bismarck Hotel downtown, hosts a get-acquainted dinner after their Sunday and Tuesday arrivals, then shuttles them each morning to Clybourn Avenue.

The merchandise exhibits, which are open from 6:30 AM to 9:30 PM, sprawl over three floors of converted warehouse space; morning meetings start at 8:00 AM sharp. Each dealer is provided a specially-designed rolling desk, stacked with order forms, which he or she pushes up and down the aisles while ordering goods. The company serves breakfast, lunch, and a candlelight dinner on-site. At a recent market, 10,451 breakfasts, 19,503 lunches, and 7,404 dinners were served; 2 and 3/4 tons of peanuts were consumed in the exhibit area between meals, along with 89,640 cans of pop and juice. Neither smoking nor alcoholic beverages have ever been permitted in the market area, but in a recent concession to human nature Cotter opened a pub, named the Clybourn Club, in vacant warehouse space. A permanent staff, headed by Leo McPhee, orchestrates each market; but John Cotter personally reviews their plans and devotes special attention to the choice of a theme. He titled one recent market, for example, "Avenues to Profit," naming each "avenue," or aisle, after a different pioneer of dealer-ownership — Hall, Stout, Herron, et al.

Cotter's attention to detail reaches throughout the company. He prescribes strict work rules for all — men must wear neckties, smoking is forbidden in office and warehouse, employees are not permitted to drink any alcoholic beverages at lunchtime, even at business lunches in restaurants — and he expects his top executives to work long hours and Saturdays, as he does. Signs throughout the distribution center warehouses read: "Locate by Number, Fill by Description. Don't Guess, Ask." An order picker should locate the specific rack or bin by number, but before grabbing an item for the order he should double-check by actually reading the description on the box. Low-cost is a fetish throughout the headquarters offices. Cotter dislikes paper clips and photocopiers for they encourage a proliferation and waste of paper. He periodically reminds members how much it costs to write a single business letter; and to set an example, he and most department managers answer most internal correspondence by scrawling a reply on the same memo or letter.

Cotter executives marvel at their boss's "tickler system." He takes notes at every meeting and conference, then files them on a calendar system timed to "tickle" his memory at the appropriate moment for follow up. Often a manager will be surprised when the chairman inquires months later about some small matter he thought everyone had forgotten about. Cotter has carried this system through to the retail level as well. Preaching constantly that "hardware is a business of repetition," he distributes a management calendar to all active members, prescribing what needs to be done in the store every day of the year.

Cotter monitors the regular dispatches and weekly letters sent to members, editing each according to his own idiosyncratic style sheet. In Cotter-speak, a warehouse is not a warehouse, it's a distribution center; a show is not a show, it's a market; and a building for manufacturing is never a plant, it's a factory. The style sheet even prescribes the proper way to staple a memo, on a 45 degree angle; and, of course, one must never, ever abbreviate Co. in the title Cotter & Company. Always spell it out. This is Cotter's tip of the hat to his employees and retail members. Pat Summerall remembers, with amazement and admiration, a small example of the chairman's incredible attention to detail. Several years after he began radio commercials, as his name and voice became well known, Summerall started closing his True Value spots with the tag line, ''Tell them Pat Summerall sent you.'' Cotter asked him to change the line to ''Say Pat Summerall sent you.'' 'Tell them' sounded too harsh, like giving an order.

This preoccupation with minutiae may seem picky or petty, and it certainly can irritate and frustrate employees. When General Power was undergoing its time of trials in the late 1970s, for example, Cotter used to visit the lawn mower factory every week. Dave Rolston would pick him up at home and drive him out. Cotter spent all day at the factory, tinkered with everything, and constantly looked over Rolston's shoulder. In this case, perhaps, his desire to know how everything works and to personally will it into operation got out of hand. Yet as Peters and Waterman point out, ''The excellent companies are marked by very strong cultures, so strong that you either buy into their norms or get out.'' Many outsiders feel Cotter works his people too hard, but few Cotter employees themselves complain. Dave Rolston still exclaims, without hesitation, ''Cotter & Company was the greatest company I ever worked for.''

Opinions differ over Cotter's ability to delegate authority. When I asked Dan Cotter to characterize his father's management style, he laughed and said: ''Authoritarian! He does delegate responsibility, but always with strings attached.'' Others confirm this. Bill Earnest states that Cotter's basic dictum reads: ''KMI — Keep Management Informed.'' On the other hand, Red Lynes reports that Cotter left him mostly on his own to shape up the various companies taken over in the 1960s. Once the takeover papers were signed, Cotter would say, "See you later," then not visit the site again for a year or more. Fundamentally, John Cotter manages by feel and instinct, not by any perfectly consistent theory. He judges each situation as it comes up.

3. Attention to People. Whether he delegated a lot or a little, John Cotter was smart enough to know he couldn't do everything himself and confident enough to surround himself with first-rate, strong managers. Other innovative distributors, such as Ace and the early dealer-owneds, tended to be one-man shows. When a Dick Hesse or a Bill Stout retired, the company's lack of "bench strength" became glaringly obvious. Cotter, however, grabbed sales managers and vice presidents away from all his old-line competition, sometimes hiring men who had previously been outspoken opponents of dealer-ownership. Since many of the executives came from dispirited, failing, or bankrupt companies, Cotter held a subtle psychological edge over them. Grateful to have a job at all and fortunate to find one with a robust, rising firm, they worked their butts off for him.

Cotter thought far into the future when making personnel decisions. Dave Rolston's experience is instructive. Rolston introduced himself to Cotter in 1959 while he was still working for Edw. K. Tryon Co. He explained that he was from Philadelphia and said, "We don't compete with you now and we won't compete with you in the future." Cotter replied, "I don't know about that; we'll see. But come out and see our warehouse. I'll show you around myself." A year later Cotter arranged to meet him at the NWHA convention, behind a pillar in the hotel lobby. He told Rolston point blank: "You're going to come to work for me. But I don't know when and I don't know what you'll be doing." Finally, in 1969, Cotter hired him to supervise the Philadelphia distribution center. As his company has grown larger, Cotter has enjoyed more leeway to make these decisions quickly. He will, occasionally, hire a manager even if he doesn't have a specific slot for him yet. A minor deviation from low-cost, lean staffing philosophy is worthwhile if he can get the right people for his company's future.

Cotter demands a lot from his managers and instills a team spirit, an upbeat, winning attitude in them. Paul Fee has summed this up well:

"His greatest strength as a manager is his ability to wring the most out of everybody who works for him in a very pleasant and stimulating fashion. And then, in a very reasonable length of time, to come to a decision. You have the feeling that your input is important and that based on that input something is going to happen.''

Perhaps his insistence on spelling out Cotter & Company is a subtle way of acknowledging the team concept.

Cotter endeavors to be firm, fair, and consistent with people; but some believe that he can be too tolerant, too indulgent. If an employee has personal problems — alcoholism, a death in the family, illness — that affects his performance, Cotter usually gives him a second chance, and a third, and a fourth. Two things he will not permit are apathy or dishonesty. Red Lynes has characterized Cotter's tolerance as ''a positive trait which sometimes produces a negative result.'' He simply doesn't like to fire people; but, fortunately, the team spirit he inspires ensures that he rarely needs to.

A CONSERVATIVE ENTREPRENEUR

First and foremost, John Cotter is an entrepreneur, an independent risk-taker who could never be comfortable working for someone else. Nor could he stand still, content to maintain the highly successful business he founded. He always has something new percolating on the back burner. He may spring a grand surprise on the industry, such as the dealer-owned paint factory or the V & S Variety Division; or he may simply experiment with something small, like the self-service Dealers' Supply warehouse he opened in Minneapolis in 1983 and closed in 1985. Like an aging gunfighter, he's still restless for one last big score, perhaps a takeover of another wholesaler. He still dreams of repeating the Hibbard coup.

Yet, paradoxically, Cotter is a very cautious, conservative entrepreneur and manager. He tells the members to plan for the future with ''guarded enthusiasm and cautious optimism'' and he preaches to them most eloquently by his example. The way he eased into the computer revolution illustrates this clearly.

The computer age had just dawned flickeringly when Cotter & Company was launched. By 1952, when Cotter's sales reached $3 million, IBM salesmen began pursuing him, but he felt that his manual systems remained low cost and easier than the bulky, unproven vacuum-tube computers. Most IBM salesmen in those days were selling inventory record keeping systems. They would argue, "Mr. Cotter, with IBM you will know at the close of each day what your inventory is." Cotter barked back, "I can't afford to look more than once a week." Still, he recognized the need to look ahead and began careful planning for eventual conversion to data processing. Joe LaRocco, one of his buyers, started working with Frank Morman on a numbering system for the inventory. They settled on a five-digit code; and then Morman adopted IBM's self-checking sixth digit, a mathematical factor of the first five, which provided an automatic check for accuracy. Many of the problems of data processing were foreseen and worked out before a single piece of computing equipment was purchased.

Finally, in 1962, with the Hibbard takeover in the works and sales growing vigorously, Cotter decided to install an IBM computer for invoicing. Les Laden, who handled data processing for a company at North Pier Terminal, heard from an IBM salesman that his former business neighbor, Cotter & Company, was finally ready to take the plunge. Laden applied for the position of data processing manager, and on his first interview, he looked over IBM's proposal and suggested a refinement to save money. IBM planned to print out a picking slip for each dealer order, then later print an additional billing invoice, listing only those items actually shipped, less any markouts. On a 100 line order, for instance, with a 5% markout rate, the computer would produce 195 lines of print, 100 on the first copy and 95 on the second. Laden suggested that the picking slip of 100 lines could be shipped with the order and then a second, or "B copy," listing just the 5 markouts could be enclosed as a credit slip. Thus only 105 lines needed to be printed, an enormous saving of computer time and paper. Cotter adopted the idea enthusiastically, even before he formally offered Laden the job. Laden thought to himself, "Here's a management willing to listen to suggestions and to do business in ways different from the accepted standard."

Laden was hired on August 13, 1962 and spent the next six months writing programs and assembling a staff. Cotter & Company took delivery of its first main frame computer, an IBM 1401, in March, 1963; and the first orders, from a few selected members in Illinois and

Indiana, were invoiced on March 25. During the first few weeks, Cotter constantly monitored the computer's performance and phoned all the participating dealers to see what problems had developed. After cleaning out the bugs, he gradually extended the service to all dealers. As IBM produced a more powerful series of machines, Cotter kept pace with the developing technology and, over the years, applied computer systems to all accounting procedures, to payroll, and to inventory control.

Though order picking and invoicing had been mechanized, True Value members still were mailing in handwritten orders throughout the 1960s, an obvious weak link in the whole system. So in 1971, an electronic order entry system was introduced, and it has since been made mandatory and universal. The member enters the order numbers on a hand-held device which looks like a pocket calculator, then transmits them via telephone at an assigned time on a specific day of the week. The orders are filled from the nearest distribution center the next day.

John Cotter expresses a healthy respect for technology, sometimes even a sense of awe. "The whole company is held together with telephone wire," he exclaims. Without the jet airplane, the WATS telephone line, and electronic data processing, nationwide wholesaling from multiple distribution centers would be impossible. With a memory that stretches back before auto and plane travel were common, he still feels amazed that he can leave Chicago on a sub-zero morning and step off a plane in Ft. Lauderdale, or at the Pomona, Cal., distribution center, before noon. Yet he adopted computer technology slowly and cautiously, letting someone else work out most of the bugs first. "We weren't trying to impress anyone; we didn't have to be first," he concludes. "Just low cost."

Cotter has shown the same conservative, wait-and-see attitude towards microfiche. About ten years ago, the trade press and the NRHA began trumpeting the convenience of replacing hundreds of pages of merchandise catalogues with a few plastic cards of microfiche. But Cotter didn't believe that dealers were ready to change: "To date, management knows of no wholesaler using microfiche which has been able to totally eliminate the illustrated catalogue and price pages," he wrote. "This means that as one goes to microfiche another system (print on paper) must be maintained at least in part. Naturally this is costly. Management is reminded of the early days of data processing.'' When Kodak salesmen delivered a sales pitch for microfiche, Cotter noticed immediately that they didn't use fiche in their own presentation, relying instead on traditional flip-boards. Cotter promptly excused them from his office. He's never the first to adopt a new technology, but he's not likely to be the last.

Cotter's paradoxical attitude towards technology typifies the man. A cautious innovator, a conservative entrepreneur, he faces the future with ''guarded enthusiasm,'' he accepts honors with ''humble pride.'' His overall philosophy can be summarized in three words: ''Order, Growth, Judgment.'' Get the basic system in order first, then take some risks to ensure growth, but exercise firm, fair, judgment consistently. Most Cotter associates emphasize his consistent, long-range outlook. Bill Earnest concludes: ''What you accomplish today at Cotter & Company is not the result of what you did yesterday, or the past month, or the past year. It is the fruit of consistent behavior.''

In the final analysis, what drives a man like John Cotter? He himself has always emphasized money and profit — a fair profit for the retail hardware dealer and enough money to support himself and his family well. Yet I suspect that money, in itself, is not very important to him; rather, it's a way of keeping score. A healthy bottom line for True Value members and handsome earnings for John Cotter signify achievement. A drive for achievement motivates him; and an ability to remain himself, to retain the contagious enthusiasm of the 12 year old boy at Dayton's Bluff Hardware, even while achieving great success, has been his greatest accomplishment.

CHAPTER FOURTEEN
THE TRANSFORMATION OF THE HARDWARE INDUSTRY

"I well remember the early postwar years when all independent merchants were considered an endangered species, but none more so than the family-owned hardware store. These operations were really up against it, trying to compete with the massive buying power and merchandising of Sears, Wards, and other chains — not to mention the discount stores then starting to appear.

Today, the independent hardware merchant is a viable, prosperous, efficient entity; with prices, advertising, and merchandising as good as any chain; with brands as well accepted as the bigger operations; and with that extra something no chain has or can ever have: the zealous commitment of an owner to his own business, and his personal rapport with the customer."

—Charles C. Horton, "John Cotter: White Knight of the Independent Merchant,"
Supply House Times, September, 1985

Nearly forty years ago, Cotter & Company began shipping hardware to 25 retail-members from 2,000 sq.ft. of warehouse space. The first year's shipments totaled $385,000. The company today counts nearly 7,000 members, in every state of the Union, and 3,000 employees, at the Chicago headquarters and in 14 modern distribution centers across the country. Revenues in 1985 added up to $1,705,730,000. The company now ships more goods in a single day than it did in any year during its first decade. The growth chart, which Cotter proudly publishes every year, graphically depicts a remarkable record, 28% average annual growth, through boom years and recessions alike (See Figure 8). True Value is the largest hardware distributor in the United States, the second largest privately held firm in Chicago, and one of the top one hundred national advertisers.

Yet numbers alone don't tell the tale. John Cotter's success story is highly personal, the story of a man who shaped a company in his own image, touched the lives of many thousands, and transformed a whole industry. A sampling of testimonials from True Value members illustrates the human aspects of Cotter's success:

—"Shirley and I took over my Father and Mother's store in 1970 after it had been gutted by fire . . . In ten short years we have nearly completed college educating three of our four children, bought a house, and are now attempting to build a new store to fulfill our dreams."

—"It seems appropriate to write this testimonial letter on Independence Day as any good word of praise for Cotter & Company is to further the independence and aid the survival of independent hardware dealers."

—"In 1954 . . . people told me not to work in a hardware store. If you do not have anything else to do you will have to dust. Well, over the years I guess I have done my share of dusting. But during that time, I have seen a business grow from doing about $75,000 annually to $500,000 . . . from employing seven people to employing fifty. Multiply this by the number of True Value Hardware Stores and you have influenced many lives because you had a dream and the guts and ambition to follow it."

Two common refrains run through Cotter's letters from grateful retailers: "We wish we had joined sooner! Why didn't you force us to join you sooner?" and "You have been the salvation of the

The World's Largest & Lowest-Cost* Wholesale Distribution, Manufacturing and Merchandising Organization Serving over 6000 Participating True Value Hardware Stores and over 700 Participating V & S Variety Stores from 14 Low-Cost Regional Distribution Centers.

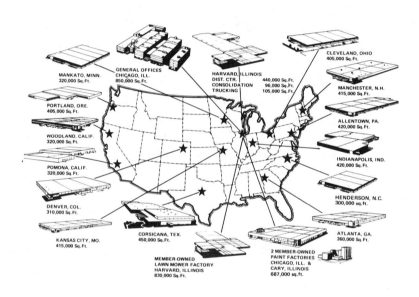

Fourteen completely stocked Regional Distribution Centers with over 32,000 items each, insure fast, low-cost delivery of merchandise.

7,568,000 sq. ft. of distributing, manufacturing and merchandising system serves Members from a $160,000,000 inventory
*when Year-End Patronage Dividends are accounted.

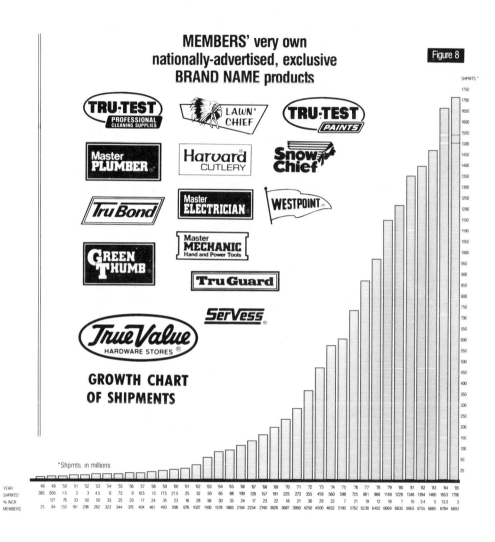

MEMBERS' very own
nationally-advertised, exclusive
BRAND NAME products

Figure 8

GROWTH CHART
OF SHIPMENTS

*Shpmts. in millions

YEAR	'48	'49	'50	'51	'52	'53	'54	'55	'56	'57	'58	'59	'60	'61	'62	'63	'64	'65	'66	'67	'68	'69	'70	'71	'72	'73	'74	'75	'76	'77	'78	'79	'80	'81	'82	'83	'84	'85
SHPMTS*	385	850	1.5	2	3	4.5	6	7.5	9	10.5	13	17.5	21.5	25	32	50	65	88	109	128	157	191	225	273	355	459	560	598	725	861	968	1149	1228	1348	1394	1460	1653	1706
% INCR		121	76	33	50	50	33	25	20	17	24	35	23	16	28	56	30	35	24	17	23	22	18	21	30	29	22	7	21	19	12	19	7	10	3.4	5	13.3	3
MEMBERS	25	84	133	181	206	262	323	344	376	404	461	493	508	676	1037	1100	1578	1885	2104	2254	2740	3026	3687	3950	4250	4500	4832	5190	5762	6238	6402	6669	6835	6903	6755	6685	6784	6893

independent hardware dealer.''

Did dealer-ownership, in general, and John Cotter, in particular, save the independent hardware retailer from extinction? The question cannot, strictly speaking, ever be answered with certainty. To attempt an answer requires what social scientists addicted to long words call ''counterfactual reasoning.'' That is, we must imagine a condition which is contrary to fact — What if John Cotter had never been born? What if no one ever thought of dealer-ownership? — and then describe the consequences of that condition. Necessarily, we can only speculate.

Certainly, hardware stores faced an uncertain future right after World War II. The competitive challenge posed by mass merchandisers and discount stores has been recounted frequently in these pages and need not be reiterated. Furthermore, the hardware store carried a bad reputation, which made it an unlikely candidate to meet the challenge. The January, 1948 issue of *Fortune* hazarded a guess ''that there are only fifteen first-class hardware stores in the U.S.'' and characterized most hardware merchandising as ''notoriously indifferent.'' Dan Cotter remembers when his father first took him out on the road as a young man, he was not impressed with what he saw. ''The hardware store was not a pretty sight. Too often it looked like a 'junk shop'.'' Even years later, after many stores had modernized, the negative image lingered. John Sullivan wrote in *Hardware Age* in 1970:

''The hardware industry has an image problem. . . . I once asked a man in a small town his opinion of hardware stores. He told me. They were small, crowded, dingy, high-priced and behind the times. This surprised me, since one of the outstanding stores in the country is located in his town . . . When I pointed this out to him, he replied, 'Why that's not a hardware store.'''

Would hardware stores have followed the dinosaur and the dodo if the dealer-owned cooperative movement had not refurbished their image with lower prices, better merchandising, and national advertising? Probably not literally. Too many people want to be their own boss, and tools carry such a powerful appeal, that some would have opened a small hardware store even if the profit possibilities seemed bleak. The famous poem, ''The Hardware Store,'' by Edgar A. Guest, sums up its primordial allure:

"There is something about a hardware store
Which, strangely, I can't resist,
And I think it's the joy I hungered for
Which somehow my life has missed.
Though under the chill of the years, I'd say
That many a passion cools,
A man will keep to his dying day
A deep-rooted love for tools."

Any hardware stores opened under such poetic inspiration, however, would have been only a marginal part of the industry and their proprietors mere hobbyists, not dynamic businessmen. Probably, if the low cost dealer-ownership movement had not revived the independent retailer, most hardware would now be sold by mass merchandisers.

Comparison with another "romantic" sector of the American economy, the family farm, throws further light on these speculations. Despite periodic political crusades to save the family farm, it has, in fact, largely disappeared as an economic entity. Only 1 in 33 Americans lives on a farm today. Seventy per cent of these are small farmers, selling less than $40,000 worth of farm products per year; but collectively they produce only 10% of the nation's food. The majority of these small farmers derive most of their income from off-the-farm jobs or pensions; they are, in short, hobby farmers. In all probability, this is the fate which John Cotter and the other pioneers of dealer-ownership saved the hardware dealer from.

These are only speculations and musings. Yet the U.S. Census of Business and hardware trade sources do provide some hard facts about the changing shape of the hardware industry in the last forty years. The number of hardware stores in the U.S. stayed steady for about ten years after the war, then fell dramatically in the 1960s. The number seems to have stabilized around 26,000, however, since 1972 (See Figure 9). For twenty-five years, sales through hardware stores failed to keep pace with the explosive postwar growth of American retailing. In the period between the 1958 and 1963 business censuses, sales actually declined. But since 1972, sales in the 26,000 independent hardware stores have matched the overall growth of U.S. retail trade (See Figure 10).

Figure 9

Number of Retail Hardware Stores in the U.S., 1948–1977

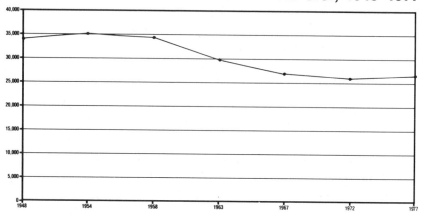

Source—U.S. Business Censuses

Figure 10

Hardware Store Sales Growth vs. Total Retail Sales Growth, Percentage Change Between Business Censuses, 1948–1982

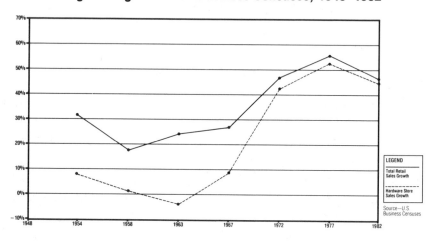

These newly vigorous hardware stores are far different from their ancestors. In 1982, 1532 of them (about 5% of the total) did over a million dollars worth of business, more than some wholesalers. A large majority recorded over $100,000 worth of trade, a sum which used to mark the threshold to large store status just a few years ago. Only 20% struggled along with less than $50,000 in annual sales. Clearly, hardware stores have reentered the mainstream of American commerce.

Before ascribing this success to dealer-ownership, let's look closely at the changes in hardware wholesaling. The number of full line wholesalers (defined by *Hardware Age* as those who "handle hardlines products in sufficient depth and breadth to serve as the major source of supply for today's hardware retailers") has undergone a precipitous free-fall since the 1950s. From 550 wholesalers in 1958, the number has plummeted to 210 in 1984 (See Figure 11). Several additional wholesalers, such as Belknap in Louisville and Salt Lake Hardware in Utah, have closed their doors since then.

Figure 11

Number of Full-Line Hardware Wholesalers in the U.S., 1950–1984

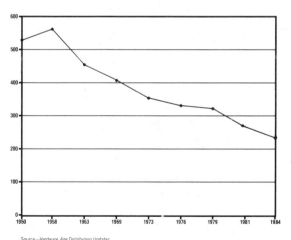

Source—*Hardware Age* Distribution Updates

More than the number of players has changed; there has also been a qualitative change, a transformation in hardware wholesaling. Wholesalers no longer sell "to" the retailer; they now endeavor to sell "through" the retailer to the consumer, with store identification, merchandising aids, and vigorous advertising. As Earl Lifshey pointed out a number of years ago, "The term 'wholesaler' has come to have a moss-covered antiquarian kind of connotation about it." The majority of wholesalers today prefer to be called 'distributors,' and these distributors are tied closely to their retail customers in voluntary chains. The whole distribution chain is more integrated, with more smoothly meshing gears.

The numbers in Table 9 and the pie-chart in Figure 12 tell the story. Currently, the dealer-owned cooperatives enjoy a 48% market share (True Value alone accounts for 19% of all hardware sales). The merchandising groups, which are federations of wholesalers that sponsor voluntary chains of retailers, account for another 34% of the market. Other franchised chains of stores record 13% of total sales. This leaves only 5% of all sales by full line wholesalers to unaffiliated wholesale houses. When John Cotter predicted the imminent demise of these tradition-bound businesses thirty years ago, he spoke the literal truth.*

Since the 1960s, when Cotter & Company's nationwide expansion finally forced recognition of the dealer-owned companies as a legitimate part of the industry, trade sources have been predicting a levelling-off in growth for the dealer-owned sector. In 1969, when dealer-owned market share stood at 24%, *Hardware Age* wrote: "There are those who know the hardware industry who believe the dealer-owned movement as we see it today has approached its peak . . . There is a limit to the number of stores that can accept the rigid buying and management disciplines required." The pundits were wrong; they underestimated the revival of the independent retailer's morale. Cotter's share rose

---

*Figure 12 does not account for all hardware sold in America, only the $7.7 billion sold by "full-line" wholesalers. The 1982 Census of Business lists a figure of $11 billion for all wholesale hardware sales in the U.S. The difference, $3.3 billion, is accounted for by numerous small specialty jobbers who sell a limited number of lines as a secondary source of supply to retailers and contractors. In addition, some unknown quantity of hardware sales by Sears and other mass merchandisers escapes this measurement completely, since it does not pass through wholesalers at all.

TABLE 9

HARDWARE DISTRIBUTION STATISTICS
1963-1984

Year	# of full-line wholesalers	Total sales (in millions)	Cotter & Company sales and market share		Total dealer-owned sales and market share	
1963	460	$1,200	$50	(4%)	$175	(14%)
1969	400	$1,900	$192	(10%)	$470	(24%)
1973	355	$3,000	$400	(13%)	$994	(32%)
1976	327	$4,500	$700	(15%)	$1,670	(36%)
1979	305	$6,200	$978	(16%)	$2,430	(39%)
1981	260	$7,400	$1,122	(15%)	$2,960	(39%)
1984	210	$7,700	$1,500	(19%)	$3,680	(48%)

Source: *Hardware Age* Distribution Updates

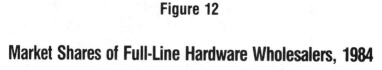

Figure 12

Market Shares of Full-Line Hardware Wholesalers, 1984

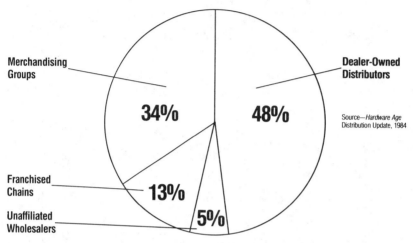

Merchandising Groups

Dealer-Owned Distributors

34%

48%

Source—*Hardware Age* Distribution Update, 1984

Franchised Chains

13%

Unaffiliated Wholesalers

5%

from 10% in 1969 to 19% in 1984, while the total share for the dealer-owned sector climbed from 24% to 48%. The growth of the dealer-owned wholesalers and the revitalization of retail hardware stores have gone hand in hand since 1972.

Sales growth in the 1980s has been even more impressive than a quick look at the raw numbers might suggest. Between 1981 and 1984, recession years for the American economy, the dealer-owneds dramatically improved their market share from 39% to 48%. They recorded nearly $700 million in additional sales, whereas the industry as a whole increased sales by only $300 million. This means that other sectors in the industry declined drastically during these recent years. Dealer-owned cooperatives are not only the largest segment of hardware wholesaling, they are the growing portion, the leading edge.

Does this mean that dealer-ownership is the "only way" to supply an independent hardware store effectively, as John Cotter so fervently preaches? Others have proposed and demonstrated different ways of assisting the independent hardware retailer. Judging by market shares, the merchandising groups appear as the principal alternative. In a merchandising group, a number of regional wholesalers retain their separate corporate identities but they federate together under the group's umbrella in order to exchange ideas, try to pool their buying power, and conduct a common advertising program. Six principal wholesaler groups — Liberty Distributors, PRO Hardware, Sentry Hardware, Val-Test Distributors, Allied Hardware Services, Associated Hardware Buyers — embrace two-thirds of the wholesalers in the country; but they account for only one-third of wholesale hardware sales.

The six groups differ greatly in size, structure, and effectiveness. The three smallest — Val-Test, Allied, and Associated — are simply loose advertising alliances, whereas the store programs of the big three — Liberty, PRO, Sentry — approximate in some ways the voluntary chains of the dealer-owneds. Sentry and PRO emphasize their advertising and merchandising aids to retailers, while Liberty makes volume buying its top priority. Until recently Liberty purchased goods for all its member-wholesalers through a system of central buying. Manufacturers billed Liberty directly, and all wholesalers in the group guaranteed payment in the event of a default by any single member. In 1985, however, S & T Industries of Louisville, a Liberty member, filed for bankruptcy; and the guarantee of S & T's debts proved very costly for all other Liberty wholesalers. Since then, therefore, Liberty has reverted to the looser billing practices of the other groups, with each individual wholesaler responsible for its own payables.

Liberty's experience illustrates a major disadvantage of the merchandising groups, their extremely cumbersome organization, with many corporations trying to act as one. This problem manifests itself in other ways as well. The affiliated wholesalers rarely agree to carry a like inventory; each stocks many different items not common throughout the group. It is extremely difficult, therefore, to hammer out an effective direct mail advertising circular for all the wholesalers to distribute.

Nonetheless, merchandising groups do seem to have carved out a market niche; they appeal most to retailers who find the greater discipline and organization of dealer-ownership repugnant. Yet their sales growth has not kept pace with that of the dealer-owned sector in recent years. Groups improved their market share only from 32% to 34% between 1981 and 1984 whereas the coops jumped from 39% to 48%. Traditionally, the market positions of merchandising groups and dealer-owned cooperatives in the grocery trade have been just the reverse of their places in hardware. In 1967, for instance, wholesale grocery groups, such as IGA, recorded a market share of about 50% while coops had only 25%. Yet the most recent business census, in 1982, shows groups, coops, and unaffiliated wholesalers about level, with one-third of the market each. Even in their strongest traditional bastion, therefore, the wholesaler merchandising groups seem to be declining.

Franchising is another alternative that has been applied to hardware distribution. Gambles, Coast-to-Coast, and the original Ace Hardware all began in the 1920s as franchised store programs. Coast-to-Coast, founded in 1929 by the three Melamed brothers — Arthur, Maurice, and Louis — inspired a high degree of dealer loyalty. The Melameds preferred to take on prospective store-owners with no previous retail experience, so they would not have to unlearn any bad habits. As long as the original founders remained in charge, Coast had a warm family atmosphere about it. The first franchisee, Otto Leudtke of Hutchinson, Minn., convinced two of his brothers to take on franchises of their own; and when Otto decided to get married, he asked Maurice Melamed for his fatherly advice and blessing first. Yet after the Melameds retired and sold their organization to Household Finance in 1961, much of the spirit and cohesiveness of Coast dissipated. The same thing happened to Gambles Stores after Bert Gamble sold the organization. From a high of about 1400 stores in 1969, Gambles shrunk to a shadow of its former self, with only 550 stores in 1984. Since then it has merged with Our Own Hardware.

Perhaps the best evidence of franchising's weakness in the hardware trade is provided by Ace Hardware's conversion to dealer-ownership. Richard Hesse and his associates announced in 1958, under apparent pressure from Cotter & Company, that in order to perpetuate their franchise organization after the passing of the founders, they would sell it to the dealers. Hesse finally carried through on this promise in 1974, shortly before his death.

Dealer ownership may not be the only way to preserve independent hardware retailers, but it has proven to be the best way, the dominant way, the most successful way. As the industry leaders, John Cotter and the other dealer-owned managers have set the standard and forced other wholesalers to keep pace. Many wholesalers who joined merchandising groups, for example, did so as a defensive measure, adopting some of the most effective methods of the dealer-owned firms, such as national radio and TV advertising. John Sullivan of the NRHA concludes: "Few know it, none will admit it, but Cotter has been good for the traditional wholesalers too. He has forced them to do a better job."

In the final analysis, does it matter that John Cotter and the dealer-owned cooperative movement have transformed the hardware industry and preserved the independent hardware store? Hardware will always be sold by someone, for it's a necessity of life. Does it make any difference whether it's sold by an independent retailer or by a mass-merchandising, corporate chain? It matters to the customer if he's interested in service and do-it yourself advice. Think of the difference between a grocery supermarket and a hardware store. Will anyone in a supermarket consult with the shopper about gourmet recipes, cooking times, or money-saving shortcuts? Of course not. Yet hardware dealers routinely map out home improvement projects with their customers. As John Cotter says, "Many hardware dealers give $2 worth of advice with a 50¢ sale."

A *Washington Post* columnist recently observed:

"It is one of the more considerable ironies of an ironic age: At a time when the base of our economy is gradually shifting from manufacturing to service, 'service' as it has traditionally been known is disappearing . . . At the supermarket you found management locked away from you in an aerie by the checkout lane . . . At the auto dealer's service department you found that they were doing you a favor to let you wait three hours in order to give them your money. At the bookstore you found a clerk who knew nothing about books and regarded special orders as an intrusion on his gum-chewing time."

Compare this with the report of a True Value dealer in the state of Washington:

"We go out of our way to provide service, everything from repairing a faucet by putting in a new stem and washer to going out to a home to solve an electrical problem. Nothing goes out of here in a box. If it's a lawn mower, we take it out, put in gas and oil and make sure it's running before the customer takes it. And we deliver free within a five mile radius.''

Service matters to the consumer, and independent ownership matters to the owner. Being your own boss is a vital part of the American system of free enterprise; anything that encourages individual ownership strengthens the system. Cotter & Company are very proud of their role in perpetuating family-owned businesses. As Herb Haller, Cotter's first sales manager, phrases it: ''You can't force a son or daughter to come into the business with you, but you can make it so attractive and profitable that they will want to.''

Let's allow John Cotter to have the last word, as he usually does: ''It seems to me that all independent merchants, who, as I've said many times before, are the very backbone of the U.S.A. and typify the very heart and spirit of this great country, are people who have *made the future happen* . . . Most True Value Members have their own money invested in their stores. Most work many, many more hours than the average jobholder. Many True Value Hardware Stores have been owned by the same family for three generations . . . Apparently, they said to themselves: 'I want more, I can do better and I'm willing to work harder to make it happen.' In short, they had faith that the future could be better.''

SOURCES

Chapter 1

There is no overall history of hardware wholesaling, or any other aspect of the hardware industry, in America, and precious little on wholesaling in general. My most important sources were: Glenn Porter, Harold Livesay, *Merchants and Manufacturers: Studies in the Changing Structure of Nineteenth Century Marketing* (Baltimore: Johns Hopkins Press, 1971); Harold Barger, *Distribution's Place in the American Economy since 1860* (Princeton, N.J.: Princeton University Press, 1955); William Henry Becker, "The Wholesaler of Hardware and Drugs, 1870-1900," (Unpublished Ph.D. dissertation, Johns Hopkins University, 1969); and Saunders Norvell's marvelous memoir, *Forty Years of Hardware* (New York: Hardware Age, 1924). Norvell's life spanned nearly all of the wholesaler's heyday. He started as a stock clerk at E. C. Simmons in 1883, worked as travelling salesman, then sales manager; became president and part-owner of Shapleigh Hardware in 1901; retired to journalism and other business enterprises in 1911. When he died in 1949 at age 85 he was writing an opinion column for *Hardware Age* under the affectionate title of "The Dean's Page."

Hardware Age magazine published a special bicentennial issue entitled "The Great American Hardware Story," on July 4, 1975. Though not a complete history of the hardware industry, it provides a fascinating look at two hundred years of hardware manufacture, distribution, and retailing. The present publisher of *Hardware Age,* Thomas L. Delph, was unfailingly helpful and cooperative, providing much timely information for this study. Likewise, Richard H. Lambert, managing director of the National Retail Hardware Association, and his staff at *DIY Retailing,* helped me immeasurably.

Two slender company histories — Clark Porteous, *The First Orgill Century, 1847-1947,* and Fred C. Kelly, *Seventy-Five Years of Hibbard Hardware, 1855-1930* — provided a few bits of information. Perry R. Duis, "Life of a Salesman," *Chicago Magazine* (May, 1985), takes a brief, vivid look at the drummer; Truman E. Moore, *The Travelling Man* (Garden City, New York: Doubleday, 1972) is a fuller study. The travelling salesman joke in the text is from chapter 3 of the book. Gerald Carson, *The Old Country Store* (N.Y.: Oxford University Press, 1954), paints a detailed portrait of old-fashioned retailers. Daniel Boorstin's section entitled "Consumption Communities," in *The Americans: The Democratic Experience* (N.Y.: Random House, 1973), bristles with insights about the beginnings of mass merchandising in America. Earl Lifshey, *The Housewares Story* (Chicago: National Housewares Manufacturers Association, 1973), provides an overall history of that industry and many insights about hardware as well. James C. Worthy, *Shaping an American Institution: Robert E. Wood and Sears, Roebuck* (Urbana: University of Illinois Press, 1984), is a definitive analysis of Sears' progress in the twentieth century.

As with every chapter in this book, my knowledge and understanding were greatly deepened by a number of intensive interviews with John Cotter. Cotter is the source of the story about Higgns, Crandall, and the Hardware Train of Progress.

My father, Edmund S. Kantowicz, served as special consultant for this book, guiding me every step of the way. I would not have attempted to write the book without him.

Chapter 2

I wrote this chapter largely from interviews with John Cotter and members of his family. Whenever possible, I verified facts in U.S. Census records, the Cotter-Garrigan family tree prepared by members of the family, and the correspondence, clippings, and memorabilia in John Cotter's personal files and scrapbooks.

Chapter 3

Much of this chapter derives from interviews with John Cotter, Steve Duffy, the second general manager of Our Own Hardware, and F. Leon Herron, Jr., former general manager of American Hardware. Two magazine articles by George Hall elucidated his ideas and operations: "This Jobber Sells Hardware at Cost of Less Than One Per Cent," *Printers' Ink Monthly* (April, 1926), and "Simplified Hardware Selling," *Nation's Business* (November, 1929).

For background on the chain store challenge, consult: Godfrey M. Lebhar, *Chain Stores in America, 1859-1962* (New York: Chain Store Publishing Corp., 1963); Theodore N. Beckman, Herman C. Nolen, *The Chain Store Problem* (New York: McGraw Hill, 1938); Paul W. Stewart, J. Frederic Dewhurst, *Does Distribution Cost Too Much?* (New York: Twentieth Century Fund, 1939); and Federal Trade Commission, "Chain Stores: Final Report on the Chain Store Investigation," 74th Congress, 21st Session, Senate Document #4 (December 14, 1934). Harold Williamson, *Winchester: The Gun That Won The West* (Washington, D.C.: Combat Forces Press, 1952) has a full description of the Winchester Stores program.

There is an extensive literature on cooperatives, much of it technical, and some of it emotional and polemical. Ewell Paul Roy, *Cooperatives: Development, Principles, and Management* (Danville, Ill.: Interstate Printers and Publishing, 1976) is a standard text. Hector Lazo, *Retailer Cooperatives: How to Run Them* (New York: Harper and Bros., 1937) is an insightful, earlier study. Raymond W. Miller, *A Conservative Looks at Cooperatives* (Athens, Ohio: Ohio University Press, 1964) is passionate, whereas Richard B. Heflebower, *Cooperatives and Mutuals in the Market System* (Madison: University of Wisconsin Press, 1980) is highly technical. John Bainbridge, *Biography of Mutual Fire and Casualty Insurance* (Garden City, N.Y.: Doubleday, 1952) provides a comprehensive history of mutual insurance. John A. Fitschen, *The Wisco Story* (Madison: 1954) is the only previously published company history of a dealer-owned hardware firm. Eugene F. Grape, "Retailer-Owned Cooperative Wholesaling in the Hardware Trade," (Unpublished Ph.D. diss. in economics, Ohio State University, 1966) is the only overall study of the movement.

Chapter 4

John Cotter, Ed Lanctot, Herb Haller, Harold Ost, and Jim Eller all shared their reminiscences of the birth of Cotter & Company, as did the members of Cotter's family, Alice Germain Cotter, Daniel Cotter, Mary Cotter Fee, Patricia Cotter Kiggins, and Michael Cotter. Unfortunately, Frank Morman died on November 5, 1983, before research for this history began.

I consulted all surviving correspondence and records dealing with the company's origins, including the original 7½ minute letter, the first dealer contracts, and a letter of reminiscence from William H. Althoff dated December 3, 1962. I have read systematically through all the weekly letters and dispatches that John Cotter sent out to his dealers, beginning with the company's incorporation in 1948.

Although I have criticized the exaggerations of George Gilder's, *The Spirit of Enterprise* (New York: Simon and Schuster, 1984), and Lee Iacocca, *Iacocca: An Autobiography* (New York, 1984), both books contain many insights into the dynamics of entrepreneurship. See also, "The Entrepreneurial Mystique," *Wall Street Journal,* May 20, 1985, pp. 2C-7C; "Hardware Entrepreneurs," *Hardware Retailing,* August, 1984, pp. 321-324; and Orvis Collins, David G. Moore, *The Organization Makers* (New York: Appleton—Century—Crofts, 1970). Thomas C. Cochran, *Railroad Leaders, 1845-90: The Business Mind In Action* (Cambridge, Mass.: Harvard University Press, 1953), and William Miller (Ed.), *Men in Business: Essays In The History Of Entrepreneurship* (Cambridge: Harvard University Press, 1952), were milestones in the serious historical study of business leaders.

Chapter 5

The background on retailing trends in the fifties was drawn primarily from the pages of *Hardware Age*, which I read systematically beginning in 1948. Every issue of the magazine contained a section featuring new ideas in hardware marketing and merchandising with case studies of specific dealers. William R. Davidson, "The End of the Discount House,"

January 11, 1962, pp. 39-42, Richard Sanzo, "What is a Discount House?", March 22, 1962, pp. 95-97, and a special issue entitled "Hardware and the Mass Merchandiser," December, 1970, provided good perspective on discounters. See also, Tom Mahoney, Leonard Sloane, *The Great Merchants* (New York: Harper and Row, 1966); "The Best of Earl Lifshey," *Retailing Home Furnishings* (October 2, 1978), section 2; and Walter Henry Nelson, *The Great Discount Delusion* (New York: David McKay Co., 1965) for more on discounters.

Interviews with John Cotter, Ed Lanctot, and Herb Haller, together with the documentary record of weekly letters, dispatches, and correspondence provided most of the information on the company's growth and struggles. Phone interviews with Bill Phair and F. Leon Herron, Jr. provided background on Bill Stout's resignation. Edmund S. Kantowicz related the toy controversy to me. A copy of the legal brief to H. G. Morison, Assistant Attorney General-Anti-Trust Division (undated, but obviously written in 1952 or 1953) furnished further details.

Ten High, Twenty High, and Fifty High Lists of Dealers, together with lists of 150 Top Manufacturers Accounts, give detailed statistics on the company's growth.

Chapter 6

John Cotter maintained extensive files on other companies in the hardware industry, which provided the raw material for Tables 4 and 5 and Figure 2. A separate file contained correspondence dealing with the annual caucus meetings. The letters exchanged between Cotter and Poole are numerous and fascinating. John Cotter, Steve Duffy, and F. Leon Herron, Jr., shared their recollections with me. Eugene F. Grape, "Retailer-Owned Cooperative Wholesaling in the Hardware Trade," (Ph.D. diss., Ohio State University, 1966), furnished useful background.

Chapter 7

The long agony of the wholesalers can be followed in detail in the editorials and the "News of the Trade" section of *Hardware Age. H.A.* also published the proceedings of NWHA and SWHA conventions. The NWHA's "Overhead Expense Reports," published annually, provide detailed cost and profit statistics. Bill Phair and John J. Sullivan, former-editors of *Hardware Age,* Bob Vereen, former-editor of *Hardware Retailing,* Rick Lambert, managing-director of NRHA, and Dave Rolston, a retired vice president of Cotter & Company, provided much useful background on old-line wholesalers.

Red Lynes and John Cotter furnished most of the details about Marshall-Wells, but I confirmed facts in the files of *Hardware Age,* the *New York Times,* and the *Duluth News-Tribune.*

Chapter 8

Both John Cotter and my father, Edmund S. Kantowicz, have extensive files on Hibbard, Spencer, Bartlett, including annual stockholders' reports, a centennial commemorative booklet, and various editions of "Hibbard Life," the employees' newspaper. I consulted the legal correspondence and the contracts concerning the Hibbard takeover. Bob Klein, long-time employee first of Hibbard's then of Cotter & Company, also offered his reminiscences and memorabilia.

Chapter 9

Red Lynes, John Cotter, Herb Haller, Ed Lanctot, and E. S. Kantowicz shared their recollections of the takeovers with me. Bill Earnest and Pat Casey added some details about Whitlock Corporation. In addition, I consulted the extensive files of trade press articles, Dun & Bradstreet reports, correspondence, and legal documents which John Cotter accumulated for each individual firm.

Chapter 10

I wrote this chapter primarily from the documentary record. John Cotter's files contain copies of all the relevant speeches and legal correspondence. Interviews with John Cotter and John J. Sullivan provided vivid detail. The cost comparisons came from the NWHA "Overhead Expense Reports" and from Cotter & Company records.

Thomas A. Fernley, III, present managing director of NWHA, commented briefly on the background of hostility between dealer-owned companies and the association but would not answer questions about the Sheffield incident. He also refused to give me the phone number of his father, Thomas A. Fernley, Jr. who was managing director in 1966. Independent efforts to locate Fernley were unsuccessful. I interviewed John W. Sheffield, Sr., by phone.

Chapter 11

About as many words have been written about advertisers as by them. For background, see the lively critical studies: Jerry Della Femina, *From Those Wonderful Folks Who Gave You Pearl Harbor* (New York: Simon and Schuster, 1970), and Daniel Boorstin, *The Image: A Guide to Pseudo-Events in America* (New York: Harper and Row, 1961); or the more sober, prosaic accounts: Martin Mayer, *Madison Avenue USA* (New York: Harper and Row, 1958), or Daniel Pope, *The Making of Modern Advertising* (New York: Basic Books, 1983).

Robert Stone, *Profitable Direct Mail Methods* (New York: Prentice-Hall, 1947) is an older study that proved useful for this chapter since it was published about the time John Cotter started his company. The following books provide background on coop advertising: Mosher Story Hutchins, *Cooperative Advertising: The Way to Make It Pay* (New York: Ronald Press, 1953); Edward C. Crimmins, *A Management Guide to Cooperative Advertising* (New York: Association of National Advertisers, 1970); Robert F. Young, Stephen A. Greyser, *Managing Cooperative Advertising: A Strategic Approach* (Lexington, Mass.: D.C. Heath, 1983). Daniel H. Hanscom, "Cooperative Advertising Allowances," *Hardware Age*, May 15, 1971, pp. 93-100, furnishes a thorough treatment of the legal rules under the Robinson-Patman Act; Michael Garry, "The Storm Over Co-op Ad Dollars," *Merchandising*, August, 1985, pp. 9-12, discusses the abuses.

John Cotter, Ed Lanctot, Pat Summerall, and Jerry Christenson discussed advertising with me at length. Ed Lanctot provided documentation of current advertising programs.

The Ace ad campaigns, and particularly the Suzanne Somers controversy, were discussed extensively in daily newspapers, tabloids, and the trade press. John Cotter kept a clipping file tracing the controversy. Perhaps the best overview, though with a pro-Ace slant, is found in two articles by Leslie Weller in *ADweek*, Sept. 21, 1981, pp. 9-10, and Sept. 28, 1981, p. 72.

Marketing & Media Decisions published a number of useful articles, particularly, "The Top 200 Brands," July, 1985, pp. 45-122, and "Do Celebrities Really Sell Products?," Sept., 1984, pp. 64-65, 120. The final quote in the chapter appeared in "National Advertising Comes to Hardware Retailing," *Hardware Retailing*, October, 1978, pp. 218-219.

Chapter 12

Thomas J. Peters, Robert H. Waterman, Jr., *In Search of Excellence: Lessons from America's Best Run Companies* (New York: Warner Books, 1982) richly deserves its national reputation. Part III, chapter 10 deals with the subject matter of this chapter.

I gathered most of the information for this chapter from company records and from interviews. John Cotter, Dan Cotter, Don Neely, Irv Rose, Dave Rolston, Glenn Alexander, Chuck Hedblom and Vern Gerdes all provided important background and furnished the necessary data. Jerry Christenson's ad agency has prepared an attractive and informative brochure, entitled "Competitive Edges," which describes the many services Cotter & Company offers the retailer. John Cotter coined the phrase, competitive edges, about 1970.

Chapter 13

John Cotter's story has been told a number of times in trade magazine articles over the last twenty years. The following articles I found most informative and insightful: Hugo G. Autz, "Ours is the Only Way," *The Sporting Goods Dealer,* (July, 1968), pp. 120-123; "Cotter & Company — Keeping That Competitive Edge Sharp," *Hardware Merchandiser,* (January, 1973), pp. 60-63; "Cotter & Company Reaches 25th Anniversary with $330 Million Sales," *Hardware Retailing,* (January, 1973), pp. 116-121; John J. Sullivan, "Cotter & Company Marks 25th Anniversary," *Hardware Age,* (January, 1973), pp. 106-111; Charles C. Horton, "John Cotter: White Knight of the Independent Merchant," *Supply House Times,* (September, 1985), pp. 37-46.

Much of this chapter was written from my own observations over the 18 months this book was in preparation. Many individuals shared their experiences with me, especially: Alice Cotter, Dan Cotter, Paul Fee, Mary Cotter Fee, Patricia Cotter Kiggins, Michael Cotter, Edmund S. Kantowicz, Le Herron, Jr., Bill Phair, John J. Sullivan, Bob Vereen, Rick Lambert, Ed Lanctot, Herb Haller, Red Lynes, Harold Ost, Dave Rolston, Les Laden, Bill Earnest, Pat Casey, Irv Rose, Glenn Alexander, Jim Eller, and John Cotter's longtime secretary, Barbara Bayer.

I drew directly on Thomas J. Peters, Robert M. Waterman, Jr., *In Search of Excellence: Lessons from America's Best-run Companies* (New York: Warner Books, 1982), and indirectly on other administrative biographies of leaders in various fields, such as, James C. Worthy, *Shaping an American Institution: Robert E. Wood and Sears Roebuck* (Urbana: University of Illinois Press, 1984); Edward R. Kantowicz, *Corporation Sole: Cardinal Mundelein and Chicago Catholicism* (Notre Dame: University of Notre Dame Press, 1983); and Arthur M. Schlesinger, Jr., *The Coming of the New Deal* (Boston: Houghton-Mifflin Co., 1958).

Chapter 14

A good theoretical overview of the themes in this chapter can be found in Alton F. Doody, William R. Davison, "Growing Strength in Small Retailing," *Harvard Business Review,* July-August, 1964, pp. 69-79.

Statistical information was drawn primarily from two sources; the U.S. Census of Business, conducted in 1948, 1954, 1958, 1963, 1967, 1972, 1977, and 1982; and the periodic hardware distribution surveys and updates conducted by *Hardware Age* in 1963, 1969, 1973, 1976, 1979, 1981, and 1984. Thomas Delph, publisher of *H.A.,* kindly provided me with reprints of the latter.

The best overview of the merchandising groups is found in *Hardware Age,* October, 1982. For information on Liberty Distributors' recent problems with the S & T bankruptcy, see *H.A.,* August, 1985, pp. 168-170. Franchising in general is discussed in Meg Whittemore, "The Great Franchise Boom" *Nation's Business,* September, 1984, pp. 20-24. The Coast-to-Coast story is well told by Charles J. Mundale, "Coast to Coast at Last!" *Corporate Report,* May, 1978, pp. 42-46, 80-84.

Statistics on family farms were quoted from Susan Sechler, Ken Cook, "It's Time to Face Facts: The Family Farm is Doomed," *Washington Post National Edition,* February 11, 1985, pp. 23-24; the quotation about service industries is from Jonathan Yardley, "An Epitaph for Service," *Washington Post National Edition,* June 17, 1985; the statement by a True Value dealer in Washington was quoted in *Hardware Merchandiser,* October, 1985, p. 61; and the final quote from John Cotter is taken from his June, 1985 Letter of the Month.

Special Acknowledgements

Karen Jumbeck, who typed the multiple drafts of this book; Ed Smith, who designed the art work and the cover; and Barbara Bayer, who managed a thousand details.

INDEX